WALT WHITMAN'S POETRY

A Psychological Journey

Riverside Studies in Literature

Riverside Studies in Literature

GENERAL EDITOR · GORDON N. RAY

Walt Whitman's Poetry

A Psychological Journey

EDWIN HAVILAND MILLER
New York University

HOUGHTON MIFFLIN COMPANY · BOSTON

New York   Atlanta   Geneva, Ill.   Dallas   Palo Alto

Ezra Pound's "A Pact" is reprinted from *Personae*, copyright 1926, 1953 by Ezra Pound. Quoted by permission of New Directions Publishing Corporation and Faber & Faber, Ltd.

Extracts from Wallace Stevens' "Peter Quince at the Clavier" and "Sunday Morning" are reprinted from *Collected Poems of Wallace Stevens*, copyright 1954 by Wallace Stevens. Quoted by permission of Alfred A. Knopf, Inc., and Faber & Faber, Ltd.

The "Chronology of Walt Whitman's Life and Work" is reprinted from *The Collected Writings of Walt Whitman*, by permission of the New York University Press.

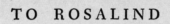

TO ROSALIND

PREFACE

Whitman's is a deeply affective poetry: it moves us emotionally and even sometimes viscerally in strange ways. Although it is difficult, perhaps impossible, to find verbal approximations of feelings, of affect, I have striven to the best of my ability to arrive at comprehensible formulations which are not merely impressionistic effusions. For Whitman's poems do have meanings, but these meanings are often emotional rather than intellectual; and his poems, despite the strictures of many critics, do have unity which we can call organic but which I prefer to term psychic. Like most poetry his greatest poems depict a journey, but to say that the journey is from darkness to light or from innocence to awareness is unsatisfactory, since it removes Whitman's journey from the psychic terrain in which it takes place and conventionalizes his insights into the human personality. For among his great American contemporaries, all of whom were in one way or another examining the nature of the self, he alone explored frankly the sexual origins of art and attitudes, the physical nature of the soul, the enduring significance of infantile needs and aspirations, and the endless quest not for intellectual consistency but for emotional security.

This essay is based upon a number of conclusions that I have reached from my study of Whitman's poetry. First, Whitman is a lyrical, autobiographical poet, as he himself admitted in his old age: "As my stuff settles into shape, I am told (and sometimes myself discover, uneasily, but feel all right about it in calmer moments) it is mainly autobiographic, and even egotistic after all — which I finally accept, and am contented so." Second, the material he writes about in his self-examination has its origins in unconscious and infantile sources; hence the results are regressive imagery, fantasy, and reactivation of infantile longings. Third, the tensions in his poems are therefore psychic, and the external world is of little importance. Fourth, this "inner drama" has an inevitable progression and its own psychic laws, for tensions and con-

vii

flicts must find some kind of resolution or release. And, finally, genius reveals itself not only by the profundity of its intuitive insights but also by its ability to put into artistic order what remains inarticulate and formless for lesser minds and sensibilities. Whitman's art has been shamefully underestimated partly because he has been judged according to irrelevant standards and presuppositions.

This "inner drama" that Whitman unfolds — which is our inner drama as well — cannot be approached from the outside, that is, by discussion of genres, traditional structure, rhetoric, and so forth. The poetry must, I believe, be approached on its own terms. Hence I have been concerned with latent and manifest content, compulsive repetitions of words and situations, psychic dynamics, narcissism, orgiastic rhythms, and the like. Which also means that in order to understand we wrestle not so much with Whitman as with ourselves, since he forces us to approximate his diagnosis of the self in painful self-analysis — to venture, in short, into "paths untrodden."

I have limited my discussion to his poetry, for a simple reason: he is one of the great English poets, but as a prose writer he is not the equal of such contemporaries as Ralph Waldo Emerson, Henry David Thoreau, and Alexis de Tocqueville. I have also confined myself to those poems which admirers and detractors agree are his greatest achievements. I can see no reason for rejecting the consensus that has been arrived at after a hundred years of discussion. I have consistently used the earliest printed versions of the poems as the basis for my commentary, although the poet prefaced the final edition of *Leaves of Grass* with a specific request: "As there are now several editions of L. of G., different texts and dates, I wish to say that I prefer and recommend this present one, complete, for future printing, if there should be any. . . ." Again my reason is simple, but admittedly debatable: the earliest readings are generally the freshest and freest expression of the original impulse from its unconscious source.

Although I am aware of Whitman's failures, I have not wasted time illustrating prolixity, affected diction, inexcusable rant, and so forth. It is easy to fault *Leaves of Grass*, but I am too grateful for, and humble before, Whitman's genius to find any gratification in censuring his weaknesses. Greatness too rarely walks among us; carping critics are a commonplace.

If this study does not send the reader back to Whitman's poetry (which is, I am aware, a commonplace), I have failed. If, on the other hand, I have been provocative, or even provoking, I shall be satisfied, since I shall then have made my modest contribution to renewing and affirming the excitement and joy of Whitman's poetry.

Finally, I want to make a number of grateful acknowledgments: to my students who patiently listened as I struggled to come to terms with Walt Whitman, but who cannot possibly know how much they helped by providing me with a sounding board; to my energetic typist, Lynne G. Bloom; and to the Arts and Science Research Fund of New York University, which over a period of several years made grants. I appreciate the privilege of using holograph materials in the magnificent collection of Charles E. Feinberg. But my greatest debts are to my long-suffering family: that the author remains not without honor in his own household is a consummation he in no way deserves.

E. H. M.

CONTENTS

CONTENTS

CHRONOLOGY
of Walt Whitman's Life and Work

1819   Born May 31 at West Hills, near Huntington, Long Island.

1823   May 27, Whitman family moves to Brooklyn.

1825–30   Attends public school in Brooklyn.

1830   Office boy for doctor, lawyer.

1830–34   Learns printing trade.

1835   Printer in New York City until great fire August 12.

1836–38   Summer of 1836, begins teaching at East Norwich, Long Island; by winter 1837–38 has taught at Hempstead, Babylon, Long Swamp, and Smithtown.

1838–39   Edits weekly newspaper, the *Long Islander,* at Huntington.

1840–41   Autumn, 1840, campaigns for Van Buren; then teaches school at Trimming Square, Woodbury, Dix Hills, and Whitestone.

1841   May, goes to New York City to work as printer in *New World* office; begins writing for the *Democratic Review.*

1842   Spring, edits a daily newspaper in New York City, the *Aurora;* edits *Evening Tattler* for short time.

1845–46   August, returns to Brooklyn, writes for *Long Island Star* from September until March.

1846–48   From March, 1846, until January, 1848, edits Brooklyn *Daily Eagle;* February, 1848, goes to New Orleans to work on the *Crescent;* leaves May 27 and returns *via* Mississippi and Great Lakes.

1848–49   September 9, 1848, to September 11, 1849, edits a "free soil" newspaper, the Brooklyn *Freeman.*

1850–54   Operates printing office and stationery store; does freelance journalism; builds and speculates in houses.

1855   Early July, *Leaves of Grass* is printed by Rome
           Brothers in Brooklyn; father dies July 11; Emerson
           writes to poet on July 21.

1856   Writes for *Life Illustrated;* publishes second edition
           of *Leaves of Grass* in summer and writes "The Eigh-
           teenth Presidency!"

1857–59   From spring of 1857 until about summer of 1859
           edits the Brooklyn *Times;* unemployed winter of
           1859–60; frequents Pfaff's bohemian restaurant.

1860   March, goes to Boston to see third edition of *Leaves of
           Grass* through the press.

1861   April 12, Civil War begins; George Whitman enlists.

1862   December, goes to Fredericksburg, Virginia, scene of
           recent battle in which George was wounded, stays in
           camp two weeks.

1863   Remains in Washington, D.C., working part-time in
           Army Paymaster's office; visits soldiers in hospitals.

1864   June 22, returns to Brooklyn because of illness.

1865   January 24, appointed clerk in Department of Inte-
           rior, returns to Washington; meets Peter Doyle; wit-
           nesses Lincoln's second inauguration; Lincoln assassi-
           nated, April 14; May, *Drum-Taps* is printed; June 30,
           is discharged from position by Secretary James Har-
           lan but re-employed next day in Attorney General's
           office; autumn, prints *Drum-Taps and Sequel,* con-
           taining "When Lilacs Last in the Dooryard Bloom'd."

1866   William D. O'Connor publishes *The Good Gray Poet.*

1867   John Burroughs publishes *Notes on Walt Whitman as
           Poet and Person;* July 6, William Michael Rossetti
           publishes article on Whitman's poetry in London
           Chronicle; "Democracy" (part of *Democratic Vistas*)
           published in December *Galaxy.*

1868   Rossetti's *Poems of Walt Whitman* (selected and ex-
           purgated) published in England; "Personalism" (sec-
           ond part of *Democratic Vistas*) in May *Galaxy;* second
           issue of fourth edition of *Leaves of Grass,* with *Drum-
           Taps and Sequel* added.

1869   Mrs. Anne Gilchrist reads Rossetti edition and falls in
           love with the poet.

1870	July, is very depressed for unknown reasons; prints fifth edition of *Leaves of Grass,* and *Democratic Vistas* and *Passage to India,* all dated 1871.
1871	September 3, Mrs. Gilchrist's first love letter; September 7, reads "After All Not to Create Only" at opening of American Institute Exhibition in New York.
1872	June 26, reads "As a Strong Bird on Pinions Free" at Dartmouth College commencement.
1873	January 23, suffers paralytic stroke; mother dies May 23; unable to work, stays with brother George in Camden, New Jersey.
1874	"Song of the Redwood-Tree" and "Prayer of Columbus."
1875	Prepares Centennial Edition of *Leaves of Grass* and *Two Rivulets* (dated 1876).
1876	Controversy in British and American press over America's neglect of Whitman; spring, meets Harry Stafford, and begins recuperation at Stafford farm, at Timber Creek; September, Mrs. Gilchrist arrives and rents house in Philadelphia.
1877	January 28, gives lecture on Tom Paine in Philadelphia; goes to New York in March and is painted by George W. Waters; during summer gains strength by sun-bathing at Timber Creek.
1878	Spring, too weak to give projected Lincoln lecture, but in June visits J. H. Johnston and John Burroughs in New York.
1879	April to June, in New York, where he gives first Lincoln lecture, and says farewell to Mrs. Gilchrist, who returns to England; September, goes to the West for the first time and visits Colorado; because of illness remains in St. Louis with his brother Jeff from October to January.
1880	Gives Lincoln lecture in Philadelphia; summer, visits Dr. R. M. Bucke in London, Ontario.
1881	April 15, gives Lincoln lecture in Boston; returns to Boston in August to read proof of *Leaves of Grass,*

being published by James R. Osgood; poems receive final arrangement in this edition.

1882   Meets Oscar Wilde; Osgood ceases to distribute *Leaves of Grass* because District Attorney threatens prosecution unless the book is expurgated; publication is resumed in June by Rees Welsh in Philadelphia, who also publishes *Specimen Days and Collect;* both books transferred to David McKay, Philadelphia.

1883   Dr. Bucke publishes *Walt Whitman,* a critical study closely "edited" by the poet.

1884   Buys house on Mickle Street, Camden, New Jersey.

1885   In poor health; friends buy a horse and phaeton so that the poet will not be "house-tied"; November 29, Mrs. Gilchrist dies.

1886   Gives Lincoln lecture four times in Elkton, Maryland, Camden, Philadelphia, and Haddonfield, New Jersey; is painted by John White Alexander.

1887   Gives Lincoln lecture in New York; is painted by Thomas Eakins.

1888   Horace Traubel raises funds for doctors and nurses; *November Boughs* printed; money sent from England.

1889   Last birthday dinner, proceedings published in *Camden's Compliments.*

1890   Writes angry letter to J. A. Symonds, dated August 19, denouncing Symonds's interpretation of "Calamus" poems, claims six illegitimate children.

1891   *Good-Bye My Fancy* is printed, and the "death-bed edition" of *Leaves of Grass* (dated 1891–2).

1892   Dies March 26, buried in Harleigh Cemetery, Camden, New Jersey.

WALT WHITMAN'S POETRY

A Psychological Journey

1

"a long foreground"

Although more than a century has passed since the appearance
of an anonymous oversized book with the strange title *Leaves of
Grass,* many people still have difficulty in coming to terms with
one of the world's great poets. Reactions to Walt Whitman continue to be extreme: glorification (sometimes approaching deification) or abuse. Such is his force that it is hard for a reader to
maintain neutrality. There have always been those who have
made Whitman into a larger-than-life figure with a mystical "mes-
sage" for the world; and others have from the beginning insisted
that he is the bard of democracy, while they declaim such banal
poems as "O Captain! My Captain!" or "I Hear America Singing."
There have always been those partisans who have taken Whitman
at his word: "This is no book, / Who touches this, touches a man."
Others have been, understandably, amused or repelled by Whitman's seductive direct address to his audience and his clamor
about masculinity. His poetic sons, like all sons — and in view of
Whitman's subject matter this is one of the ironies of literary
history — are ambivalent, and like Ezra Pound make the inevitable "pact" reluctantly:

1

> I make a pact with you, Walt Whitman —
> I have detested you long enough.
> I come to you as a grown child
> Who has had a pig-headed father;
> I am old enough now to make friends.
> It was you that broke the new wood,
> Now is a time for carving.
> We have one sap and one root —
> Let there be commerce between us.

Whitman is indeed a difficult "father," partly because in his life and in his poetry he attempts to be both comrade and father, a rough and a bard. Almost alone among the world's great poets, he has enjoyed a first-name familiarity with his readers. Yet the familiarity is in part illusory: Whitman embraces all men, but his greatest and most characteristic poems depict him as a solitary singer, an isolate; he "undrapes" but at the same time conceals; he gives himself to comrades, but then directs them not to press too close, to pursue their own paths alone. As a democratic poet he craves the love and acceptance of a mass audience, with whom he identifies as he never does with aristocratic intellectuals, in life or in art; and at the same time he aspires to be a leader or a hero, a man endowed with insight not granted to ordinary mortals. Without complete awareness, although he acknowledges his mountainous inconsistencies, Whitman plays both roles, sometimes even simultaneously, as evidenced in the sudden transformations of the poetic "I" from active to passive postures, from assertiveness to self-protective dependency. Thus he remains a kind of brother and a bearded father-figure whom, basically, we know but do not know. He eludes his friends, his biographers, and his critics — and not without conscious artfulness and disingenuousness.

Despite his pose of olympian detachment from the often intemperate sallies of his adversaries, from the beginning he gave silent blessing to the Whitman cult, and graciously accepted the accolades of his idolaters. When William Sloane Kennedy listed those "for" and "against" the poet,[1] he but drew the battle lines after Whitman's example. William Douglas O'Connor, a fiery champion with an extraordinary command of invective, stated publicly, in "The Good Gray Poet" and "The Carpenter," the messianic pretensions implicit in the poetry, when Whitman dismisses the "cautious old hucksters," Socrates, Jesus, and the others, and proclaims himself, in effect, a man-god. So that the lunatic fringe which has always surrounded the poet is traceable to the poet himself. His admirers have always acted as though his power remained unrecognized, as though he were a martyr of philistinism or of the establishment; but very few years were to pass after the appearance of *Leaves of Grass* before Whitman was heralded as a new voice and force in England, Denmark, Germany, France, and Russia. D. H. Lawrence, in his own prose "yawp," proclaimed Whitman the first American "original," and Henry Miller was not the earliest to claim that Whitman's impact has been in some respects comparable to that of Dante in the Middle Ages. Whitman, in short, has never been without recognition. The excessive and sometimes foolish claims of idolaters given to doctrinaire pronouncements have, however, often misrepresented Whitman's greatness: polemical sound and fury may satisfy partisan prejudices but lead to little understanding of the poet's achievements.

In their understandable but sometimes wild-eyed reaction against the authoritarian impersonality of the Eliot school and in their sometimes feverish (perhaps hysterical) idolatry of Whitman's "personalism," many of Whitman's recent imitators have reestablished the either-or categories, but they have mistranslated their teacher. "Barbaric yawp" is not exactly translatable as "howl." The "open road" is not a journey down an endless road of neon-lighted motels to nowhere. If he were alive today, Whitman would no doubt revel in the modern supermarket, but with the unrestrained delight and excitement of a child, not with the overeducated ennui of writers recklessly baptizing themselves in self-destructive sensations. Although it is Whitman's destiny to be periodically invoked in the ever old-new assault upon the establishment, his followers rarely approximate his sanity or balance of tensions. The Whitmanites in our time have frequently committed the errors of the eighteenth-century followers of Milton who aped his metrical technique but lost his vision. Moreover, the idolaters have forgotten the "pig-headed father's" injunction: "He most honors my style who learns under it to destroy the teacher."

Unlike some recent poets who have apparently wanted to "outbid" Whitman in matters of sexual frankness, many readers, in their embarrassment, prefer a Sunday-school version of the poet of the body. They want, despite the brilliant insights of Freud, to believe that sex is sex and art is art, and never the twain shall meet.

To deny the sexual component in art is to indulge in cultural castration. There is no passage to Whitman if one denies the sexual basis of his art. To Horace Traubel, Whitman in his old age observed, "Sex is the root of it all: sex — the coming together of men and women: sex: sex."[2] There is no passage to the essential Whitman if one denies the sexuality inherent in the artistic experience itself — "I hear the trained soprano," Whitman writes in the first version of "Song of Myself," "she convulses me like the climax of my love-grip." Hence there is evasion in the depiction of Whitman as the bard of democracy, the apostle of the brotherhood of man, and a mystic. Unfortunately, for decades American elementary schools have imposed a distortion upon the minds of the young, who too often grow to man's estate knowing no poem of Whitman's except "O Captain! My Captain." Teacher and student, it sometimes seems, cannot resist the worst of Whitman: his predilection for evangelistic utterance, his facile chauvinism, and his sentimental invocations of motherhood, family, democracy, and the like. The mass audience which Whitman sought and naively expected to have a century later can apparently respond only to the conventional rhythms of his banalities. Where Whitman reflects the national devotion to megalomania and vapid moralisms, he has reaped the rewards of self-betrayal.

Yet this is an overstatement. As Walter Whitman — the more familiar "Walt" appeared for the first time in "Song of Myself" in 1855; even his letters were signed Walter until after the appearance of *Leaves of Grass* — he had been a hack indistinguishable from countless others. He had not been a loafer, although he liked to fancy himself one, for he had supported himself from the time he left home at the age of fourteen. For a period he drifted from job to job, but when he tried journalism he soon mastered the trade and held editorships when he was in his twenties. In fact, as a self-taught and self-made man he was doing well by himself, at least in the world's terms. As an editor, however, he showed little originality or brilliance, his writings conforming to the journalistic mentality, which observes according to established standards of realism and reflects the truths its audience wants to hear. Similarly, when Whitman began to write prose tales in the 1840s, he aped the melodramatic style and content of the successful hack writers of the era and was as conventional and banal as they were. In other words, the "long foreground," which puzzled Emerson, revealed nothing at all of the original genius that was to be unfolded in the 1855 edition of *Leaves of Grass:* Whitman had displayed a not uncommon facility in writing, but certainly no indications that he had the capacity to grapple with psychic truth, that he had the courage to "undrape" the complex self, or that he was capable of creating an artistic vehicle for his insight.

Placed next to his earlier writings, *Leaves of Grass* appears to be the work of another author, but the truth is that the "original" did not permanently leave behind the platitudes of his editorial days or of his short stories. For five years, from 1855 to 1860, he explored and depicted a new inner landscape in an extraordinary series of poems, in an extraordinary outburst of creativity. He fearlessly and even at times gaily looked into the mirror at the perplexing self; almost effortlessly, or so it seems, the subject matter found appropriate poetic form. The fantasy of the poetic overman and the almost manic exhilaration of the first edition, however, he could not sustain either artistically or emotionally. The overman had feet of clay, and exhilaration gave way to honest expression of doubt and uncertainty. Thus in the third edition of *Leaves of Grass,* in 1860, the exuberance of the "flowing savage" in "Song of Myself" must be set beside the impotency and fear expressed in such new confessional poems as "As I Ebb'd with the Ocean of Life" and the "Calamus" sequence. His freely offered and in many ways heroic assistance to wounded soldiers in hospitals during the Civil War was one of the most meaningful experiences in his personal life, but, unfortunately for his poetry, too frequently the war elicited the sincere but embarrassingly chauvinistic rant of Walter Whitman. His ardent involvement with dying soldiers was a tribute to his humanity but not a stimulant to creativity. After the composition of "When Lilacs Last in the Dooryard Bloom'd," which in many respects is a (magnificent) restatement of his earlier themes, he did not write poetry of the first order. As the years passed and as he struggled, somewhat anxiously, to establish his reputation, more and more the voice was that of Walter Whitman. His announcements to the press were intended to humanize the "original," to make the revolutionary poet into a warm personality, almost a highly indulgent grandfather. Walter and Walt were, in short, in conflict from the beginning, or, perhaps more accurately, were facets of a perplexing personality.

These generalizations are sustained by the verse itself if one examines a pattern in his poems which is too little observed because readers tend to be taken in by the egomaniacal outburst: the poetic

"I" occupies for only a brief time a dominant role before he retreats, sometimes precipitately, into a dependent position. The protagonist in "The Sleepers" marches for a moment as the "boss" of a group of "blackguards," or Dionysians, only to become their "pet" and accept their "stretched arms." Always there are the "stretched arms" of a motherlike figure or of death itself, which is a matriarchal deity, to shield the "I" from realities he cannot cope with. For the artistic fantasy cannot hide the emotional needs of its creator, even when the poet is compensating for his passivity in what he chooses to call "barbaric yawp." His aggressive egomania, unlike Ahab's, occurs usually in a defensively comic context, as in Section 24 of "Song of Myself," where the "I" sheds his anonymity to become "Walt Whitman, an American, one of the roughs, a kosmos" — in one of the wittiest passages in American literature. One can say in jest, which is an acceptable social vehicle for the expression of aggression, what modesty forbids in serious discussion. But the comic brilliance which Richard Chase has correctly pointed out in "Song of Myself" is rarely evident in Whitman's poetry after 1855 and 1856: understandably, the anguish audible in the autobiographical chants of "Calamus," the desire to be considered a "religious" poet, and the assumption of the mantle of "the good gray poet" proscribed comedy.

In *Leaves of Grass* Whitman attempts to create a "modern personality," or poetic image, and succeeds — Walt Whitman is insistently there — but at the same time, with almost equal zeal, he created a colorful newspaper personality, or prose image — Walter Whitman. Not only did he write reviews of his own poetry, beginning in 1855 and continuing almost until his death in 1892, on the incontestable principle that he was the best judge of his own poetry, but also throughout his career he utilized his newspaper background and his journalist friends to have almost every personal happening or offhand opinion, regardless of its significance, duly noted in the papers and magazines. Although his admirers and the poet himself were given to depicting him as a martyr, scorned by publishers and editors, the simple truth is that Whitman received more newspaper coverage than most poets have ever enjoyed, then or now. In 1879, when he journeyed as far west as Colorado, he was not only accompanied by a Philadelphia newspaper publisher, but also was repeatedly interviewed by journalists in St. Louis, Denver, and elsewhere. Some of these interviews he himself edited and sent to Eastern publications. Or when he was in Canada in 1880, Canadian newspapers printed his long (and dull) accounts of his travels and impressions, and he sent the same article to ten or more newspapers here and in Canada. Camden and Philadelphia papers printed countless notices of his activities during the last two decades of his life, mostly written by America's most celebrated journalist-poet.

Moreover, he was personally responsible for large parts of the biographical and critical accounts which his friends John Burroughs, William Douglas O'Connor, and Dr. Richard Maurice Bucke wrote of him. Burroughs invariably sent an advance copy of comments on Whitman to the poet for correction and accepted his editing; O'Connor was supplied by him in great detail with the material to be included in a tirade against Whitman's detractors; and Bucke's biography (1883) was so closely supervised and edited by the poet that in a letter Bucke acknowledged what was plainly the case: Whitman was coeditor of the longest study of himself to appear in his lifetime. This self-created public image, then, Whitman manipulated furtively throughout his life; and, as he with his innate shrewdness was no doubt aware, he was molding all future portraits with "facts" and distortions of his own manufacture. In part, of course, his publicity cult boomeranged. His distortions gave ammunition to the hostile, who with misguided self-righteousness pointed to the "pose," forgetting that all human beings are to some extent poseurs. Further, the public image, with its emphasis upon "normality," tended to obscure the "original" who was anything but a well-rounded democratic man. Finally, Whitman, like Shaw and Hemingway, has had to pay a price for his insatiable craving for publicity: to many people the man is more interesting than the poet.

But this statement, too, is somewhat misleading. For Whitman wanted to be the comrade, the great democrat, almost as much as he wanted acceptance as a poet. The direct address in his poetry — the seductive caress he offers to his readers — is a calculated attempt to personalize the relationship between poet and audience. So that in one sense the poetry and the self-publicity express the same need to love and to be loved — which is but another way of explaining why the "I" in the poetry frequently assumes within a few lines the role of the admired poet-orator and the role of the dependent child. The craving for admiration, of course, may also

stem from feelings of deprivation, real or imaginary, for beneath
the verbal ardor, which is sometimes almost strident, lurks fear,
I suspect. But then I do not hear, as many commentators apparently do, a consistently prophetic voice in Whitman's poetry. Personal need and confusion account at least in part for the uneven-
ness of his verse as well as for the acute evocations of psychic
depths.

Whitman was inordinately proud of the praise he received from
two of the most venerable literary figures of his age, Emerson and
Tennyson. He shamelessly exploited the "greeting" the former had
sent to him in 1855 by quoting it without authorization on the
spine of the second edition of *Leaves of Grass* in 1856 and by
releasing it to a journalist. He abetted the efforts of William
Michael Rossetti, the brother of the poet, in all kinds of ways when
Rossetti proposed to issue selections from *Leaves of Grass* in
England in 1868. In the late 1870s he submitted willingly to the
adulation of literary groups and clubs when he visited New York,
and he virtually supported himself for a number of years by the
sale of the expensive 1876 edition to poetry lovers in England and
in this country. But although his livelihood and critical success
depended upon the favors of intellectuals, his heart belonged, as
his verse and his letters testify, to the ordinary man. In one of his
early reviews of his own book Whitman observes that he "would
leave a select soiree of elegant people any time to go with tumul-
tuous men, roughs, receive their caresses and welcome, listen to
their noise, oaths, smut, fluency, laughter, repartee — and can
preserve his presence perfectly among these, and the like of these."
Later in the same review he describes himself as "a person singularly beloved and looked toward, especially by young men and the
illiterate — one who has firm attachments there, and associates
there — one who does not associate with literary people."

The most cursory reading of his letters confirms this point. To
his equals he was matter-of-fact and detached. To the youths he
befriended throughout his life, particularly the Civil War soldiers,
his letters are affectionate and sometimes even impassioned, so
much so that one young man, Thomas Sawyer, was puzzled and
perhaps frightened by Whitman's ardor. However, Burroughs,
who was as dedicated a follower as the poet could desire and a
man as famous in his day as the poet himself, complained on one
occasion of the prosaic letters he received from Whitman. Bur-

roughs was not unfair in his comment; he simply did not understand Whitman's attachment to the "roughs."

Whitman wanted to be received as a comrade by these illiterate young men and went about it slyly. As their letters reveal, he did not inform the soldiers he nursed in Washington hospitals that he was a poet, and we can assume that he followed the same course in his casual contacts with hundreds of men, usually under twenty years of age, whose names, occupations, and ages he recorded in his notebooks throughout his life. From firsthand experience in his own family he knew that they were incapable of understanding his poetry, and that in their eyes poets were anomalous and usually effeminate. Thus he concealed his literary interests in order to cement friendships with people of very different interests. Yet the concealment revealed too his sensitivity to the nature of human relationships in that he did not destroy or evade them by insisting upon his own importance and superiority as an artist. He delicately — and despite his "yawp" and his egocentricity Whitman's was a delicate sensibility — communicated as a poet in verse and as a human being in his correspondence and prose.

Whitman's fondness for the "roughs" is not difficult to explain, if for a moment we regard him as a man, not as a bard. When he was creating his public image, he gave himself an idyllic family life centering in an angelic mother. This portrait has the irresistibility of untruth. It diverts attention from the truths revealed in the poems: that he was a lonely, unappreciated child who was in deep conflict with his parents and whose adjustment, the crossing of the "bridge" to manhood, was especially difficult, as "The Sleepers" makes clear. The idyll is wish, the reality is reflected in the tensions of his poems. For if his youth had been happy in the large Whitman family, he certainly would not have made the poetic "I" into an only child, almost an Ishmael. If the emotional bonds with the parents had been satisfactory, the poetic protagonist would not have been an outsider in search of familial security. If the early environment had gratified the young Whitman, he would not have created in his poetry a landscape from his private dream world. And if as a young man he had received intellectual and artistic encouragement from his parents, he would not have depicted the kind of boy-poet that appears in "Out of the Cradle Endlessly Rocking."

Yet the fact remains that Whitman was more comfortable among people who resembled his family. The "roughs" he befriended were not muscular brutes or even athletes, but uneducated, emotionally unstable young men not unlike his own brothers and sisters. Peter Doyle and Harry Stafford, the two "comrades" about whom we know a great deal, were weak, insecure youths who, probably on an unconscious level, recalled the poet's unhappy childhood. When Whitman became a father-comrade to these lads, he was creating a relationship between father and son which had not been successful in his own life.

Although the "I" becomes a father or "wound-dresser" to mangled and dying soldiers in the *Drum-Taps* poems, in the first three editions of *Leaves of Grass* Whitman is frequently the singer of an "athletic reality," as he puts it in one of the "Calamus" poems. This almost meaningless phrase discloses his longing for the company of virile comrades, blackguards, swimmers, and athletes. He wants to roam with them down "the open road" and "in paths untrodden." This, of course, is wish fulfillment, not reality. If he had been secure in the company of athletes, or even secure in his masculinity, he would not have had to proclaim in "Song of Myself" in 1855: "Walt Whitman, an American, one of the roughs, a kosmos."

This key line underwent significant changes in later editions. In 1867 it reads: "Walt Whitman am I, of mighty Manhattan the son"; and in 1881: "Walt Whitman, a kosmos, of Manhattan the son." He was willing in the final version of the line to reassert his cosmic pretensions, but he partly disowned "the rough" after the Civil War. The intimacy with Peter Doyle, the great love affair in the poet's life, began a year after the war ended, but in 1865 he had lost a governmental post because the Secretary of the Interior was offended, or pretended to be, by the sexual passages in *Leaves of Grass*. O'Connor created "the good gray poet" in answer to this scandal and inaugurated (unfortunately) the cult of deification. When an English edition of selections was under consideration — the sexual poems were, with the poet's consent, to be excluded — Whitman insisted upon his refinement and even his personal cleanliness in a letter which he prepared for O'Connor to copy before forwarding it to his English admirers. To attract readers shocked by some of his subject matter, Whitman was willing to modify the poetic image. Although he often maintained that he never altered his verse, after the war he frequently,

if sometimes reluctantly, compromised: in 1881 he was willing
to accede to some of the deletions demanded by the Boston censors
so long as the printed pages looked as though no alterations had
been made. Whitman was neither so brave in defying priggish
critics nor so "rough" as he liked to think, but in this he was no
different from most men.

The desire to establish an intimate relationship with an unknown reader, even with an audience a century later, is not the
gesture of a "rough," but of a shrinking temperament. In "A Song
for Occupations" (1855) his opening declaration of love is un-
conventional but symptomatic of a thwarted emotion:

Come closer to me,
Push close my lovers and take the best I possess,
Yield closer and closer and give me the best you possess.

This is unfinished business with me . . . . how is it with you?
I was chilled with the cold types and cylinder and wet paper between
    us.

Whitman attempts — and for many readers "Walt" succeeds —
in converting type-face into a sensory mechanism. In one of the
poems in the *Sequel to Drum-Taps* he writes: "(As I glance upward out of this page, studying you, dear friend, whoever you
are . . .)." These lines from "So Long!" have had an extraordinary
effect upon some readers:

This is no book,
Who touches this, touches a man,
. . . .
It is I you hold, and who holds you,
I spring from the pages into your arms —

a statement which on one level is one of the most startling erotic
proposals in American literature but on another and more significant level suggests the poet's disguised desire to return to a secure,
infantile relationship in the "arms" of the beloved. Simultaneously
the lines express aggression and dependency. He wants to be "the
tenderest lover," as he puts it in "Calamus," but also he seeks to
be the passive beloved who is sheltered from reality. Almost all his
poems, except those in which he expresses his patriotic evangelism,

are love poems to an anonymous audience, at least on the surface, but at the same time are elegies lamenting the separateness that is his lot and man's as well.

Although Whitman's desire to transcend "cold types" in order to transcend man's despair is Faustian (and infantile) in its confusion of artifact and life, he, unlike most men, does not shrink from truth, nor does he allow truth to poison his world view. The personal poems in "Calamus" reveal the conflict of the artist with the man as well as the poet's reluctant confession of the inadequacy of artistic sublimation:

I am indifferent to my own songs — I will go with him I love,
It is to be enough for us that we are together — We must never
    separate again.

Art did not (for it cannot) completely fill the vacuum in the personal life of the "outsetting bard of love," although he was to succeed better than most men in reconciling himself to the anguish of loneliness. Out of this loneliness Whitman wrote some of the world's loveliest lyrics.

For Whitman is a great lyric poet. When he rants and bathes himself in patriotism, sincere though he unquestionably is, he is a dull preacher and a bad poet. The explanation is simple. Ideology, political or otherwise, is the harried mind at work vainly seeking to fill emotional needs through cerebral evasions of these needs. Lyricism is the natural vehicle of a lonely, introspective, sensitive individual such as Whitman. The lyricist is a passive contemplator, an observer who more successfully than most men handles his emotional needs by honestly searching for self-understanding. Whitman's noisy evangelism is an unsuccessful attempt to transcend these needs by assuming a role that he as man and lyricist was unable to fill. Whitman's characteristic mode is meditation. When he meditates on the self, love, and death, he speaks to man timelessly and profoundly.

Although these three subjects appear in his earliest writings, he treats them there with the conventional sentimentality and evasiveness of his age. Exactly when Whitman became dissatisfied with such falseness and such traditional forms, we cannot know, but it must have been about 1850, when he was thirty-one. The miracle that is *Leaves of Grass* is the result of his search for an artistic form in which to express the "truth" about himself in ways Huck Finn (or Mark Twain for that matter) never dreams of. The process was not only an artistic but also a painful human experience. Painful because the journey to understanding of the enigmatic self opens old wounds and unveils long-repressed desires. To "undrape," to use Whitman's word, was a courageous personal act and ultimately a courageous public act, since the confession of man's physical desires and needs was without precedent in American literature or in American life, which for centuries had so accustomed itself to expressions of man's spiritual ordeals that it had tried to forget, or, more accurately, to repress, man's animalistic nature. In one of the "Calamus" poems ("O Living Always, Always Dying") Whitman writes: "O to disengage myself from those corpses of me, which I turn and look at, where I cast them!" Although he did not succeed in abandoning the "corpses," or the imposed norms of his society, he freed himself more successfully than any of his contemporaries from "tight mental allegiance given to a morality which the passional self repudiates," to quote D. H. Lawrence's astute comment on our classical literature.

For purposes of discussion it may be useful to divide Whitman's life into six phases or periods, as long as we keep clearly in mind that any such division is partially invalidated by the fluidity of human existence, which, fortunately, is neither so consistent nor so neat as our rubrics.

The first thirteen years we can term phase one. This is the phase that Whitman presents lyrically in "There Was a Child Went Forth," which, despite its surface simplicity, is a brilliant evocation of childhood; in the early parts of "The Sleepers," where he wrestles symbolically with oedipal conflicts; and in "Out of the Cradle Endlessly Rocking," where the boy-poet learns to accept the loss of relationships.

The second phase began at age fourteen and extended, roughly, to age thirty. At fourteen, in puberty, Whitman left his family to make his way in the world. Undoubtedly at the time he thought that he was a completely emancipated youth. But his seeming freedom was illusory and was marked by a number of false starts as he wandered from job to job. It was illusory because it was an evasive act, an attempt to run away from the real self and accept the standards of the world, or, in his own imagery in "The Sleepers," to circumvent the "bridge" from childhood to manhood.

Although Whitman achieved success, particularly as an editor, success did not provide the gratification he sought. His psychosexual arrestment in this phase provided him with the core of many of his most successful poems, such as "The Sleepers" and "Calamus."

When his latent dissatisfaction with the "corpses" began to trouble him seriously, the third phase began. This, significantly, took place when he returned home and worked with his father as a housebuilder in the 1850s. At this time he seems to have superseded his ineffectual father not only in business but also as the economic prop of his family. Whitman, then, had to go home again in order to seek out and confront the sources of the self, just as in Henry James's tale "The Jolly Corner" Stephen Brydon cannot be a "bride" until he returns to the ancestral home after years of floundering in foreign countries. Superficially it seems paradoxical — actually it is too commonplace and universal to be paradoxical — that Whitman could take his gigantic step toward freedom only in the protective shelter of the family itself, particularly in the presence of his mother. There, not unlike Marcel Proust (and there are many similarities between these two artists), Whitman conjured up his youth and its difficult relationships with the family and the external world. Like the boy-poet in "Out of the Cradle Endlessly Rocking," he faced the earliest trauma of loss — the death of the mother-child relationship — and, like his poetic counterpart, became "extatic" with the advent of understanding. It is not without significance that the "word" which the boy-poet discovers emerges from the "hissing melodious" of "the savage old mother," the sea.

The fourth phase, from 1856 to 1860, saw the results of Whitman's discovery of the sources of poetry in his greatest poem, "Song of Myself." The most important event in this period was the death of Whitman's father one month after the "birth" of *Leaves of Grass* in June 1855. Although biographers have generally followed the poet in slighting the significance of his father, the human fact (and no other facts are ultimately important) is that the loss of a parent is no small matter; Whitman's later silence about his father speaks loud, of guilt, ambivalence, and denial. (Coincidentally perhaps, although coincidences usually are not without explanations, the anonymously printed first edition of *Leaves of Grass* contained a notice on the verso of the title-page that it was "entered . . . by Walter Whitman," whereas all sub-sequent editions were "entered . . . by Walt Whitman.") Not only did Walt upon his father's death become the principal male in a family which included a feeble-minded boy and two alcoholic brothers, but also, as a cursory comparison of the daguerreotype in the first edition of *Leaves of Grass* and the photographs taken around 1860 demonstrates, physically he began to look like a venerable father-figure rather than a bohemian rake. More impor-tant, though no one appears to have noticed its significance, is the fact that one of his major themes — "adhesiveness" or male friend-ship — was introduced for the first time in the 1856 edition. Homosexual undertones are present in the 1855 edition, but they are so unobtrusive as to be almost unrecognizable. So long as his father was alive, Whitman could not bring himself to public con-fession of his deviant sexual drives, presumably because of fear of paternal censure.

The 1860 edition, in which the "Calamus" poems first appear, contains his frankest statement of the deviant nature of his passion but also his first admission of feelings of guilt and inadequacy. The "flowing savage" in "Song of Myself" bestrides an amoral universe in which his lust is love and any activity is permissible. So, too, the "I" in "The Sleepers" assumes various roles without moral compunctions. But the protagonist in "Calamus" is at one point "conscience-struck!" and he attempts to reconcile himself to a sexually unfulfilled life. The almost compulsively confessional nature of "Calamus" reveals despite some evasiveness the gnawing despair and guilt of a man unable, for all his physical counterfeit-ing of the bearded-father role, to assume the basic functions of paternity. To wish to be the "father" of comrades a century hence was a transparent rationalization of sexual inadequacy. Similar anguish and despair, for which there is no precedent in the first two editions, appear in "As I Ebb'd with the Ocean of Life," also new in the 1860 edition. In this poem the "I" in his uncertainty and loneliness seeks to establish an affectional rela-tionship with an ineffectual paternal symbol, the land, which is overpowered by the maternal sea. Psychologically, it is of interest that in two major poems written about the same time, "Out of the Cradle Endlessly Rocking" and "As I Ebb'd with the Ocean of Life," the protagonists identify themselves with father-figures over-whelmed by powerful feminine forces. Unconsciously, it seems

clear, Whitman was identifying himself with his father's subordination to the awesome dominancy of Louisa Van Velsor Whitman — there was a real, though probably unrecognized, bond
between father and son — but at the same time in these two
poems he reestablishes the longed-for infantile relationship between mother and son.

The change in Whitman's poetry is clearly visible if one com-
pares these two poems with the conception of the "savage" in
"Song of Myself." When the "I" transforms himself into an overman, he is the male orphan of fantasy who moves without check
in an environment where women are invariably submissive to his
potency and where he establishes a kind of patriarchy. Uninhibitedly, he sounds his "barbaric yawp over the roofs of the
world," the world, however, of wish fulfillment. When he departs,

I bequeath myself to the dirt to grow from the grass I love,
If you want me again look for me under your bootsoles.

Although the conclusion of "Song of Myself" has intimations of
"Out of the Cradle Endlessly Rocking," the reconciliation with the
maternal principle is much less explicit.

In the fifth phase, the Civil War, Whitman enacted in life the
role he gave to himself in poetic fantasy. After the Civil War he
repeatedly overestimated its impact both upon himself and upon
his art. Occasionally he made it appear as though he had been in
Washington from the outbreak of hostilities to the conclusion of
the war, when in actuality he did not go to Washington until
December 1862, and for six months in 1864 was in Brooklyn
supervising the publication of *Drum-Taps.* He gave himself more
battlefield experiences than his two brief visits to the front war-
ranted. The legend that his later physical disabilities stemmed
from his exposure to hospital infections is questionable: his
paralysis occurred almost eight years after the war. And although
Whitman sometimes liked to link the war and *Leaves of Grass,* as
though the poetry sprang from the conflict, the dates of the first
three editions, which contain almost all of his greatest poems,
refute him.

Like most people, Whitman attached too much importance to
an external event in his maturity, failing to recognize that for him
the significance of the war was its reactivation of earlier experience
as well as the opportunities it afforded for satisfying deep-seated

personal needs going back to childhood. In the Washington hospital, as a father-mother to temporary orphans in need of the solace of an affectionate heart and of the soothing hands and kisses of a parental substitute, Whitman reenacted his own youth and, momentarily at least, supplied to the soldiers the affection he had not enjoyed in his own childhood. The artificial conditions of war afforded Whitman an acceptable outlet for his "Calamus" emotions, and he freely conceded in his disarming honesty that his relationships with wounded soldiers were more meaningful to him than to them. (He did not state, publicly at least, what was obviously true: when the veterans returned to their homes, life duplicated the transitory and unfulfilled relationships recorded in the "Calamus" chants.) There was a price exacted, however: Whitman's ardent involvements with wounded and dying young men, the daily sights of horrible wounds and crudely performed amputations without anesthesia, and horrifying death scenes, took their toll of a once healthy body. As medical examinations at the time indicated, Whitman's physical collapse in 1864 was not primarily the result of careless exposure to infection in unhygienic hospitals; the body manifested physiologically the symptoms of the anxieties and emotional turmoil set off by his almost daily exposure to the agonies of the dying. The transcendence of tragedy that he achieves in his poetry, the calm and peace that come to his protagonists after their exposure to a harsh reality which Whitman never glosses over — this reconciliation he could not always effect in life.

His greatest poem of the war years, "When Lilacs Last in the Dooryard Bloom'd," sums up Whitman's emotional involvement in the strife. More than most men he sensed the mythic and psychological dimensions of the fratricidal conflict: that the estrangement of brothers from each other and from motherland closely parallels man's personal estrangement which can be healed only through reconciliation with the mother. With its three dominating images, "Lilacs" has a threefold subject: the death of Abraham Lincoln, the death of comrades (soldiers who were, as the similar imagery suggests, "Calamus" friends), and the poet's acceptance, as in "Out of the Cradle Endlessly Rocking," of the "Dark Mother," "encompassing Death — strong Deliveress!"

Lost in the loving, floating ocean of thee,
Laved in the flood of thy bliss, O Death.

The subject of the poem, then, is Walt Whitman, who accepts his and the nation's loss and places death once more in the perspective of the natural cycle, the unifying center of which is the eternal mother, the giver and receiver of life.

The last phase, which may be said, loosely, to include the rest of the poet's life, is marked by personal contentment but also by a rapid decline in poetic achievement. Despite occasional "perturbations" — "corpses" do not stay buried, and "Calamus" relationships are subject to vicissitudes — Whitman's later life was apparently as serene as man has any reason to expect. Although Whitman was not wont to expose personal anguish publicly in later life, the olympian detachment and the almost godlike radiance which Thomas Eakins captures in his magnificent portrait, and which observers repeatedly noted, were more than a pose: Whitman was at peace with himself.

Inner peace exacted an artistic price. Increasingly Whitman, to borrow once more from Lawrence, "mentalized" his emotions, as in "By Blue Ontario's Shore," where he depicts the healing of the nation's wounds in characteristic images which are, however, devoid of felt emotion:

I know now why the earth is gross, tantalizing, wicked, it is for my sake,
I take you specially to be mine, you terrible, rude forms.

(Mother, bend down, bend close to me your face,
I know not what these plots and wars and deferments are for,
I know not fruition's success, but I know that through war and crime your work goes on, and must yet go on.)

The "risings and fallings," which constitute the underlying erotic rhythms and tensions of doubt, uncertainty, rationalization, and affirmation, disappear. Eros gives way to "the good gray poet."

The division of Whitman's life into these stages, arbitrary and crude as it is and must be, is useful only insofar as it helps to explain the circular journey recorded in Whitman's poetry. His art centers in the child's relationship to the family: the infant's early dependency upon the mother, the loss (or death) of this relationship, the flight from the family in pursuit of a false concept of freedom, and the eventual return of the "prodigal son" and reconciliation. His poems are meditations on the anxieties of the search for identity and for a unifying principle in the seeming chaos of existence. Beyond their artistry, the successful poems operate upon the reader at an unconscious level because Whitman explores the psychic depths and evokes the traumas of Everyman. The reconciliation he seems to achieve satisfies the universal hunger for order and meaning.

Three extraordinary secular meditations appeared in the 1850s: *Moby-Dick, Walden,* and "Song of Myself." As Melville meditates on the nature of the ambiguous whale and Thoreau on the desperateness of desperate men, so Whitman meditates on the nature of the isolated self in the nineteenth-century world. These meditations, originating in deep personal dissatisfactions and cultural inhibitions, take the form of literal or symbolic journeys in search of a unifying principle that will simplify and harmonize the disparities of life. Disguised or undisguised, these journeys are regressive in nature, as indeed they must be, and constitute a return to the peace and security of an earlier existence — in short, a return to a womblike state. The three writers retreat from civilization, to the sea, to Walden, or to the contemplation of a "spear of summer grass." That water imagery, with its complex associations, is prevalent, fulfills the pattern of the regressive search for an ultimate source. That the three books present, at least figuratively, orphans friendless in an indifferent environment, dramatizes the emotional vacuum in the lives of their creators as well as illustrates the lonely protestant pilgrimage of our heritage — the quintessentially American quest.

More than Melville and Thoreau, Whitman had to make a relatively explicit confession and even to indulge in exhibitionism, but because he was less given to intellectual evasions of basically emotional problems, he was a more acute self-analyst than either of his contemporaries. He ventured into the amoral depths of the psyche more fearlessly than Ahab pursues Moby Dick. Where Melville disguised and "mentalized" the personal conflict by spinning a symbolic yarn about an extraordinarily ambiguous whale, Whitman "undraped" the awesomely mysterious self with a directness unequaled in our literature. Furthermore, he refused to conform to the desexualization of man that his age insisted upon; Thoreau and Melville were not so courageous. Whitman recognizes in his poetry that knowledge, in the ancient biblical sense, is sexual growth; that coming to man's estate entails the crossing of a bridge (itself a veiled sexual symbol) between childhood and manhood that poses formidable difficulties for youths in puberty, and afterward, if it is not crossed successfully; and that art has a sexual base and is a sublimation of libidinal drives.

Whitman's epiphany — the metamorphosis of a conventional, fearful hack writer into America's greatest and most courageous "original" — is symbolically unfolded in the fifth section of "Song of Myself." This is the crucial passage in Whitman's poetry and probably the greatest moment in American verse. This much-discussed section is not to be explained away or conventionalized by vague descriptions in terms of an even vaguer mysticism.

The scene is a startling, audacious portrait of an artist who has retreated from the artificialities of society to contemplate a "spear of summer grass." Alone, nude, searching for a "reality" that is true to the self, not a cultural imposition upon the self, he opens his atrophied senses to the natural rhythms of the universe. No longer is his body checked in its natural desire for tactile sensation, his ears hear "the belched words of my voice," and his nose greedily absorbs the "perfumes" of the woods. For with his clothes he has shed value judgments and guilt in order to "possess the origin of all poems." Freed from chronological time and from sexual fears and inhibitions, he is ready for the regressive journey to the depths of his being.

I believe in you my soul . . . . the other I am must not abase itself to
    you,
And you must not be abased to the other.

Loafe with me on the grass . . . . loose the stop from your throat,
Not words, not music or rhyme I want . . . . not custom or lecture, not
    even the best,
Only the lull I like, the hum of your valved voice.

I mind how we lay in June, such a transparent summer morning;
You settled your head athwart my hips and gently turned over upon me,
And parted the shirt from my bosom-bone, and plunged your tongue to
    my barestript heart,
And reached till you felt my beard, and reached till you held my feet.

Swiftly arose and spread around me the peace and joy and knowledge
    that pass all the art and argument of the earth;

And I know that the hand of God is the elderhand of my own,
And I know that the spirit of God is the eldest brother of my own,
And that all the men ever born are also my brothers . . . . and the
    women my sisters and lovers,
And that a kelson of the creation is love;
And limitless are leaves stiff or drooping in the fields,
And brown ants in the little wells beneath them,
And mossy scabs of the wormfence, and heaped stones, and elder and
    mullen and pokeweed.

Although the section takes superficially the form of the ancient allegory of the soul and the body, Whitman magically transforms the confrontation. The soul is corporeal: its voice, when the "stop" is released, is a "lull" or a "hum," like the sound of the mother's soothing, wordless lullaby; there is no suggestion of the nonhuman music of the spheres. Nor is there a debate between these ancient antagonists. The body is the passive, perhaps feminine, receiver of the soul's aggressive, perhaps masculine, sexual force. In other words, the fearful body is eroticized by contact with the soul, which is not bound by the repressiveness of the artificial civilization described in the opening section of the poem. In the consummation of frankly inverted sexuality, the agitated and guilty body achieves calm and peace, as Whitman's indescribably lovely lines reveal better than paraphrase. For natural harmony has been restored through redefinition of the soul and through the destruction of the artificial and inhuman separation of body and soul, reason and feeling, decreed by Western society.

The scene is played out in regressive sexual imagery. The orality — "plunged your tongue to my barestript heart" — evokes the child at the mother's breast, "heart" being associated with the phallus and the breast. In "going under" Whitman, unconsciously, approximates the child's phallic picture of the mother. The tongue is the means of the child's earliest contact with the world, his bridge, in a literal and figurative sense, to something outside himself as well as a source of physical comfort. At the same time, for we are in the world of a child's associative processes, the tongue like the breast is phallic in its fecundating powers.

The roles Whitman assumes in his later poetry are traceable to this regressive scene. As a poet-orator he sees himself gifted with an omnipotent tongue (phallus) which will fertilize a receptive world — hence the erotic assault upon the ears of his auditors.

As a lover he seems to be strangely satisfied with a passing glance or a fleeting kiss, but the strangeness disappears when one recalls the importance of infantile oral gratification as well as the child's blithe disregard of social taboos surrounding touch. Whitman's regressive imagery reflects the childlike confusion of bodily organs, which accounts for the displacement evident here in the "heart" reference and in the difficulties and apparent obscurities in a poem like "Scented Herbage of My Breast."

In this crucial episode Whitman's images are predominantly oral and tactile. Many commentators have termed Whitman's orality and tactility abnormal, failing to recognize that the very nature of Whitman's art rests upon his evocation of the polymorphously perverse in his own and human nature. The source of his impact upon his readers, at least upon those who do not protect themselves by normalizing Whitman, is that he taps subterranean currents that we have tried to forget when we put away childish things. Human beings hunger for the oral and tactile gratifications which Whitman candidly acknowledges.

So too his vision of an emancipated, affectional society could not be advanced until he had retreated in order to recapture the child's construction of reality. At the same time this is the limitation of Whitman's love vision. As the body, or the "I," quiescently accepts the soul's sexual invasion, so his vision cannot go beyond his (feminine) passivity and his dependent nature. Except for a few flamboyant passages of erotic aggressiveness, Whitman establishes a passive relationship with his imaginary and real lovers. Even in art Whitman could not escape his fearful shrinking from normal sexuality, or cross "bridges" he was unable to cross in life.

The epiphany recorded in Section 5 takes the pictorial form of a cross:

You settled your head athwart my hips and gently turned over upon me,
. . . .
And reached till you felt my beard, and reached till you held my feet.

As Professor Allen notes in his study of Whitman's biblical imagery, the poet was particularly attracted to "the crucifixion scenes of the Christ-drama."[3] It is understandable why Whitman, perhaps unknowingly, chose to dramatize the scene in terms of a crucifixion. For at least in one sense the old Whitman dies and a new one is born: the conventional, prosaic Walter Whitman is succeeded by the Walt Whitman announced in the first edition of *Leaves of Grass.* The crucifixion also suggests the death of the ancient dualism (body and soul) and the resurrection of a single whole being. The body is reborn without the Judaeo-Christian mortification of the flesh: the soul accepts the entire body, "felt my beard, and reached till you held my feet," for all organs of the body are equally important and all sensations are equally good. Since the eyes as the organ of spiritual insight restrict man to intellectual gratification, Whitman resurrects the body, or, to put it another way, makes the soul sensual once again, as it was in the beginning of the child's life before society imposed conscience and "thou-shalt-nots."

"Peace and joy and knowledge" come, not through asceticism, but through orgasm. And, figuratively, the artist is no longer a lonely recluse: he has found the illumination that is to be his art, his comrade. For with self-understanding Whitman was no longer an idle drifter; he was ready to burst forth in assured song, to "itch" at the ears of his audience. So, too, Stephen Dedalus abandons his "corpses" and his guilt, and is filled with a mysterious serenity as he accepts his artistic and mythic calling. Whitman's epiphany has the virtue of shunning Joycean intellectualization and self-conscious mythicism, as he symbolically reenacts the primal scene, which gives birth to the child, who turns in upon himself in order to emerge as an artist. Neither poet nor man can be free, Whitman in effect asserts, until he lets the child come forth.

2

"There was a child"

I, a child, very old, over waves, toward the house of maternity.

— "Facing West from California's Shores"

The portrait of Whitman which emerges from the poetry, with the author's characteristic indirectness, is singularly different from that of "the good gray poet" or the heroic bard. The poems give us truths about the facets of Whitman's complex personality which cannot be substantiated by the facts carefully assembled by the biographers. Whitman in his fame related trivia about his youth, pointless facts about his ancestry, inaccurate accounts of his reading, and so on. He urged his biographers to collect and print strings of anecdotes as Bucke did in *Walt Whitman* in 1883. Yet, with not unusual inconsistency, in an early passage in "Song of Myself" Whitman pointedly ridicules anecdotes and external facts as avenues to understanding of the self:

Trippers and askers surround me,
People I meet . . . . the effect upon me of my early life . . . . of the
ward and city I live in . . . . of the nation,

24

The latest news . . . . discoveries, inventions, societies . . . . authors
  old and new,
My dinner, dress, associates, looks, business, compliments, dues,
The real or fancied indifference of some man or woman I love,
The sickness of one of my folks — or of myself . . . . or ill-doing . . . .
  or loss or lack of money . . . . or depressions or exaltations,
They come to me days and nights and go from me again,
But they are not the Me myself.

The poet made no important revelations about his personality to
Horace Traubel in their nightly conversations in the late 1880s,
which the idolatrous young man unselectively and monotonously
recorded. *Specimen Days,* his longest work in prose, presents only
the skimmings from the surface, as Whitman admitted.

The poems, however, on one level are literally a "song of
myself," a sustained meditation on the nature of a "modern personality," Walt Whitman. Nowhere in the hundreds of pages in
Leaves of Grass does he attempt analysis of another individual.
This omission can be justified: because his is the insight of genius,
his self-analysis is by extension a commentary on Everyman. In
"Assurances" he admits: "I do not doubt there is more in myself
than I have supposed . . . . and more in my poems than I have
supposed" — a passage which he later excised. Nor is he being
falsely modest when he writes in "You Felons on Trial in Courts,"
"(O admirers! praise not me! compliment not me! you make me
wince, / I see what you do not — I know what you do not. . .) ."
In his poetry Whitman is truthful but sometimes evasive; in his
prose pronouncements and conversations after fame had come, he
is frequently inaccurate and often deliberately misleading.

Whitman's poetry, as we have seen, was an act of liberation.
When he says at the beginning of "Song of Myself," "I will go to
the bank by the wood and become undisguised and naked," he is
not proposing nudity, as some of the narrowminded early reviewers
suggested; he is seeking the reality beneath the public image. Or,
as he puts it in "O Living Always, Always Dying," "O to disengage
myself from those corpses of me." Repeatedly he acknowledges the
confessional nature of his poetry:

I loosen myself.
                                ("I Sing the Body Electric")

O all untied and illumined! . . .
O to have the gag removed from one's mouth! . . .
O to escape utterly from others' anchors and holds!
                                   ("One Hour to Madness and Joy")

From this hour I ordain myself loosed of limits and imaginary lines,
. . . .
Gently, but with undeniable will, divesting myself of the holds that
    would hold me.
                                   ("Song of the Open Road")

I will play a part no longer. . . .
                                   ("Native Moments")

I am determined to unbare this broad breast of mine. . . .
                                   ("Scented Herbage of My Breast")

Passages such as these — and others can easily be found — clearly
indicate that he sought release and freedom from tensions and
anxieties in his poetry, that, in short, his verse is, as Dr. Gustav
Bychowski's sensitive study[1] makes clear, a sublimation of his
personal despair and gnawing loneliness.

Although Whitman made many seemingly contradictory statements about his intentions in *Leaves of Grass,* depending upon the
exigencies of the moment and his whims, in a letter to William D.
O'Connor in 1882 he makes what I consider his definitive statement about his book:

The *worry* of Ruskin . . . with *Leaves of Grass* is that they are *too
personal,* too emotional, launched from the fires of *myself,* my spinal
passions, joys, yearnings, doubts, appetites, &c &c. — which is really
what the book is mainly for, (as a type however for those passions, joys,
workings &c *in all the race,* at least as shown under modern & especially American auspices) — Then I think he winces at what seems
to him the *Democratic* brag of L. of G. . . . R[uskin] like a true
Englishman evidently believes in the high poetic art of (only) making
abstract works, poems, of some fine plot or subject, stirring, beautiful,
very noble, completed within their own centre & radius, & nothing to
do with the poet's special personality, nor exhibiting the least trace of
it — like Shakspere's great unsurpassable dramas. But I have dashed
*at the greater drama going on within myself & every human being —
that is what I have been after —*[2]

As a commentator on the drama of democracy Whitman sounds more like a Fourth of July orator than a perceptive critic or poet: he was a poor historian and a naive prophet of the future. Sidney Lanier's attack on this aspect of Whitman's thought was more than justified.

But where are these roughs, these beards, and this combativeness? Were the Adamses and Benjamin Franklin roughs? was it these who taught us to make ruffianly nominations? But they had some hand in blocking out this republic. . . . it may be fairly said that nowhere in history can one find less of that ruggedness which Whitman regards as the essential of democracy, nowhere more of that grace which he considers fatal to it, than among the very representative democrats who blocked out this republic. In truth, when Whitman cries "fear the mellow sweet," and "beware the mortal ripening of nature," we have an instructive instance of the extreme folly into which a man may be led by mistaking a metaphor for an argument. . . .

In the name of all really manful democracy, in the name of the true strength that only can make our republic reputable among the nations, let us repudiate the strength that is no stronger than a human biceps, let us repudiate the manfulness that averages no more than six feet high.[3]

Nowhere in his poetry does Whitman explore industrial discontents, the problems of urbanization, the impact of the dynamo, or the religious doubts fostered by new scientific theories. Where he is successful, and gloriously successful, is in his rendition of the inner drama of the self searching, now fearfully, now joyfully, for its identity. Whitman's example lends strong support to the contention that in our literature the appropriate subject is not the geographical frontier, which Natty Bumppo desperately seeks only to lose it to so-called civilization, but the frontier within, which the great writers of the nineteenth century scrutinized with an intuitive clairvoyance that has made them accurate harbingers of twentieth-century dilemmas. They, but particularly Whitman, recognized that the self was the only uncertain stability in an unstable world. Thus Gertrude Stein is fatefully correct: American writers are the oldest in the Western world. They were among the first to learn that to free himself man must journey back into the child's terrain.

"There Was a Child Went Forth" is one of the most sensitive

lyrics in the language and one of the most astute diagnoses of the emergent self. Whitman recaptures the awakening consciousness of the child-poet and the lovely but lonely landscape in which the American child matures. The opening line with its biblical cadence evokes the edenic past and presages the future of the boy who "received with wonder or pity or love or dread." At first he perceives only beautiful natural objects — the lilacs, the grass, the morning glories, the clover. Gradually sounds intrude — "the song of the phœbe-bird" and "the noisy brood of the barnyard." With wonder the child observes the miracle of birth in the barnyard — "the sow's pink-faint litter." Quietly he moves to the "pondside," where he sees "the fish suspending themselves so curiously below there . . and the beautiful curious liquid."

With deceptive understatement Whitman introduces a pivotal symbol in the poem and in his writings. When the boy looks into the water, he is, of course, reenacting the Narcissus myth, like Eve in the Garden of Eden. Unlike Milton, since he is not given to moral judgments or to didactic oversimplifications, Whitman recognizes that love originates in self-love before its evolution into outgoing love, and that only negation stems from self-hatred. In other words, he perceives that narcissism with its creative aspects is a complex phenomenon in the growth process. Whitman's "doting" on the self, which has so frequently and simplistically been labeled egocentricity, is better explained in Marcuse's formulation in *Eros and Civilization:*

The striking paradox that narcissism, usually understood as egotistic withdrawal from reality, here is connected with oneness with the universe, reveals the new depth of the conception: beyond all immature autoeroticism, narcissism denotes a fundamental relatedness to reality which may generate a comprehensive existential order. In other words, narcissism may contain the germ of a different reality principle: the libidinal cathexis of the ego (one's own body) may become the source and reservoir for a new libidinal cathexis of the objective world — transforming this world into a new mode of being.[4]

Somewhat like Proust dipping the madeleine into the teacup, except that Whitman keeps the incident within the framework of a child's limited perception, the boy sees in miniature the totality of his and human life. Unknowingly he journeys to the source, for as he watches the fish in "the beautiful curious liquid" he is observing the fetus in the amniotic fluid, the eternally creative womb of life and art. The fish also introduce the phallic motif, which is invariably present in Whitman's most successful poems: the grass in "Song of Myself," the calamus plant in his love songs, and even the lilacs in "When Lilacs Last in the Dooryard Bloom'd." Here the phallicism leads to the "fatherstuff" in the child's account of his own birth.

In this tightly structured poem, psychologically and artistically, the pond is crucial to the emotional and intellectual development of the child protagonist and to the progression of the poem itself. Similarly, the boy-poet in "Out of the Cradle Endlessly Rocking" discovers the "word," the unifying principle, near the "hissing" sea; and the protagonist in "As I Ebb'd with the Ocean of Life" will have doubts about his identity along the shore. In the "Calamus" poem "In Paths Untrodden," the "I" listens to "tongues aromatic" near the "margins of pond-waters," "away from the clank of the world." In Whitman's verse, then, the pond serves a complex function, as, coincidentally, it does in *Walden;* and Melville's Pierre writes enigmatically: "Not yet had he dropped his angle into the well of his childhood, to find what fish might be there; for who dreams to find fish in the well?" (Book XXI).

The child in Whitman's poem now wanders blithely in a world filled with animals, "field-sprouts," and "appletrees," when suddenly his idyllic world is shattered. For the first time another human being, significantly an adult, appears, and with his appearance comes fear: "And the old drunkard staggering home from the outhouse of the tavern whence he had lately risen." The drunken motion of the man clashes with the natural order, but at the same time may be the human equivalent of the jerky, darting movements of the fish. Here Whitman's associations are subtle, since the drunkard is linked both with the father who is to be introduced shortly and with the boy himself. The disgusting appearance of the drunkard is to be paralleled in the boy's disgust with his father's craftiness, and both adults evoke fear in the child's heart. The "staggering" parallels the crude description of the father who "had propelled the fatherstuff at night." The drunkard, we are told, "had lately risen" "from the outhouse," and the father from the marital bed. (If Whitman's father was, as some would have it, a drunkard, these associations take on added significance.) But the lonely lot of the besotted man is also that of the child, for as the man makes his uncertain way home alone, so the child sees a group of happy schoolchildren from afar and is not part of the group.

Now the poet turns to the most mysterious and haunting event in his life — his own conception. With fascination and perhaps dread he alludes to "the fatherstuff at night [that] fathered him" and to the mother who "conceived him in her womb and birthed him." Next there is a picture of the mother "with mild words . . . . clean her cap and gown" — one of Whitman's idealized maternal figures. Perhaps the phrase "a wholesome odor falling off her person and clothes as she walks by" is to be contrasted with the somewhat odorous drunkard. From this portrait of the mother we move abruptly to the repellent one of the father, who, as already indicated, embodies the intemperateness and dread associated in the child's mind with the drunkard:

The father, strong, selfsufficient, manly, mean, angered, unjust,
The blow, the quick loud word, the tight bargain, the crafty lure. . . .

It matters little whether this passage is autobiographical and literally true, since truth in family relationships is usually the emotional response of the participants. What is important is the self-revelation — the emphasis, perhaps overemphasis, upon the mother's purity and perfection and the ambivalence toward the father, whose genital prowess the boy reluctantly admires but whose "crafty" disposition he scorns.

The section on the family, rightly the longest in the poem, for Whitman is almost invariably correct in his psychological values, is followed by a passage reflecting the uncertainty of the child's "yearning and swelling heart":

The sense of what is real . . . . the thought if after all it
should prove unreal,
The doubts of daytime and the doubts of nighttime . . . the curious
whether and how,
Whether that which appears so is so . . . . Or is it all flashes and
specks?
Men and women crowding fast in the streets . . if they are not flashes
and specks what are they?

Here the doubts and deep-seated fears of the boy are understated, unlike the painful confessions later in the "Calamus" sequence.

Just as in life Whitman left home at an early age, presumably
because the family provided neither emotional nor intellectual
security, so in this poem the child seeks his own answers to his
"curious whether and how" when he begins what is to become a
familiar journey motif in Whitman's poetry, as he wanders along
urban streets and observes teams of horses moving along peopleless
streets and ferries crossing the river. In the course of the journey
— and the pattern established in "There Was a Child Went Forth"
is characteristic of most of his poems — the child-man in some
mysterious way overcomes the paralysis of doubt and arrives at
certainty.

Ascending images gradually lead to "light falling on roofs and
gables of white and brown," and, finally, to

The strata of colored clouds . . . . the long bar of maroontint away
    solitary by itself . . . . the spread of purity it lies motionless in,
The horizon's edge, the flying seacrow, the fragrance of saltmarsh and
    shoremud;
These became part of that child who went forth every day, and who
    now goes and will always go forth every day. . . .

The reader's eye follows the child-poet in the ascent to cosmic
peace and harmony. Here as elsewhere Whitman makes a "leap,"
as it were, from despair or uncertainty to affirmation. The abrupt
transition is perhaps rationally unconvincing, but emotionally there
is satisfaction in Whitman's expression of the personal and cultural
hunger for an edenic state. Such is the subterranean appeal that
we forget that the protagonist finds reality and identity far from
the troubling movements of life (the drunkard's "staggering" and
coitus), and that, like Melville's Ishmael, the child-man is alone
at the beginning and the end of the poem. He, like "the long bar
of maroontint" or "the flying seacrow," is "away solitary by itself,"
a solitary singer in a vast landscape. Thus Whitman creates a
lovely rationalization, or sublimation, of human loneliness, which
the protagonist (and the poet himself) will endure without a
whimper.

To put it another way, the journey comes to its conclusion with
a leap that restores the idyllic landscape of the child; the movement, in short, is circular. For the imagery at the conclusion of the
poem suggests retreat to the womb. "Purity" and "fragrance" recall
the mother's cleanliness and "wholesome odor"; and "the spread

of purity it lies motionless in" refers back to the fish in the pond, the fetus in the amniotic fluids. Paradise is regained — through the restoration of the shattered infantile relationship with the mother.

It has been said too loosely and too often that Whitman is the first of the urban poets. Despite the brilliance of lines like "the blab of the pave" and the graphic, but fleeting, pictures of city life in "Song of Myself" and elsewhere, the settings of his greatest poems are almost invariably rural. "The open road" may lead the "I" through city streets, and comrades may be found in "A populous city," but the road invariably leads to rustic sites, and love is consummated, or companionship temporarily found, while "the waters roll slowly continually up the shores" ("When I Heard at the Close of the Day"). As in "There Was a Child Went Forth," harmony and peace come out of earshot of the city's "dark" or the dynamo's whirring.

Understandably so, since in his evocation of childhood Whitman recreates not only the child's relationship to the family but also the physical environment the child knew. Whitman lived most of his life in Brooklyn, Washington, and Camden, but in his first years, at Huntington, Long Island, he had never been far from the "hissing" of the Atlantic Ocean, and he had roamed freely in a rural setting. His art, like Proust's, is a remembrance of things past. It is more than coincidence that he did not begin to recover from the debilitating paralysis of 1873 and the death of his mother in May of that year until he found at the Stafford farm in Kirkwood, New Jersey, an approximation of his childhood environment on Long Island, and in the impoverished and barely literate Staffords, mother, father, and children, the equivalent of his own family.

Grace Gilchrist, the daughter of the woman who journeyed to America out of her impassioned desire to marry the poet, records Whitman as saying that "the time of my boyhood was a very restless and unhappy one: I did not know what to do."[5] There is no way of verifying the accuracy of Miss Gilchrist's recollection, but poems like "There Was a Child Went Forth" tend to corroborate her report, for the visual setting in Whitman's poetry is ordinarily not unlike that of the solitary shepherd in the painter's landscape, where lovely colors, like Whitman's beautiful language, keep us from pondering upon the character's isolation. The protagonist in

"Song of Myself" withdraws from the intoxicating "distillation" of his artificial or social environment in order to observe "a spear of summer grass." The first line of "Starting from Paumanok," in the 1860 edition, characterizes the poet as "Free, fresh, savage," but the last line in the opening section belies the description and reveals the true state, "Solitary, singing in the west, I strike up for a new world"; Whitman had again "withdrawn to muse and meditate" alone. By a significant addition in 1871, he qualifies his paeans in "A Song of Joys," when he speaks of "Joys of the free and lonesome heart, . . . / Joys of the solitary walk." The original opening line of "As I Walk These Broad Majestic Days" is quite different from its later title: "As I walk, solitary, unattended." In "As I Ebb'd with the Ocean of Life," there is a line as appropriate to the despairing mood as a similar one in *The Waste Land,* "I, musing, late in the autumn day." Even in the rejuvenation of another season, in "These I Singing in Spring," the poet is "Far, far in the forest, . . . / Solitary."

Repeatedly he refers to "lonesome walks" ("Recorders Ages Hence") during which "I stand and look at the stars" ("Night on the Prairies") or "I sit and look out upon all the sorrows of the world" ("I Sit and Look Out") or "I sit alone, yearning and thoughtful" ("This Moment Yearning and Thoughtful"). Whitman sings of union and companionship and sees himself as the comrade of people unborn, but the song comes from the yearning depths of a solitary observer, of a withdrawn child who, as a man, still reflects the child's estrangement in lines like these from "Not Heaving from My Ribb'd Breast Only":

Not in many a hungry wish, told to the skies only,
Not in cries, laughter, defiances, thrown from me when alone, far in
the wilds. . . .

Although Whitman sometimes creates a marvelous fantasy of a joyous overman or "savage" speaking with a "barbaric yawp" — an American Pan, as it were, who impregnates the earth with his poetry — the wish gushes forth from a withdrawn soul; like Thoreau's, his Pan is an imaginative fiction. "I am not to speak to you," Whitman writes in "To a Stranger," "I am to think of you when I sit alone, or wake at night alone." Or in "Poets To Come," the celebrator of comrades cannot permit himself the simple gratification of social contact: "I am a man who, sauntering along, without fully stopping, turns a casual look upon you, and then averts his face." But why avert his face? And why must this liberator of the senses write like a latter-day disciple of Puritan duty and asceticism in "All Is Truth": "Meditating among liars, and retreating sternly into myself"? "Sternly" conjures up duty and deep-rooted repressions. "Retreating sternly into myself" is an evasive act out of fear. The fear the drunkard arouses in "There Was a Child Went Forth" anticipates the avoidance of human interaction in Whitman's writings. (Except for the accounts of his experiences in wartime hospitals, *Specimen Days* consists mostly of ramblings about nature; people appear infrequently.) The fear is generally submerged or disguised, since Whitman attempts to deny it in order to play the role of the comrade or lover, but as in dreams we cannot ignore the latent content. This fear is not unlike that which keeps Henry James's most autobiographical characters, Ralph Touchett and Lambert Strether, from acknowledging their affections and entering normal human and sexual relationships. Although critics intent upon neat categories like to make James and Whitman antithetical, this kind of oversimplification will not withstand scrutiny. Just as most of Whitman's protagonists retreat to the forests to meditate upon existence, so the Lambert Strethers retreat to the United States to live out their lonely lives of virtue and self-reliance. For despite James's depiction of class structure and his dramatization of the emergent consciousness in a social context, his heroes and heroines, if death does not snuff them out, have at the conclusion of his fable only the self — no "connections."

In many of Whitman's poems there are crowds of people, particularly in his inventories of occupations and his kaleidoscopic catalogues of urban and rural activities. In "There Was a Child Went Forth," it will be recalled, the child sees the drunkard

And the schoolmistress that passed on her way to the school . . and the friendly boys that passed . . and the quarrelsome boys . . and the tidy and freshcheeked girls . . and the barefoot negro boy and girl. . . .

But at no point in the poem does the child speak to these people or interact with them. The "I" in "Song of Myself," although he speaks forcefully and amorously to an anonymous audience, does not converse with even one of the innumerable people who appear in more than 1,300 lines. Sometimes he talks to himself, as in this passage:

Speech is the twin of my vision . . . . it is unequal to measure itself.
It provokes me forever,
It says sarcastically, Walt, you understand enough . . . . why don't you
    let it out then?

The rest is monologue with deceptive trappings of dialogue. So, too, Henry James creates *ficelles* to relieve the monologue of the unraveling consciousness with a dialogue that is more illusionary than real, since for the Isabel Archers, Christopher Newmans, Lambert Strethers, and Merton Denshers — and the Huck Finns, for that matter — the territory ahead is the silence of monologue.

Though Whitman sympathizes with prostitutes, criminals, hunted slaves, and abject failures, at no time does he do more than express sympathy and suggest in general terms their anguish. More often than not, he confines himself to descriptions of the life-and-death heroics of firemen or soldiers, nude male swimmers in danger or in sportive play, mothers nursing or tending their children, parents honored by their children. But the brave fireman, unlike the Greek warrior of whom he is the modern counterpart, is never given the dignity even of a name, and is simply one of the "divine average," an anonymous and previously unsung hero.

Whitman, then, describes people externally and superficially, as representatives of meaningful activities in a democratic society. These descriptions are often Michelangelesque in their fascination with the muscular movements of the beautiful male bodies, as in this well-known passage in "Song of Myself":

The butcher-boy puts off his killing clothes, or sharpens his knife at
    the stall in the market,
I loiter enjoying his repartee and his shuffle and breakdown.
Blacksmiths with grimed and hairy chests environ the anvil,
. . . .
The lithe sheer of their waists plays even with their massive arms,
. . . .
The negro holds firmly the reins of his four horses . . .

. . . .

His blue shirt exposes his ample neck and breast and loosens over his
   hipband,

. . . .

The sun falls on his crispy hair and moustache . . . . falls on the black
   of his polish'd and perfect limbs.

The throbbing flesh reduces these men from human status to
anatomical functions. They are movements, not humans. Except
in "Faces," the people are even faceless, Whitman's eye being
drawn to the flesh as though fearful of eye-to-eye contact.

The people in Whitman's poems are like those of Maurice
Prendergast, another lonely, isolated American artist. With lovely
color and exquisite delicacy Prendergast fills his canvases with
people promenading in parks, congregating at beaches, participat-
ing in various social functions. Always crowds of people in every-
day activities, yet when one looks closely, often there are no faces,
only bodies (or colors) in motion. The hedonism evoked by the
beautiful pastel colors vanishes as one becomes aware of the artist's
shrinking temperament, gregarious in fantasy but painfully timid
and withdrawn.

Though Whitman is the greatest singer of love in nineteenth-
century American literature, almost always he chants of unrequited
love or asserts his love of collective democratic man. The lover
portrayed in his poems is for the most part a passive, timid individual who avers his satisfaction with the passing glances of a
stranger or a fleeting touch in a crowd. (What little sexual aggression there is resembles autoerotic fantasy.) The beloved, who is
neither named nor individualized, is a stranger whose sudden disappearance the lover seems to welcome, for it is easier (and safer)
to lament the loss of love than to consummate it. It is also easier
to make love to an unknown audience, except that to do so is
scarcely to make love at all.

Whitman's fear of personal involvement is part of the hidden or
"indirect" meaning of "There Was a Child Went Forth," since the
poem records the failure of basic relationships. Whitman, it will
be recalled, notes the child's "yearning and swelling heart" and
his search for "what is real," but whatever the child discovers he
discovers for himself through his own observations of nature,
strangers, and parents. There is no interaction between the youth

and his parents, only the summarizing statements about the
mother's gentleness and the father's harshness. They do not fulfill
their parental roles of offering guidance and affection to the boy.
In view of their failure, it is scarcely surprising that the child does
not interact with other people, that he retreats "sternly" into himself. It is also significant that, although Whitman was the second
of seven children and grew up in a large household, the child in the
poem has neither brothers nor sisters. In fact, it can be said that
Whitman, like Proust and James, acknowledged the reality of
sibling rivalry by having his poetic expression of childhood follow
two patterns: either the youth enjoys, as in "There Was a Child
Went Forth," an exclusive relationship with parents as an only
child, which is a kind of paradise, or the boy is more or less an
"orphan" who, in his fantasy, enjoys the illusory freedom of a
parentless world. The latter situation is more frequent — "Out of
the Cradle Endlessly Rocking" and "The Sleepers" are examples —
but the only child and the orphan invariably find at the end of their
journeys the same haven — the protective maternal figure.

The mature man depicted in "Song of Myself" leaves "Houses
and rooms . . . full of perfume," but apparently no family, and in
his meditation creates a vision of the free and fulfilled self. However, he establishes no enduring connections:

I am a free companion . . .

I turn the bridegroom out of bed and stay with the bride myself,
And tighten her all night to my thighs and lips.

He is, ironically, "free" to roam, to revel in natural and human
beauties, and to gather to himself a large group of admirers, but he
is not "free" to establish lasting relationships, except imaginary
ones. Although it can be argued that Whitman follows the protestant tradition in his insistence that each man is the determiner of
his own lot — and this is certainly a partial explanation — it is
also true that his fear of personal involvement was such that in his
poetry he woos his readers and then holds them off through barriers
which he erects between himself and his (imaginary) admirers.
When the idolaters in "Song of Myself" become too insistent, he
reminds them, "He most honors my style who learns under it to
destroy the teacher." No one must approach too close. Only the
superficial egocentricity of "Song of Myself" keeps us from recog-

nizing Whitman's sometimes strained attempts to hide feelings of inadequacy and fears of rejection.

For a century detractors have heaped contempt upon Whitman for ignoring or at least minimizing the existence of evil. So-called evil appears everywhere in his writings, although he refuses to stand in judgment or to insist upon the human bond of shared responsibility. His position seems to me to be tenable. Man's great problem is not the world's evils; it is the absence of relationships, or love. Man may think that he is troubled by the world's evils, but his greatest horror is of an emotional lack, of utter loneliness in an indifferent universe. For Whitman heaven or joy is relatedness, real or imaginary; hell or agony is its absence. And so Whitman dwells at length on the difficulties of becoming human through the establishment of what E. M. Forster calls "connections." Thus Whitman's poetic journeys lead from the self to relatedness to nature and man, at least on the verbal level. The qualification must be introduced, since, as close examination reveals, at the conclusion of a poem the protagonist frequently has achieved only sublimation through art or attributes too much to a future union, or relationship, with "unborn admirers." But, although his conclusions are evasive, he wrestles honestly and bravely with *"the greater drama going on within myself & every human being."*

The tensions in Whitman's poetry stem from the shifting moods of the narrator as fear and joy vie with each other, the one now dominant, then the other, until resolution, or reconciliation, is achieved. Despite the quiet mood of "There Was a Child Went Forth," these alternations are present: the joy in natural phenomena, the momentary fear of the staggering drunkard, the lonely glances at the children, the ambivalence toward "fatherstuff," the reverence for the mother and the fear of the father, and then the peace the child finds at the end of his journey. The phrase "the yearning and swelling heart" succinctly describes the shifts of mood. Perhaps even better is "the curious systole and diastole within." For Whitman's verse does not so much correspond to a symphony or to the waves of the sea, comparisons he and his interpreters are fond of, as to inner tensions, contractions in fear and release into joy and peace. The tensions closely approximate, as the eroticism in his poetry testifies, the sexual rhythm of desire, frustration, and release through consummation or sublimation.

This tension-and-release is brilliantly explained in Jean Delay's *The Youth of André Gide:*

> Like anguish, ecstasy is a purely affective state, hence an ineffable state. One is fear without any apparent object, the other joy without any apparent object. Both are states of panic — that is, total — but one is panic fear and the other panic joy; they resemble one another and are in opposition to one another. Both are spontaneous states of intoxication, "intoxication without wine." . . . But in anguish the suffocation is painful and accompanied by a constriction; whereas in ecstasy the constriction is replaced by voluptuous anhelation, an expansion of the whole being, an elation. Both, although felt *hic et nunc,* seem outside of space and time, which are abolished, and give the person possessed the impression of being transported outside himself (*ek-stasis*) or of being lifted up, carried away, overcome by an "inner sea" which submerges the consciousness.[6]

The difficulties in Whitman's poetry are like those in Shakespeare's sonnets: the consciousness of the poet is so wayward, so realistically unstable, that we as readers, with our understandable desire to place people in rigid (and inevitably falsifying) categories, are baffled. The human mind craves simplification, not complexity. Montaigne uses the analogy of a seesaw to characterize the flux of the contradictory personality and to describe his essays. In Whitman's day Melville was dissatisfied with the depiction of fictional characters and restlessly sought to find an adequate literary vehicle to express ambiguous and shifting emotional moods, particularly in the experimentation present in *Pierre* and *The Confidence-Man.* In our time D. H. Lawrence employed the term "the unstable ego" to designate the ego in a state of flux. Whitman is saying the same thing when he speaks of the "fluid" personality which changes from moment to moment but retains its identity. In this respect, too, Whitman's commentators, friendly and hostile, have overlooked the realistic core at the center of his writings.

Although it is difficult to take seriously Whitman's visions of democracy — their fatuous pastoralism is pathetically attractive to the socially maladjusted and almost tragically irrelevant in modern industrial civilization — "There Was a Child Went Forth" is a more moving and acute analysis of the problem of being an American than is de Tocqueville's. The Frenchman explains by means of intellectual distinctions which omit the all-important emotional components. Whitman, on the other hand, unfolds the universal terrain, which is neither aristocratic nor democratic, but simply and profoundly human. In hindsight he does not obliterate the fears and loneliness of the child, even though the womb imagery represents nostalgia for a most elementary form of security. The violation of the child augurs the violation of the American man. The inability to interact reflects the cultural situation evident as early as the family portraits of John Singleton Copley and as recently as Sherwood Anderson's *Winesburg, Ohio* or James Baldwin's *Another Country*. The absence of affection — emotional poverty — is the unacknowledged price paid by the affluent society. Whitman seeks a way out by a return to the primeval, the infantile source of life:

These became part of that child who went forth every day, and who
    now goes and will always go forth every day,
And these become of him or her that peruses them now.

3

"fathered him . . . and birthed him"

Is it wonderful that I should be immortal? as every one is immortal,
I know it is wonderful . . . . but my eyesight is equally wonderful . . . .
  and how I was conceived in my mother's womb is equally wonderful,
And how I was not palpable once but am now . . . . and was born on
  the last day of May 1819 . . . . and passed from a babe in the
  creeping trance of three summers and three winters to articulate
  and walk . . . . are all equally wonderful.

And that I grew six feet high . . . . and that I have become a man
  thirty-six years old in 1855 . . . . and that I am here anyhow —
  are all equally wonderful. . . .

The childlike qualities of these lines from "Who Learns My Lesson
Complete?" (1855) disarm the critic. For we do not expect the
mature man to dwell upon the wonders of birth and growth, subjects too trivial for profound reverie, although we pay close attention to those who dwell, even excessively, on the agonies of existence. Yet to insist upon man's evilness is as sentimental as to

41

overassert his innate goodness. Self-pity is no less egocentric than
self-love. A "waste land" is no less an intellectual and human
distortion than rosy-colored faith in progress. Both attitudes are
ideological stances marked by uncritical predispositions to see what
one wants to see.

Now in these lines Whitman insists, perhaps overinsists, that
life is "wonderful," but the repeated use of the word hints, at least
to our skeptical ears, that he is endeavoring to reassure himself of
his identity and his uniqueness. Further, as the next line of the
poem reveals, the isolated poet is even forced to rationalize his
separateness as "wonderful":

And that my soul embraces you this hour, and we affect each other
    without even seeing each other, and never perhaps to see each other,
    is every bit as wonderful. . . .

But our skeptical ears perhaps err in a fundamental respect.
Whitman has a childlike interest in life and revels in the simplest
of miracles as few people do, not because he is a simplifier of complexities and an evader of ambiguities, but because he retains in
maturity much of the child's overexcited interest in so-called trivi-
alities which are "wonderful" to the expanding consciousness of
youth. Yet at the same time there is a kind of fixation, to use our
ugly word, upon the primary events in his life, his birth and his
relationship to his mother and father.

In "There Was a Child Went Forth" the boy is troubled and
frightened by the ill-tempered acts of the father, and he identifies
himself with the gentle mother. In "Out of the Cradle Endlessly
Rocking" the situation at first sight appears to be reversed when the
child-poet identifies with the he-bird whose mate has suddenly and
mysteriously vanished. The boy listens to the bird voicing in song
his grief in the face of inexplicable finalities like that of death itself.
The bird is overwhelmed by uncomprehending despair. The child,
however, harkens to the cryptic murmuring of "the fierce old
mother," the sea. Like a mother soothing a baby at her breast, the
sea engulfs the future poet:

Hissing melodious, neither like the bird, nor like my aroused child's
    heart,
But edging near, as privately for me, rustling at my feet,
And creeping thence steadily up to my ears,
Death, Death, Death, Death, Death.

When the boy learns from the eternal mother that she rocks the cradle and the coffin, that from her womb issues life and to her womb all life returns, despair vanishes and he is healed.

The two climaxes in "The Sleepers," so far as Whitman allows the reader to penetrate the dreamlike screen, involve disguised oedipal conflicts — the familiar psychological trio, mother, father, and child. Identities and even sex are confused and the movements of the phantoms are unexpected and indefinite, because the poet is delving into the dangerous realm of incestuous attachments as he recreates the bewilderment and agony of the journey from childhood to manhood. Another (strange) trio appears in the frustrated lines of "From Pent-up Aching Rivers":

> the sight of the perfect body,
> The swimmer swimming naked in the bath, or motionless on his back lying and floating,
> The female form approaching — I, pensive, love-flesh tremulous, aching. . . .

The ambiguous syntax conceals and at the same time reveals that although the woman is apparently approaching the swimmer, she is also approaching the "I," who, although he seems to be observing from the shore, has identified with the male. The scene, then, may be a depiction of the anguish of chastity, "pent-up aching rivers," or a veiled oedipal fantasy. In either case, the male is the passive participant in the sexual act. This scene parallels one in "The Sleepers" in which the protagonist helplessly watches, from the shore, "a beautiful gigantic swimmer swimming naked through the eddies of the sea," and then sees "ruffianly red-trickled waves"

> bear him away . . . . they roll him and swing him and turn him:
> His beautiful body is borne in the circling eddies . . . . it is continually bruised on rocks,
> Swiftly and out of sight is borne the brave corpse.

Placed together — the situation and the image of the nude swimmer justify it — the eternal mother, the sea, is again seen in its twofold role of creator and destroyer. In the amniotic fluids a child is born, and to the waters the man is "borne."

In his poetry Whitman, then, frequently recreates the child's central and difficult relationship to his parents. Hence much of his imagery is regressive. The "indirections" he speaks of are in large part attributable not to his desire to be "modern," but to the personal, infantile material he deals with and must present obliquely. Perhaps, although the context is not entirely clear, the problem of the child's relationship is summed up in this line from "One Hour to Madness and Joy": "O the puzzle — the thrice-tied knot — the deep and dark pool! O all untied and illumined!"

But not always does he untie the "knot" and find illumination and catharsis. "Out of the Cradle Endlessly Rocking" depicts the emergence of "the outsetting bard of love," but in "As I Ebb'd with the Ocean of Life," composed about the same time, the poet-protagonist admits that he is "baffled, balked." His poems are "loose winrows, little corpses / Froth, snowy white, and bubbles." While the child-poet in "Out of the Cradle Endlessly Rocking," figuratively, becomes the assured "savage" in 'Song of Myself," an artist-overman who sounds his "barbaric yawp" over the world's rooftops, the poet in "As I Ebb'd with the Ocean of Life," like Eliot's Fisher King, is left with fragments which his "musing, late in the autumn day," cannot transcend.

We, capricious, brought hither, we know not whence, spread out
      before You, up there, walking or sitting,
Whoever you are — we too lie in drifts at your feet.

In the confessional lines of this poem Whitman not only admits defeat but also ridicules his own arrogant pretensions:

O baffled, balked,
Bent to the very earth, here preceding what follows,
Oppressed with myself that I have dared to open my mouth,
Aware now, that, amid all the blab whose echoes recoil upon me, I
      have not once had the least idea who or what I am,
But that before all my insolent poems the real ME still stands un-
      touched, untold, altogether unreached,
Withdrawn far, mocking me with mock-congratulatory signs and bows,
With peals of distant ironical laughter at every word I have written or
      shall write,
Striking me with insults till I fall helpless upon the sand,

O I perceive I have not understood anything — not a single object —
      and that no man ever can.

"Helpless upon the sand," overcome by feelings of insignificance, he unconsciously assumes the role of a helpless, wayward child who sees the parents from a childlike perspective as overpowering forces — "You oceans both!"

I perceive Nature here, in sight of the sea, is taking advantage of me,
    to dart upon me, and sting me,
Because I was assuming so much,
And because I have dared to open my mouth to sing at all.

Though it has been suggested by Schyberg that Whitman refers here to his father's contempt for his poetry and for idle poets, such a narrow biographical reading does not do justice to the rape imagery or to the fact that no one in the Whitman family, including the mother, ever demonstrated any intelligent sympathy for or interest in Walt's poetry. The poem centers not only in the explicit guilt the protagonist feels "because I have dared to open my mouth to sing at all," but also in the implicit guilt he feels because at least in his poetry, particularly in the overman he creates in "Song of Myself," he has dared to divorce himself from his family and to see himself as a colossus. In the poem the "I" asks for chastisement in order to assuage his guilt and, more important, in order to be forgiven. "Be not too rough with me," he begs like a child; and also like a child he asks for the caress that follows punishment: "I submit — I close with you." He accepts his insignificance, his infantile relationship:

I too am but a trail of drift and debris,
I too leave little wrecks upon you, you fish-shaped island.

The "fish-shaped island" becomes "my father," a stern parent whose love and protection the protagonist desperately seeks.

I throw myself upon your breast, my father,
I cling to you so that you cannot unloose me,
I hold you so firm, till you answer me something.

Kiss me, my father,
Touch me with your lips, as I touch those I love,
Breathe to me, while I hold you close, the secret of the wondrous
    murmuring I envy. . . .

The plea to the father-figure becomes almost a shriek in the lines which Whitman removed from the 1867 edition of *Leaves of Grass:*

For I fear I shall become crazed, if I cannot emulate it, and utter myself as well as it.

Sea-raff! Crook-tongued waves!
O, I will yet sing, some day, what you have said to me.

But, like most paternal figures in Whitman's poetry, the father is ineffectual; and, though fearful of the "Crook-tongued waves," the protagonist attempts to reestablish the security of the child-mother relationship:

Cease not your moaning, you fierce old mother,
Endlessly cry for your castaways — but fear not, deny not me,
Rustle not up so hoarse and angry against my feet, as I touch you, or gather from you.

Superficially, the despondency evident in "As I Ebb'd with the Ocean of Life" may be in part attributable to the fact that, except for Emerson's greeting "at the beginning of a great career," the first two editions of *Leaves of Grass* had not excited a great deal of attention. But the confession of failure in the poem stems from more fundamental and personal matters than the reception of his poetry, and the intensity of the lines points to deep-seated personal dissatisfaction. First, there is awareness that the poet-hero in "Song of Myself" and the cosmic harmony he affirms in many of his poems are unsatisfactory sublimations (or repressions) of the despair and isolation he endured from day to day. As he makes clear in "Calamus," art cannot completely fill the emotional void. Second, Whitman realized, despite the sentiments expressed in many poems and in *Democratic Vistas,* that his "insolent poems" further estranged him from his family and from the common people he most admired. Third, "As I Ebb'd with the Ocean of Life" confirms what is also evident in more affirmative poems: despite the repeatedly expressed desire to be the poetic spokesman of democracy, the "real I" is more passive than active, and the real subject matter is the restoration of infantile relationships. When the poet says to the "fierce old mother," the sea, "I mean tenderly by you," he presumably means, "Be tender with me, an insolent child."

For "As I Ebb'd with the Ocean of Life" is a kind of self-chastisement and fulfillment of the psychological cycle of guilt and punishment. To punish himself the arrogant national poet places himself again in his childhood, where he reexperiences long-familiar feelings of insignificance and inferiority. The island-father refuses to embrace and enlighten the child-poet, just as the rancor of Walter Whitman apparently chilled and infuriated his son. The sea-mother fails to "gather" her castaway to her breast, just as the egocentric indifference of Louisa Van Velsor Whitman repelled her son but made him hunger for affection. Out of these "fragments," reflected in one of Whitman's most forthright statements of his fluctuating moods and his continuing uncertainty:

Buoyed hither from many moods, one contradicting another,
From the storm, the long calm, the darkness, the swell,
Musing, pondering, a breath, a briny tear, a dab of liquid or soil,
Up just as much out of fathomless workings fermented and thrown,
A limp blossom or two, torn, just as much over waves floating, drifted
    at random . . . ,

he "gathers" the material for the diverse poems which make up his book. In acknowledging his feelings of inadequacy and lostness, Whitman may tarnish somewhat the portrait of the American bard he often imagines himself to be and may cast doubt upon the sainthood which his followers foolishly bestowed upon him, but neither the bard nor the saint is human. And what is admirable about Whitman is his humanity and his humility. The avowal of uncertainty is the courageous act of a man honest with himself. His acceptance of his aloneness makes the reader's loneliness easier to endure, for art is one of man's refuges against futility.

Almost every commentator has noted what Whitman himself makes abundantly clear in his personal letters and in his public statements — that he was the dutiful son of an adored mother. With few exceptions, critics have accepted Whitman's statements at face value, and Mrs. Whitman has become virtually the personification of American motherhood. Whitman's praise, however, should be examined for latent ambivalence, just as the silence about the father in his letters and his recollections should not lead one to conclude simplistically that Whitman found his male parent anathema. The treatment of parental figures in the poetry does not point to such easy conclusions.

It was alleged by the poet's friend John Burroughs that the father was an alcoholic, and some biographers have implied that he was responsible for the alcoholism of two of his sons, Jesse and Andrew Jackson. Though it is true that the two boys had this weakness, the Zolaesque pattern is not so important as the indeterminable answer to the question why they turned to drink in the first place. If the father escaped periodically into an alcoholic world, he apparently also escaped into another (perhaps similar) world of dreams of patriotism and power when he named Andrew Jackson, Thomas Jefferson, and George Washington Whitman. At any rate, Walter Whitman was not overly successful as a contractor, and, partly because of his failure but also because of her aggressive nature, Mrs. Whitman dominated the family. (That the father and two sons sought escape in the male society of taverns and that Walt ordinarily depicts passive males are consequences, I suspect, of the mother's emasculating rule of the family.)

If this reconstruction of life in the Whitman family is correct, one begins to comprehend the ambivalences present in Whitman's poetry. His silence about his father may indicate shame and grief: he was humiliated by his father's inability to assert himself and by his subordination to his wife; and he longed, as he makes clear in "Out of the Cradle Endlessly Rocking" and "As I Ebb'd with the Ocean of Life," for a meaningful male figure with whom to identify. Though the mother looms large in his poetry, Whitman was also searching for the lost father. It is a fact that Whitman left home at fourteen in order to make his own livelihood, but it is not a fact, as Schyberg supposes, that he left because of impossible relations with his father. It is more likely that, though he found the capricious behavior of an alcoholic father difficult, he found equally difficult the matriarchy which Mrs. Whitman had established in the household.

Though one must not attach too much significance to the banal stories which Whitman published in the 1840s,[1] one must not make the mistake of dismissing them because of their triteness and sentimentality. It is highly suggestive that similar situations recur in tale after tale in which a young boy, as in the later poems, is exposed to life's vicissitudes. In six stories, for example, a father or a substitute father brutally mistreats a youth. The child that goes forth in "Death in the School-Room," "The Child and the Profligate," and "The Last Loyalist" is a poor orphan, who is handed over to three tyrants, a schoolteacher, an employer, and an uncle, respectively. In "Bervance: or, Father and Son" the father prefers the older son and has the second-born placed in an institution; and the overpowering father in "Wild Frank's Return" favors the older son above Frank, who is the favorite of his mother and who is melodramatically strangled at the end of the tale. In "Reuben's Last Wish" Father Slade, a drunkard, strikes one son in an alcoholic rage and exposes another son, Reuben, an invalid, to the rain. Reuben dies holding out a temperance pledge to his father! A mother or surrogate is important in only one of these six tales.

Two of the six, it should be noted, center on the father's preference for the first-born son. Since Walt was the second-born, perhaps these are autobiographical references to Jesse's relationship with the father. Little is known about Jesse except that he was alcoholic and syphilitic and died, presumably of paresis, in an asylum in 1870. A few of Mrs. Whitman's letters written during the Civil War refer to his violent temper outbursts. It may be of some importance that Whitman apparently never referred to his brother's death. It is, however, even more significant that in "My Boys and Girls," a curious tale in which he refers to some of his brothers and sisters by name, Jesse is not mentioned. (It is not implausible that rivalry with Jesse contributed to Whitman's early departure from home.) More noteworthy still is the fact that in "My Boys and Girls" Whitman's parents do not appear at all, and that the opening sentence reads: "Though a bachelor, I have several girls and boys that I consider my own" — a sentiment, expressed when he was twenty-five, that curiously anticipates his later life.

Undoubtedly the most poignant aspect of these early stories is the fact that the youthful protagonists receive real affection in only two stories, and then not from parental figures. In "The Child and the Profligate" the lad finds respite from the taskmaster's cruelty in his friendship with a beautiful young man, and "The Madman," an unfinished tale, presents a sudden and intense friendship between Richard Arden and Pierre Barcoure. In other words, almost twenty years before the appearance of the "Calamus" poems and the enunciation of "adhesiveness," Whitman's life experience permitted the depiction of successful affectional relationships only in terms of male friendship.

These early tales, despite their similarities to popular literature of the era, are significant since Whitman, consciously or unconsciously, chose to present in them almost without exception a young man in a loveless environment where his only expectations are physical violence and the release of early death. No mother appears to shelter the child from the father's ire. Of course the mother is usually dead, since we are discussing orphans, or she is associated with death, as in "Bervance: or, Father and Son," in which the penitent father at last waits for "that repose in the bosom of our great common mother" — another anticipation of a major poetic theme. It is an inescapable conclusion, I think, that only a man from a similar environment, who saw himself as an orphan, could be so repetitively attracted to such subject matter — to the extent even of conceiving himself as the father-mother of his brothers and sisters.

The father is dealt with more indirectly and less melodramatically in the poetry than in the prose. For with the exception of "There Was a Child Went Forth" and the oedipal rivalry in "The Sleepers," the child-poet is not confronted with terrifying father-figures. One interlude in "The Sleepers" deals with the father of the country, George Washington, whom Whitman had extolled in 1842 in "The Last of the Sacred Army." In "The Sleepers" the benign Washington sheds "weeping drops" during a battle at Brooklyn as "He sees the slaughter of the southern braves confided to him by their parents." Just as in "Out of the Cradle Endlessly Rocking" the abandoned he-bird is powerless except to sing his dirge of despair while the "fierce" sea hisses an answer to life's riddle, so in "The Sleepers" the powerlessness of the great general is contrasted with the murderous power of the sea, which in the two preceding scenes has destroyed a middle-aged swimmer and a ship. At the conclusion of "The Sleepers," after the protagonist has emerged from his journey into the "heart of darkness" and discovered "A show of the summer softness," the pervading aura of harmony is furthered by the following description, or wish fulfillment: "The father holds his grown or ungrown son in his arms with measureless love . . . . and the son holds the father in his arms with measureless love." The depiction of the mother in the next line is almost emotionless: "The white hair of the mother shines on the white wrist of the daughter."

Another august father appears in "I Sing the Body Electric," the only particularized portrait in a poem which is for the most part a catalogue of American types:

This man was a wonderful vigor and calmness and beauty of person;
The shape of his head, the richness and breadth of his manners, the
    pale yellow and white of his hair and beard, the immeasurable mean-
    ing of his black eyes. . . .

After dwelling upon the respect the elderly man receives from his children and his grandchildren, Whitman writes, almost plaintively: "You would wish long and long to be with him . . . . you would wish to sit by him in the boat that you and he might touch each other." The longing for tactile contact (one of the most recurrent desires in Whitman's poetry) is an unconscious longing for the symbolic laying on of hands, the ritual that will permit the child to sever the dependency of youth and to enter into man's estate. In the poem the ritual is almost reenacted when in succeeding sections the protagonist achieves a kind of amorous contact and consummation in the description of the bridegroom's sexual mastery over the "divine nimbus" of "the female form":

Ebb stung by the flow, and flow stung by the ebb . . . . loveflesh
    swelling and deliciously aching,
Limitless limpid jets of love hot and enormous . . . . quivering jelly
    of love . . . . white-blow and delirious juice,
Bridegroom-night of love working surely and softly into the prostrate
    dawn,
Undulating into the willing and yielding day,
Lost in the cleave of the clasping and sweetfleshed day.

But it must be noted that Whitman presents sexual union in allegorical rather than in personal terms, between "Bridegroom-night" and "sweetfleshed day."

The most thoroughly developed fatherly figure in Whitman's poetry is the overman in "Song of Myself." With the advent of the "friendly and flowing savage" in Section 39, the vacillations and uncertainties of the protagonist disappear, and the poem moves triumphantly to its conclusion. The savage, primeval man, released from the encrustings of "civilization and its discontents," walks sensuously among sensuous men and women.

Wherever he goes men and women accept and desire him,
They desire he should like them and touch them and speak to them and stay with them.
Behaviour lawless as snow flakes . . . . words simple as grass . . . .
uncombed head and laughter and naivete;
Slowstepping feet and the common features, and the common modes and emanations,
They descend in new forms from the tips of his fingers,
They are wafted with the odor of his body or breath . . . . they fly out of the glance of his eyes.

In this role the "I" is the beloved "teacher" of all men, more ardently admired than the grandfather in "I Sing the Body Electric."

My lovers suffocate me!
Crowding my lips, and thick in the pores of my skin,
Jostling me through streets and public halls . . . . coming naked to me at night,
Crying by day Ahoy from the rocks of the river . . . . swinging and chirping over my head,
Calling my name from flowerbeds or vines or tangled underbrush,
Or while I swim in the bath . . . . or drink from the pump at the corner . . . . or the curtain is down at the opera . . . . or I glimpse at a woman's face in the railroad car;
Lighting on every moment of my life,
Bussing my body with soft and balsamic busses,
Noiselessly passing handfuls out of their hearts and giving them to be mine.

Like a man-god (or a grandfather) he declaims:

Come my children,
Come my boys and girls, and my women and household and intimates,
Now the performer launches his nerve . . . . he has passed his prelude on the reeds within.

But the "performer" enacts his role of august paternity by abbreviating the "prelude" and by concealing his evasions in lovely bombast and intense eroticism. For the overman has come to manhood without crossing the "bridge" of sexual maturity. The savage is more often the passive receiver than the giver, the beloved rather than the lover. He is a child receiving affection — "Bussing my body with soft and balsamic busses." The deeds he performs and the adulation he enjoys are the long-suppressed daydreams of an unhappy youth who envisages himself as a hero in order to gain attention and to alleviate his feelings of impotency. In short, the poet in maturity supplies the affectional needs of the emotionally frustrated child. In strange ways is the child father to the poet.

During the Civil War years Whitman found in life an outlet for the imaginings expressed in his poems. (In "A Song of Joys," where he fancies himself the impregnator of democracy, he takes a fatherly delight in "my brood of tough boys.") Now paternal in appearance, prematurely gray and heavily bearded, he became the loving father to the wounded soldiers from all the states. When they wrote to him in their illiterate and youthful scrawls, they addressed him as "father" or "comrade." Both titles were correct since Whitman played two roles. On the one hand the forty-year-old man resembled the idealized image of a father as he walked through the crude and unhygienic wards of army hospitals, sat by the bedsides of lads in pain, or comforted the dying. On the other hand his indulgence in horseplay and puerile chatter with the boys was an attempt to make himself one of them. So too was the invitation extended in letters to boys who had returned to their homes to come and live in Washington with him and some of the other ex-soldiers. Yet in the hospitals Whitman himself was both the giver and the receiver of his affections: he was both Walter Whitman and Walt Whitman, father and son in the kind of warm relationship he had always longed for.

Undoubtedly the same confusion existed in the seven-year friendship with the young Confederate veteran Peter Doyle, a relationship which began in 1866 when the poet casually laid his hand on the knee of the previously unknown motorman. As their letters reveal, Whitman at times was a "pal" to a boy often bewildered about himself and life. Like a parent, Whitman took pleasure in ordering clothes for Pete, clothes identical with his own attire, and when the young man was ill and depressed, even voicing suicidal tendencies, Whitman was ready to establish a household for him — in Baltimore, not in Washington where the Doyle family lived. Later, in his involvement with Harry Stafford, the eighteen-year-old son of poor New Jersey farmers, Whitman, then almost sixty and a semiparalytic, paternally directed the activities of the boy, instructing him in composition and finding jobs for him. Like a father with a child, the poet at times had the young man sit on his lap, but, as Burroughs' diary and Harry's letters reveal, Whitman also romped with Harry like an adolescent. On a trip to New York Whitman passed him off as "a nephew" and insisted that they share the same bedroom. When the poet gave the young man a ring, symbolically there was a marriage which is best described in a line from "Whoever You Are Holding Me Now in Hand": "I am the new husband, and I am the comrade."[2]

This confusion of roles is never completely resolved in his poems, even in his projection of himself in the role of the democratic bard or of the prophetic leader. In the preface to the 1855 edition of *Leaves of Grass*, in the poems called "Chants Democratic" in the 1860 edition, and in *Democratic Vistas*, he outlines the role of the poet, the imperturbable sage who is the Whitmanesque equivalent of Emerson's poet. Particularly in "By Blue Ontario's Shore" (1860 version) the poet becomes a man-god.

Of mankind, the poet is the equable man,
Not in him, but off from him, things are grotesque, eccentric, fail of
    their full returns,
Nothing out of its place is good, nothing in its place is bad,
He bestows on every object or quality its fit proportions, neither more
    nor less,
He is the arbiter of the diverse, he is the key,
He is the equalizer of his age and land,
He supplies what wants supplying — he checks what wants checking,
In peace, out of him speaks the spirit of peace, large, rich, thrifty,
    building populous towns, encouraging agriculture, arts, commerce,
    lighting the study of man, the Soul, health, immortality, govern-
    ment,
In war, he is the best backer of the war — he fetches artillery as good
    as the engineer's — he can make every word he speaks draw blood;
The years straying toward infidelity, he withholds by his steady faith,
He is no arguer, he is judgment,
He judges not as the judge judges, but as the sun falling round a help-
    less thing;
As he sees the farthest he has the most faith,
His thoughts are the hymns of the praise of things,
In the dispute on God and eternity he is silent,

He sees eternity less like a play with a prologue and denouement,
He sees eternity in men and women — he does not see men and women
    as dreams or dots.

This father-poet, like the protagonist in "There Was a Child Went
Forth," passes beyond human foibles, troubling emotions, and difficult personal relationships — to a stasis in a womblike Eden. The
search for the father, or the identity crisis, culminates in a retreat
to the eternal mother — which, as we have seen, is the basic movement in much of Whitman's poetry.

That Whitman was deeply attached to his mother is a commonplace. In the preface to the 1876 editions of *Leaves of Grass* and
Two Rivulets he speaks of "my dear Mother, the most perfect and
magnetic character, the rarest combination of practical, moral and
spiritual, and the least selfish, of all and any I have ever known —
and by me O so much the most deeply loved." In *Specimen Days*
he describes her death as "the saddest loss and sorrow of my life."
Yet his picture of the loving and lovable mother is not corroborated
by the nagging querulousness present in the hundreds of extant
letters Mrs. Whitman wrote to her children, which are filled with
self-pity and hostility toward anything that disrupted her way of
life. She opposed the marriage of her son George, then about forty
years old, because she was living with him at the time and did not
wish to be supplanted by a daughter-in-law. To be sure, she doted
upon Walt, but he had the good sense not to marry.

Without any intention of impugning Whitman's sincerity, since
he unquestionably considered his encomia sincere, it must be said
that his portrait of his mother appears to be as much a wish as a
reality. Mrs. Whitman's letters make somewhat suspect Walt's
excessive praise. But in hundreds of letters to members of his
family, not once is he critical of her obvious self-centeredness and
willfulness. His letters to her, particularly during the Civil War,
are models of sensitivity and tenderness.[3] Yet his ambivalence
(never verbalized so far as I can discover) is evident in his failure
during the years when he was a government employee to act upon
her repeated suggestions that she come to Washington and establish a home for him, though he was ready to have Peter Doyle and
various soldiers move in with him. It is also significant that the
mother-figures in two of his most autobiographical poems, "Out of
the Cradle Endlessly Rocking" and "As I Ebb'd with the Ocean of

Life," are "fierce" women who, miraculously, become tender when
the child's bond with the mother is restored.

That the relationship between Whitman and his mother was
abnormal is confirmed by at least two additional facts. For years
after her death he slept on her pillow, a grief reaction which, with
its unresolved oedipal undertones, does not testify to a healthy
relationship. Second, it is unusual (and of course significant)
that mothers, but not women, dominate his poetry, and that
maternal love receives more extensive treatment than heterosexual
love. (That, in Peter Doyle's words, he never got "bothered up by
a woman"[4] reveals psychic arrestment, particularly for the self-
styled "outsetting bard of love.")

Although some commentators emphasize the "athletic" or
"manly" qualities of Whitman's poetry, generally regarding the
"Calamus" poems as a statement of ideal friendship, not as a
poignant account of sexual confusion and frustrations, Burroughs,
who was usually hampered in his criticism by his intense attachment to Whitman as a person, once observed very acutely: "He
was not an athlete, or a rough, but a great tender mother-man, to
whom the martial spirit was utterly foreign."[5] As one should
expect, Whitman himself puts it very well in "Song of Myself":
"Maternal as well as paternal, a child as well as a man." Or in a
later poem:

Me imperturbe,
Me standing at ease in Nature,
Master of all, or mistress of all — aplomb in the midst of irrational
        things. . . .

And perhaps Whitman's offhand remark in a letter to a friend has
implications beyond those of which he was conscious at the
moment of writing: "I think sometimes to be a woman is greater
than to be a man."[6] Equally revealing, I believe, despite its face-
tiousness, is his well-known comment to Edward Carpenter:
"There is something in my nature *furtive* like an old hen! You see
a hen wandering up and down a hedgerow, looking apparently
quite unconcerned, but presently she finds a concealed spot, and
furtively lays an egg, and comes away as though nothing had
happened! That is how I felt in writing 'Leaves of Grass.' "[7] For
he, unconsciously, assumes in his writing a feminine more often
than a masculine role, even his vision of a race of democratic com-

rades a century hence being more a maternal than a paternal wish.

As Kenneth Burke points out in an astute article, Whitman frequently depicts the mother in images that well out of the unconscious and recall a child's genital confusion, as in these lines in "By Blue Ontario's Shore" (revised version):

(Mother! with subtle sense severe, with the naked sword in your hand,
I saw you at last refuse to treat but directly with individuals.)

The opening lines of "Song of the Broad-Axe" —

Broad-axe, shapely, naked, wan!
Head from the mother's bowels drawn!
Wooded flesh and metal bone! limb only one and lip only one!
Gray-blue leaf by red-heat grown! helve produced from a little seed
    sown! —

are haunting because they revive the child's wonder about the birth process and his confused equation of all objects with the phallus. Similarly, not unlike the fifth section of "Song of Myself," the extraordinary imagery in "Pioneers! O Pioneers!", which appeared for the first time in *Drum-Taps* (1865), rests upon the confused association of the breast and the phallus:

    Raise the mighty mother mistress.
Waving high the delicate mistress, over all the starry mistress, (bend
    your heads all,)
Raise the fang'd and warlike mistress, stern, impassive, weapon'd mis-
    tress,
          Pioneers! O pioneers!

And in "Delicate Cluster" (1871), a poem resembling the "Cala-mus" chants in its latent genital imagery but never included in that series, the flag is "my matron mighty! / My sacred one, my mother." Coincidentally, Henry Fleming in *The Red Badge of Courage* plays out an oedipal drama not unlike those depicted by Whitman: this formerly fearful young man has the illusion of security when he becomes the standard-bearer of the regiment with a flag which "was a goddess, radiant, that bended its form with an imperious gesture to him. It was a woman, red and white, hating and loving, that called him with the voice of his hopes" (Chap. XIX).[8]

Although Whitman occasionally, and sometimes comically, describes the poet as an impregnator of the hearts of men, perhaps even more frequently he associates the poet with the womb. In "Salut Au Monde!" he writes: "What widens within you, Walt Whitman?" and in "Ages and Ages Returning at Intervals": "bathing my songs in sex, / Offspring of my loins." In "A Broadway Pageant" (1865) he aptly mentions "The nest of languages," and in some trial lines, presumably composed before 1855, he writes:

Afar in the sky was a nest,
And my soul flew thither and squat[ted], and looked out
And saw the journeywork of suns and systems of suns,
And that a leaf of grass is not less than they. . . .[9]

The wonderful rhythm of the following lines was to be further developed in "Out of the Cradle Endlessly Rocking" and "As I Ebb'd with the Ocean of Life":

Unfolded out of the folds of the woman, man comes unfolded, [and] is always to come unfolded,
. . . .
Unfolded only out of the inimitable poem of the woman, can come the poems of man — only thence have my poems come,
Unfolded out of the strong and arrogant woman I love, only thence can appear the strong and arrogant man I love. . . .

Even in the description of male friendship in the "Calamus" poems, womb imagery is intermingled with the basic phallicism. In the first poem, "In Paths Untrodden," Whitman speaks of "this delicious Ninth Month, in my forty-first year," a reference not, as one commentator suggests, to a love affair in September 1859 (which was not the ninth month of his forty-first year), but to the "birth" of a series of poems describing his attraction to his own sex. The fantastic, almost surrealistic imagery of "Scented Herbage of My Breast" is surely a displaced womb analogy:

Scented herbage of my breast,
Leaves from you I yield, I write, to be perused best afterwards,

Tomb-leaves, body-leaves, growing up above me, above death,
Perennial roots, tall leaves. . . .

As the poem progresses, womb, heart (or breast), and phallus are
bewilderingly confused:

> Grow up out of my breast!
> Spring away from the concealed heart there!
> Do not fold yourselves so in your pink-tinged roots, timid leaves!
> Do not remain down there so ashamed, herbage of my breast!

Later in the series, in "Roots and Leaves Themselves Alone," he
mentions the calamus plant (his basic phallic image) and other
flowers of March, which he characterizes as "Love-buds" — "Buds
to be unfolded on the old terms." The last line, omitted in the
1867 revision, reads: "They have come slowly up out of the earth
and me, and are to come slowly up out of you."

Included in *Drum-Taps* is a two-line poem entitled "Mother and
Babe" —

I see the sleeping babe, nestling the breast of its mother;
The sleeping mother and babe — hush'd, I study them long and
    long —

which at first sight seems unrelated to the war poems in the
volume, until one recalls Whitman's deep attachment to helpless
wounded veterans whom he nursed as the mother nurses the
"babe," even to the farewell kiss of which Whitman made too
much. To the poet the maternal breast is a source of fertility and,
perhaps more important, the child's first contact with the external
world. So that the journey "toward the house of maternity" is
regression to the security of the mother's bosom. "I loosen myself
and pass freely," he writes in "I Sing the Body Electric," "and am
at the mother's breast with the little child." In "On the Beach at
Night Alone," alone with "the old mother [who] sways to and fro,
singing her savage and husky song," he declares:

I am not uneasy but I am to be beloved by young and old men, and to
    love them the same,
I suppose the pink nipples of the breasts of women with whom I shall
    sleep will touch the side of my face the same,

But this is the nipple of a breast of my mother, always near and
  always divine to me, her true child and son, whatever comes.

In these revealing lines (deleted in the extensive expurgations of
1867) the poet cannot conceive of love or of physical contact
except in the earliest associations of the child at the mother's
breast. Whitman also excised the third line of "Out of the Cradle
Endlessly Rocking," "Out of the boy's mother's womb, and from
the nipples of her breast," and this line from "By Blue Ontario's
Shore," "Have you sucked the nipples of the breasts of the mother
of many children?"

In the "Calamus" poem "Whoever You Are Holding Me Now
in Hand," the title itself and these lines are descriptive of an infantile relationship:

        Let go your hand from my shoulders,
Put me down, and depart on your way.

Later in the same poem he says of himself, "I am the new husband,
and I am the comrade." In the passage immediately following,
Whitman returns to the mother-child relationship:

Or, if you will, thrusting me beneath your clothing,
Where I may feel the throbs of your heart, or rest upon your hip,
Carry me when you go forth over land or sea;
For thus, merely touching you, is enough — is best,
And thus, touching you, would I silently sleep and be carried eternally.

Except for the brief moment when the poet sees himself as the
"husband," the young man is the mother-comrade to an older man
who in turn remains a dependent child.

And what is Whitman imagining in his first version of "So
Long!" (1860) other than an enduring mother-child relationship
between his poetry (and therefore himself) and his readers?

Lift me close to your face till I whisper,
What you are holding is in reality no book, nor part of a book,
It is a man, flushed and full-blooded — it is I — *So long!*
We must separate — Here! take from my lips this kiss,
Whoever you are, I give it especially to you;
So long — and I hope we shall meet again.

He might have substituted the previously quoted line from "Who-ever You Are Holding Me Now in Hand": "And thus, touching you, would I silently sleep and be carried eternally."

The oral imagery in Whitman's poetry, like that in Melville's prose, has rarely been examined, yet it is unmistakably part of his preoccupation with the breast. The orality of the union of the body and soul in the fifth section of "Song of Myself" is reminiscent of the child and the mother. The sea in "As I Ebb'd with the Ocean of Life" has "Crook-tongued waves!" and in "This Compost" he asks the sea "to lick my naked body all over with its tongues." He writes in "Starting from Paumanok" of "My tongue . . . formed from this soil," and in "Salut Au Monde!" (1856) he describes the orator "that turns states by the tip of his tongue." Of poets it is said in "Chants Democratic" in the 1860 edition of *Leaves of Grass,* "Strong and sweet shall their tongues be"; they are char-acterized as "full-lung'd and limber hipp'd," possessed of "a loosened throat"; and they sing "American mouth-songs!" In "Song of Prudence" Whitman refers to "the divinity of his [the poet's] mouth," and to the "Soul of love and tongue of fire" in "By Blue Ontario's Shore" (revised version), in which he also asks: "Will it absorb into me as I absorb food, air . . . ?"

Sexuality is often described in terms of feeding. His genitals, in an excised passage in "A Song of Joys," are "love-root! love-apples!" In "A Woman Waits for Me," "the man . . . avows the deliciousness of his sex," and insemination bears "fruits of the gushing showers" when "for loving crops from the birth . . . I plant." Sexual frustration is "the hungry gnaw that eats me night and day" in "From Pent-up Aching Rivers," and "That greed that eats me day and night with hungry gnaw" in "Spontaneous Me." The madness of (imagined) sexual delight is described in similar images: "O to drink the mystic deliria" and "To feed the remainder of life with one hour of fulness and freedom!" in "One Hour to Madness and Joy." Comradeship, as is to be expected, is revealed in the same oral terms, whether in "Scented Herbage of My Breast" or in "In Paths Untrodden":

> the Soul of the man I speak for, feeds, rejoices only in comrades;
> Here, by myself, away from the clank of the world,
> Tallying and talked to here by tongues aromatic. . . .

In "When I Heard at the Close of the Day":

my dear friend, my lover, was on his way coming, . . .
O then each breath tasted sweeter — and all that day my food nourished me more. . . .

And when, after dwelling upon personal anguish, he changes "the
strain" to sing of the joys of comradeship in "Roots and Leaves
Themselves Alone," he begins: "Calamus taste."

Though rarely observed, the regressive nature of Whitman's
imagery is clear. His protagonists are ingesting experiences —
"absorbing" is one of his favorite words — in a manner suggestive
of the child at the mother's breast. One need only translate his
imagery into pictorial equivalents to perceive the point, as in this
line from "Vocalism": "After a loosened throat — after absorbing
eras, temperaments, races." His imagery, of course, is consistent
with the evocation of the polymorphously perverse landscape that
is an integral part of his "faint clews & indirections." Under these
circumstances it is scarcely surprising that the poetic "I" is basically
passive, acted upon rather than acting, in his quest to remain
"aplomb in the midst of irrational things" ("Me Imperturbe").

The poetic "I" as the passive recipient of experience remains
constant in the poems even though after the Civil War Whitman
gives more emphasis to the renewed union of the states than to the
trials of the self, and in his early and later poems the return to the
protective shelter of the mother is the goal of the protagonists. In
"Faces" (1855) the "I" examines with terror the faces of those
who have willfully destroyed themselves. Then he witnesses (and
absorbs) a strange sexual encounter:

This is a fullgrown lily's face,
She speaks to the limber-hip'd man near the garden pickets,
Come here, she blushingly cries . . . Come nigh to me limber-hip'd
    man and give me your finger and thumb,
Stand at my side till I lean as high as I can upon you,
Fill me with albescent honey . . . . bend down to me,
Rub to me with your chafing beard . . rub to my breast and shoulders.

Such is the irony of the unconscious that the passive male has this
experience "near the garden pickets," that the woman would
"blushingly" be the aggressor, and that in the last line she would
become a mother with a bearded child. The "I" after this encounter is still restless, perhaps because of the threat to his sexual

adequacy, but when he encounters the "old face of the mother of many children," he exclaims: "Whist! I am fully content." Now sheltered by a matriarchal deity in American homespun, with her "quaker cap," he rediscovers

The melodious character of the earth!
The finish beyond which philosophy cannot go and does not wish to go!
The justified mother of men!

In a later poem, "The Return of the Heroes" (1867), emotional "content" is achieved, without struggle, in the opening stanza:

For the lands and for these passionate days and for myself,
Now I awhile retire to thee O soil of autumn fields,
Reclining on thy breast, giving myself to thee,
Answering the pulses of thy sane and equable heart,
Tuning a verse for thee.

"By Blue Ontario's Shore" (1856), which versifies many of Whitman's views of American poetry expressed in the preface to the first edition, was drastically altered in 1867. In the revision the democratic poet is directly associated with the fate of the United States in the postwar years, "As I mused of these warlike days and of peace return'd, and the dead that return no more." In the second section, in 1867, he introduces a new unifying thread in the first of a series of parenthetical passages — asides, as it were, which give the poem topical and social relevancy:

(O Mother — O Sisters dear!
If we are lost, no victor else has destroy'd us,
It is by ourselves we go down to eternal night.)

In Section 14 he describes the maternal aspects of his work as a hospital nurse:

(Upon this breast has many a dying soldier lean'd to breathe his last,
This arm, this hand, this voice, have nourish'd, rais'd, restored,
To life recalling many a prostrate form;)
. . . .
(Say O Mother, have I not to your thought been faithful?
Have I not through life kept you and yours before me?)

This is followed in the next section by that extraordinary bisexual image previously cited, "Mother! . . . with the naked sword in your hand," in which the "fierce" power ordinarily associated with the male warrior is transposed to the maternal figure. For a moment the poet voices confidence in his prowess (Section 17):

I will not be outfaced by irrational things,
I will penetrate what it is in them that is sarcastic upon me,
I will make cities and civilizations defer to me,

. . . .

(Democracy, while weapons were everywhere aim'd at your breast,
I saw you serenely give birth to immortal children, saw in dreams your
      dilating form,
Saw you with speading mantle covering the world.)

But in the next section his courage falters before "you terrible, rude forms," and he implores the security of the protecting mother:

(Mother, bend down, bend close to me your face,
I know not what these plots and wars and deferments are for,
I know not fruition's success, but I know that through war and crime
      your work goes on, and must yet go on.)

Only then, such are the logic and consistency of his imagery — which surely are traceable to Whitman's own psychic needs — is he prepared to equate the fertility of his verse with the fertility of motherland — and, more important, motherhood.

I thrill'd with the power's pulsations, and the charm of my theme was
      upon me,
Till the tissues that held me parted their ties upon me.

The poet is woman.

Like many men in his time, when everyone, it sometimes seemed, including even Emerson, talked (too much) of manliness, Whitman searched vaguely to reestablish meaningful affectional relationships in an age which was beginning to worship the (male) monster, the dynamo. The new synthesis, which Whitman never succeeded in elaborating successfully, although he was fond of imagining America a hundred years hence, was, of course, an ancient social and political organism, a matriarchy. As a thinker Whitman is too fragmentary and too amorphous to convince any except those already convinced, but his awareness of a deep conflict in democracy, deeper than that which led to the war, is acute, even if his solution is too simplistic perhaps to be acceptable.

Whitman's meditation upon the lives of "desperate men" is little different from Hawthorne's, if we may assume that Hester Prynne reflects her creator's carefully qualified hope that the future is woman:

She assured them [the women of the community], too, of her firm belief, that, at some brighter period, when the world should have grown ripe for it, in Heaven's own time, a new truth would be revealed, in order to establish the whole relation between man and woman on a surer ground of mutual happiness. Earlier in life, Hester had vainly imagined that she herself might be the destined prophetess, but had long since recognized the impossibility that any mission of divine and mysterious truth should be confided to a woman stained with sin, bowed down with shame, or even burdened with a life-long sorrow. The angel and apostle of the coming revelation must be a woman, indeed, but lofty, pure, and beautiful; and wise, moreover, not through dusky grief, but the ethereal medium of joy; and showing how sacred love should make us happy, by the truest test of a life successful to such an end! (Chap. xxiv)

And Hawthorne leads to Henry James, whose Alice Staverton is the "staff" upon which man must lean, as Arthur Dimmesdale leans upon Hester in mounting the scaffold. And Henry Adams expresses the Whitmanesque vision in his historical re-creation, which is one of the most splendid imaginative achievements in our literature, when he lovingly (and unhistorically) depicts the "boudoir" of the Virgin.

In *The Guardians of Tradition* Ruth Miller Elson quotes from a schoolbook published in 1872: "Mother, Home, and Heaven . . . are three of the most beautiful words in the English language."[10] Serious writers were but expressing the same thought, perhaps without such obvious sentimentality. As Whitman puts it in "For You O Democracy" —

O mother! have you done much for me?
Behold, there shall from me be much done for you.

4

"The doubts of daytime and . . . nighttime"

In "There Was a Child Went Forth" Whitman recaptures, in the appropriate diction of a simple, questing child, youth's eternal uncertainty about the nature and meaning of reality:

> The sense of what is real . . . . the thought if after all it should prove unreal,
> The doubts of daytime and the doubts of nighttime . . . the curious whether and how,
> Whether that which appears so is so . . . . Or is it all flashes and specks?

The youth in the poem grapples with the universe lying beyond his own narcissism and resolves the eternal questions much too easily perhaps, since he discovers his "sense of what is real" without the paralyzing "doubts of daytime and . . . nighttime."

Although the journey to self-awareness, and therefore to reality, has a long literary history, the past furnished Whitman with no usable models, just as Greek tragedy and Aristotelian theories contributed little to Shakespeare's drama. As he makes clear in the preface to the 1855 edition of *Leaves of Grass,* Whitman wanted to present a modern personality in nineteenth-century America. He knew that this personality could not be rendered in an academic imitation of another time, another place. Like Columbus, with whom he was to identify himself in a poem written in the 1870s, Whitman had to find a new route, a style and form appropriate to his vision. He refused to doff his hat — just as his *"vale"* became the idiomatic "so long" — to ancient and foreign precedents, although few of his contemporaries had his "nerve," or, for that matter, his faith. Whitman accepted the challenge of a new land and a new man with a nonchalance that often irritated his critics and with an originality for which he is given inadequate credit.

Unlike most of our nineteenth-century writers (Cooper, Hawthorne, and James, for example), he wasted no time in lamentations over the absence of classes and traditions, universally accepted absolutes, or an intellectual elite. Without blather or self-pity he accepted certain facts as self-evident. He lived in a universe of flux, not in the orderly Ptolemaic world of Dante or, for that matter, in the schematic universe of the Puritan divine. American democracy and capitalism were rapidly completing the task of toppling the closed walls of the feudalistic social order. Hence Shakespeare's world, which Whitman constantly labeled feudalistic, was not his, or the modern, world, although he did not lack appreciation of Shakespeare's humane genius. The United States was peopled with heterogeneous people who mixed reluctant respect for authority with Machiavellian schemes for self-aggrandizement, who too frequently took the law into their own hands while they in effect legislated an absolute conformity, and who were united not so much by their faith in democratic principles, which they rarely hesitated to brush aside when these conflicted with their own interests, as by their faith in energy — the human and mechanical dynamo. America was a new kind of garden of engines, embryonic assembly-line techniques, and ingenious gadgetry of fertile imaginations — in which Milton's sonorous line was an anachronism. "Made in America" was not an idle boast of an industrious people, for the United States was shortly not only to abandon its agrarian past (and then to hunger for it) but also to

lead the world into an age of technocracy which terrified not only
Henry Adams but others before him, Whitman, it must be confessed, included.

When Whitman struck his first chords in 1855, American art
and architecture for the most part singularly failed to express the
American reality, partly because popular culture and the popular
imagination cling obstinately to artistic stereotypes. Banks were
cloaked with almost comic neoclassical façades to conceal their
materialistic function, just as today their aseptic interiors testify
to a lingering (unstated) belief that there is something dirty about
money. American colleges, almost unbelievably confused as to
their function in a utilitarian society according to Henry Adams,
covered their confusion with neo-Gothic arches. Railroad engines,
the perfect symbols of the extraordinary energy of Americans,
pulled into stations that were masterpieces of architectural irrel-
evancy. The capitol of an aggressive, disorderly nation revealed
the ungratified hunger for an order and symmetry that America's
undirected energy made a mockery of.

Some of Whitman's literary contemporaries were struggling to
express the new continent, but not so successfully as he. Cooper
looked back to an older order and craved eighteenth-century
decorum and rationality in place of the turbulent nineteenth-century disorder, represented best perhaps by the Bushes in *The
Prairie*. (After all, Natty Bumppo, Cooper's supreme creation,
is a "sensible" man from another century lost in a new society
which he troubles little to understand.) Hawthorne, although he
was one of our most perceptive psychologists, chose for his purposes the chiaroscuro of romance, and in its ambiguous shadows
shielded himself from the raucous modern world. Melville, for
all his genius, struggled to achieve a style as well as an audience,
and, more important, wrestled endlessly with his Bartleby-like
alienation from American society, for Melville's quarrel was not
only with God but with life itself. Only Whitman flourished
amid the dissonances of democracy and the excitements produced
by the wonders of a technological civilization. Perhaps Whitman
alone could revel in the power of the locomotive without conjuring
up a "celestial railroad" or becoming Dantesque about "the Tar-
tarus of maids." That the materials of American life were coarse
and rude did not shock his sensibilities — in fact, he delighted in
the "rowdy" aspects of the contemporary scene — for he refused

to measure the present in terms of a past that had served its purpose but was now dead: for Whitman, as for most of the American people, there was only tomorrow, and tomorrow was promises. And, finally, Whitman's vision and views, until he became "the good gray poet," were not predicated upon established value judgments, moral or social. Like Nietzsche, Whitman goes beyond good and evil as popularly defined and beyond tragedy, without the doubts and uncertainties that plagued Hawthorne and Melville.

Under these circumstances and in a "strange new world" — as Emerson observes, "America is formless, has no terrible and no beautiful condensation"[1] — Whitman's poetry could not be shaped into the architectonic splendors of *The Divine Comedy*. Dante's "star," however refulgent in its era and its universe, no longer shone, except as an artistic monument, in protestant, democratic America. There was no contemporary architectural equivalent of Whitman's "form," although the delightfully eccentric views of Horatio Greenough reveal similar aspirations and goals; only later would Louis Sullivan and Frank Lloyd Wright in architecture and Charles Ives in music confirm Whitman's quest.

Dante's journey rests on gigantic metaphors and ancient literary analogues, patterned and rationally organized, that reflect a schematic theology in a schematic universe, stasis rather than flux. For Whitman, traditional metaphors and sophisticated literary parallels are inexpressive and irrelevant. For his protagonists journey through terrain unlike the geography of Dante's Inferno or even the limited boundaries of an Eden. There is in Whitman's poetry a fluidity, sometimes expressed in extraordinary bisexual transformations, that antedates the imposed logic of patriarchal stratification, as well as a kind of timelessness that, as we shall observe, is more characteristic of preliterate societies than of so-called civilization.

Dante's is an aristocratic, authoritarian voice, of the father, earthly and divine, who exemplifies order, control, discipline, and logic. Whitman's is a democratic, permissive voice, of the mother who caresses and hints, who accepts equally all her children without moral evaluations or rational gradations. Where Dante is clear and precise, Whitman is vague and illogical: he troubles not at all to define the divine potential of Everyman, he believes it simply because he believes it. In a time of crisis Dante reasserts the patriarchal concepts of the Mosaic tradition; in another time of

crisis, when religion and, more important, the basic family structure were under assault, Whitman reintroduces in his fluid poetry
and in his undiscriminated emotional effusions the more ancient
love of the all-encompassing mother. Yet both present in their
different ways divine comedies.

Dante undergoes his awesome journey with a constant companion, who exemplifies the continuity of established precedents and
traditions, and with whom he carries on a meaningful dialogue.
With a good deal of amusement, and no little aggressiveness, Whitman sweeps out the cobwebs of "the old cautious hucksters," as he
steadfastly refuses to filter experience through an intellectual or
literary tradition. Whitman's protagonists invariably are alone in
a world where there is almost no interaction between human
beings. So that, although there are traces in a poem like "The
Sleepers" of the rites of ancient races, there is no established social
unit or visible human solidarity. The child enters an enigmatic
universe alone: the custodians of the rites have disappeared. Whitman's "I" anticipates the lot of "modern man" who must, according
to existential critics, exist in a society that is not a society, and who
must carry the burden, not of Christian's religiously decreed sins,
which are part of a waning patriarchal system, but simply of being
human and alone. Whitman's faith, however, in a rejuvenated
democracy, under the aegis of the "eternal mother," is rarely shared
by his successors.

Although critics in their neat antitheses, and simplifications, like
to set off Hawthorne and Melville against Whitman, in a sense
subscribing to Melville's superficial dualism, "No gentry" and
"Yes gentry," it is certainly more than coincidental that at approximately the same time the three authors were examining
similar landscapes and emotional crises in roughly similar terms
— in Robin Molineux, Redburn, and the protagonist of "The
Sleepers." The three young men, in puberty, it will be noted,
undergo similar rites. Robin, when he enters the boat that takes
him to the city and its horrors, plays out the oedipal conflict
simultaneously on personal and political levels — the separation
from the familial father and the separation of the American colonies from England — in an intricate web of symbols that have
only been appreciated and comprehended in our era of anthropo-
logical and psychological knowledge. The fatherless Redburn
seeks the dead parent by crossing the sea in order to experience at
first hand, with the aid of an inherited guidebook, his father's

early life in Liverpool, only to discover that the past provides no useful models for present behavior. Hawthorne's tale ends with Robin accepting, or possibly rejecting, the guidance of a father substitute; since, characteristically, Hawthorne is evasive, we cannot be certain that Robin will not return to his family. After a series of rejections, including the humiliation of having the once-revered Captain Riga cheat him of his wages, Redburn returns to his home, his arrogance chastened but the emotional void unfilled; characteristically, Melville's conclusion is inconclusive, and the search must continue in *Moby-Dick* and even in *Billy Budd*. Whitman employs the same materials and the same "bridge" but arrives at a joyful, affirmative conclusion — only, however, through a kind of Kierkegaardian leap.

Where Whitman differs notably from his contemporaries is in his explicit acknowledgement that the identity crisis of adolescence is associated with sexual awakening and in the importance he attaches to sexual energy, its frustration and its sublimation. Hawthorne and Melville were actually as much preoccupied with the "passional self" as Whitman, but their fear of social censure, as D. H. Lawrence correctly avers, inhibited their art. Robin's eager interest in the seductive "red petticoat" (who, of course, since Hawthorne refuses to be precise, may be the Whore of Babylon) is, cautiously, understated. Despite the presumed freedom of male society aboard a ship, Redburn exhibits in word and deed no sexual interest of any kind, although he is, as extravagantly inflated descriptive passages reveal, strongly attracted to handsome young men.

One of Whitman's most original contributions to our (and world) literature is his depiction of the narcissistic universe of the child and adolescent, not in the irrelevant terms of angelic youth with or without "intimations of immortality," but in terms of the dynamics of relationships (or their absence) and sexual maturation. When Whitman insists that the soul cannot be separated from the body, he is alleging that man is fated to live by and with his body with all its insistent and frequently contradictory and anxiety-producing desires — as well as with its sensuous delights, which neither Hawthorne nor Melville permits to his fictional creations. Whitman does not displace the libido, in other words, in the fashion of Emerson, Thoreau, Hawthorne, and Melville (or, for that matter, Twain and T. S. Eliot later). When he writes, in "Song of Myself,"

Divine am I inside and out, and I make holy whatever I touch or am
  touched from;
The scent of these arm-pits is aroma finer than prayer,
This head is more than churches or bibles or creeds,

he is protesting the human and emotional damage that results from
a culturally imposed rejection of tactility and infantile sensuousness. Casting aside, more successfully than any other American
writer of the century, the dark dress of American puritanism and
Western inhibitions, he "undrapes" and dances like a Dionysian,
or one of the "monsters" in Hawthorne's curiously ambivalent tale
of "The Maypole of Merry Mount," to the very brink of Henry
James's "abyss," and finds it good because it is human.

Long enough have you dreamed contemptible dreams,
Now I wash the gum from your eyes,
You must habit yourself to the dazzle of the light and of every moment
  of your life.

Although Whitman's "open road" is not so open as he sometimes
asserts, and although his "faint clews & indirections" protect by
obscuring his meaning — his "indirections" are infinitely less
secretive and evasive than those of Hawthorne and Melville —
Whitman at least rises above the half-truth that afflicted the
brooding minds of his contemporaries: he perceives not only the
"inferno" but also the "paradiso" granted to those not afraid of
"the dazzle of the light and of every moment of your life."

"The Sleepers," that strange, haunting, and in places baffling
poem which until recently has been neglected and misunderstood,
is not only a confession, one of Whitman's most personal revelations, but, more important, a reenactment of ancient puberty rites.
The landscape, in which obscure symbols disguise the latent content and the universal taboos, and in which the protagonist undergoes sudden and seemingly inexplicable personal and sexual transformations, is dreamlike, even surrealistic at times, because it
evokes vague memories of almost forgotten rites of cultures which
provided meaningful communal ceremonies to celebrate the individual's journey to adulthood, as a modern industrial society

does not. Unlike a dream, the poem does not end inconclusively, but as in a rite of adolescence the protagonist experiences the terrors of anticipated initiation, with its physical pain, as well as the attendant joys of entrance into manhood and into society — except that the drama in Whitman's poem, of necessity, is played out in the protagonist's consciousness, and that the conclusion is sublimation.

At the beginning of the poem the "I" is wandering "confused . . . . lost to myself," as "with open eyes" he observes the sleepers: the wretched who have destroyed themselves, "the gashed bodies on battlefields," the fulfilled lovers, the unrequited lovers. In his bewilderment he sees only the waste of human life, the loneliness of those destined to isolation. Overcome with despair, he stands "with drooping eyes," between wakefulness and sleep, between an oppressive reality and a vision of what may be called a truer reality. Quietly, almost unnoticed, he passes his "hands soothingly to and fro a few inches from" the unhappy people. Almost at once a magical transformation takes place:

The earth recedes from me into the night,
I saw that it was beautiful . . . . and I see that what is not the earth is
    beautiful.

I go from bedside to bedside . . . . I sleep close with the other sleepers,
    each in turn;
I dream in my dream all the dreams of the other dreamers,
And I become the other dreamers.

I am a dance . . . . Play up there! the fit is whirling me fast.

I am the everlaughing . . . . it is new moon and twilight,
I see the hiding of douceurs . . . . I see nimble ghosts whichever way
    I look,
Cache and cache again deep in the ground and sea, and where it is
    neither ground or sea.

With the mind's eye the protagonist sees only superficially and at a distance. With the intuitive eye and with physical contact he enters empathetically into the pangs and joys of the sleepers. For like a child he "sees" through all the senses, particularly the tactile sense. When he is metamorphosed into the "everlaughing," not only is he a child who has abandoned Apollonian reason and cultural repression but also, in his uninhibited dance, a Dionysian in the realm of irrationality, undirected eroticism, and sensuous freedom.

The movement of the hand is pivotal in the development of the poem as well as characteristic of the tactility present in Whitman's poetry. The hand at various times is linked with the mother soothing a child, the father conferring a blessing upon a son, or with autoerotic gratification. The hand brings comfort in "To One Shortly to Die": "Softly I lay my right hand upon you"; and again in "The Wound-Dresser" in *Drum-Taps*: "The hurt and the wounded I pacify with soothing hand." In his idealization of the poet, Whitman endows him with a hand like that of Michelangelo's Jehovah as he reaches toward Adam. "Salut Au Monde!" begins, "O take my hand, Walt Whitman!" and concludes like a benediction: "I raise high the perpendicular hand — I make the signal." The poet in "Starting from Paumanok" has "a flowing mouth and indicative hand," and his power, in "Song of Prudence," is in "the shaping of his great hands." In "By Blue Ontario's Shore" Whitman declares, "I lead the present with friendly hand." In place of the chilled separateness of contemporary America, he foresees, in "For You O Democracy," "There shall be countless linked hands." (Gatsby, in a later age, when the "green light" is almost blacked out, futilely raises his "right hand" to confer futile blessings.) The hand is also linked with adolescent sexual explorations. The "journeymen divine" in "The Sleepers" accept the protagonist amorously "with stretched arms." At the conclusion of an autoerotic dream, "My hands are spread forth . . I pass them in all directions," a passage paralleled by one in "Spontaneous Me": ". . . the hot hand seeking to repress what would master him." Of his beloved he concludes in "Of the Terrible Doubt of Appearances": "He ahold of my hand has completely satisfied me." Or in "I Sing the Body Electric" (1860 version): "The curious sympathy one feels, when feeling with the hand the naked meat of his own body, or another person's body."

The hand, then, is directly linked with the three roles the "I" in "The Sleepers" will play in his frequent physical and sexual metamorphoses — mother, father, and adolescent. It is also visually expressive of his deepest emotional needs; he seeks the soothing, protective hand of the mother, sometimes in oedipal rivalry and eventually in a return to the womb; he craves the guidance of

a father, the symbolic "laying on of hands," which will free him
from dependency and permit him to enter adult sexuality; and,
finally, as a young man entering puberty and genital awareness he
is baffled by his strange reactions to his parents but elated by the
excitement his hands contribute to his sexual awakening.

Immediately in his night journey the "hero" begins a series of
transformations which express his emotional needs and his sexual
confusion — in short, the trauma of every adolescent. At first
he appears to be "the everlaughing," an aggressive overman or
"boss" of "those journeymen divine," a dominant masculine role
which he assumes for a moment as he moves at the head of this
"gay gang of blackguards" with "wildflapping pennants of joy" —
in unrestrained phallic splendor. But since he has presumed to be
the initiator rather than the initiate of the rites, he simultaneously
retreats to the role of a dependent youth protected by adults:

> they make me a pet besides,
> And surround me, and lead me and run ahead when I walk,
> And lift their cunning covers and signify me with stretched arms,
> and resume the way. . . .

The "blackguards" — the term is used affectionately by one
emulous of the "roughs" — coax their "pet" to abandon his self-
consciousness and adolescent fears of sexuality and "uncover" in
order to enter man's estate.

Before the protagonist can assume a masculine role, however,
he must reexperience the bisexual desires of adolescence and relive
the oedipal conflict. Upon the disappearance of the "blackguards,"
he declares: "I am the actor and the actress" and "the wellformed
person . . the wasted or feeble person"; and in the first extended
dream, beginning with line 46, he plays all the parts in a three-
character drama: the amorous woman who "folded her hair ex-
pectantly," her "truant love," and the erotic "darkness."

> Double yourself and receive me darkness,
> Receive me and my lover too . . . . he will not let me go without him.
>
> I roll myself upon you as upon a bed . . . . I resign myself to the dusk.
>
> He whom I call answers me and takes the place of my lover,
> He rises with me silently from the bed.

Darkness you are gentler than my lover . . . . his flesh was sweaty and
    panting,
I feel the hot moisture yet that he left me.

My hands are spread forth . . I pass them in all directions,
I would sound up the shadowy shore to which you are journeying.

The drama has the confused aspects of a sexual dream in which
the dreamer achieves yet fails of the consummation he craves because the craving springs from deep-rooted but forbidden desires
which a cultural inhibition decrees must be played out in shadows.
The protagonist is both "the actor and the actress," the father as
well as the mother. The action represents both sides of the oedipal
ambivalence: the "I" is the woman receiving her "lover," the father,
and is the "darkness" that is "gentler than my lover" and replaces
the father; thus he is the father's rival for the mother, and at the
same time he substitutes for the mother in the primal act.

The woman fades away, and the "I" awakens from this descent
into the ambivalences of the human drama — "O hotcheeked and
blushing! O foolish hectic!" "Where shall I run?" he asks. He
blushes because he dimly perceives, although he dare not verbalize
them, his secret desires, and his guilt again compels him to seek
protection. This time he wants to run to the "Pier that I saw dimly
last night when I looked from the windows." Obviously, but
"dimly" to the troubled youth, the pier represents the security of
a child-adult relationship, and is apparently like the flag in "Delicate Cluster," a bisexual symbol — "Pier out from the main, let
me catch myself with you and stay . . . . I will not chafe you."
"Chafe" suggests some kind of physical involvement. If the pier
is construed as a male symbol, at least two interpretations are
possible: the "I" seeks again the relationship he has enjoyed as the
"pet" of the "blackguards" — "chafe" suggesting muscular and
sexual overtones — and the flight may represent the guilty boy's
search for the father. If, on the other hand, the pier is to be
linked with feminine water imagery, then "chafe" may refer to the
child at the mother's breast or to the fetus in the amniotic waters.
The latter construction is supported by the last line in the preceding
erotic dream of the woman — "I would sound up the shadowy
shore to which you are journeying" — and by the womblike state
depicted in the concluding lines of the poem.

Both constructions are valid and applicable in view of the previously noted sexual transformations and the oedipal ambivalences. At the same time the young man is, literally, awakening from an erotic dream and is perplexed and frightened by his aroused sexuality:

I feel ashamed to go naked about the world,
And am curious to know where my feet stand . . . . and what is this flooding me, childhood or manhood . . . . and the hunger that crosses the bridge between.

Here with sensitive insight Whitman recreates a young man's feeling of shame, about which Erik Erikson has written most perceptively:

Shame is an infantile emotion insufficiently studied. . . . Shame supposes that one is completely exposed and conscious of being looked at: in one word, self-conscious. One is visible and not ready to be visible; which is why we dream of shame as a situation in which we are stared at in a condition of incomplete dress, in night attire, "with one's pants down." Shame is early expressed in an impulse to bury one's face, or to sink, right then and there, into the ground.[2]

For the protagonist, since he is alone, only imagines his public exposure, and reveals, as in his earlier retreat into the arms of the "blackguards," that he is not ready to be seen as a man. (Perhaps it is oversubtle to point out what appear to be unconscious associations of "pier" and "peer," both in terms of sight and relationships.)

The involuntary orgasmic spasm, which duplicates the involuntary movement of the hand at the beginning of the night journey, introduces the second crucial symbol — "the bridge." The sexual context in which the word appears reveals that it is more than simply a means of crossing from childhood to manhood, and seems better explained by Marie Bonaparte's psychoanalytic commentary: a bridge is "a representation of the penis which the male infant cannot and the male adult must not use as a means of sexual intercourse with the mother, but also a symbol of the 'extroverted mother . . .' or vagina dentata."[3] The obscurities of the following stanza become more comprehensible when we recognize the bisexual fantasy and what may be traces of the ancient puberty rites which Bruno Bettelheim analyzes in *Symbolic Wounds*.

The cloth laps a first sweet eating and drinking,
Laps life-swelling yolks . . . . laps ear of rose-corn, milky and just
   ripened:
The white teeth stay, and the boss-tooth advances in darkness,
And liquor is spilled on lips and bosoms by touching glasses, and the
   best liquor afterward.

It is, of course, obvious and significant that the "I" visualizes
genitals and sexuality in oral images — that, in other words, the
protagonist, according to Bettelheim's description of an ancient
ceremony, "may also be mastering great fear of or desire for the
vagina through oral incorporation."[4] At the same time the passage
reveals the boy's misunderstanding of the female genitals, when
Whitman employs the (now) classic symbol of "white teeth."
("Boss-tooth" recalls the earlier reference to "boss.") The youth's
conception of coitus retains the infantile association of sexuality
and physical assault, just as the earlier line, "Double yourself and
receive me darkness," is more reminiscent of masturbation than
of mature sexuality. And the last line in this extraordinary passage
is a strange combination of masturbatory and sexual imagery
which at the same time suggests that the child is still at the
mother's breast.
   Despite Whitman's evocation of psychic depths, artistically he
is in firm control of his material, since this first poetic climax corresponds with the autoerotic climax, which, in turn, fuses the
tactile imagery ("touching glasses"), the phallicism, and the regressive sexual fantasies. The movement of the poem, like the
orgiastic crescendoes and decrescendoes in the music of Richard
Wagner, captures the protagonist's sexual tensions and anxieties,
the release or autoerotic gratification, and the relaxation of the
sexual afterglow ("and the best liquor afterward"). Only with
this sexual expenditure is the protagonist at peace with himself
and the universe: "I descend my western course . . . . my sinews
are flaccid." The disturbing subterranean excitement in some
of Whitman's best poems comes in large part from this orgiastic
movement.
   With seeming serenity the protagonist now continues his quest
in order to make the choice between "childhood or manhood,"
but since the choice has already been made — in his retreat
among the "blackguards" and in his search for the protection of

the "pier" — the quest is basically illusory. New situations are only variations upon earlier situations, and the "I" invariably retreats to the protected position of the child or of the fetus. The destination is indicated in his transformations into a grandmother darning "my grandson's stockings" and into "the sleepless widow" — the one looks after the child and the other mourns her husband, whose role the "I" immediately assumes. At the conclusion of the brief second section the "I," significantly, is in the "coffin" and is enjoying the warm protectiveness of the "dark grave." (Here we have the linkage of the cradle and the coffin which is to be elaborated later in "Out of the Cradle Endlessly Rocking.") That the sexual bed in the preceding scene becomes the death bed is inevitable: "Sinews . . . flaccid" with sexual satiety find their ultimate place of rest, and the veiled oedipal desire has no resolution except in death. For in this episode the "I" is the widow and the shroud, husband and wife, father and mother — the grave is the "solution" for the boy who wishes the father dead, and wishes himself dead for having the wish. In death there is release from guilt and torment: "it is not evil or pain here . . . . it is blank here, for reasons."

In the third section the "I" is on the shore observing "a beautiful gigantic swimmer" "in the prime of his middle age" — a figure that immediately calls to mind the middle-aged poet himself who, as we have noted, "dotes" upon the beauties of his body. The swimmer, we are told, has "courageous arms" which, however, cannot save him from the "swift-running eddies." His vigorous muscular movements are as futile as the protagonist's verbalization of his hatred for the "ruffianly red-trickled waves." In fact, the swimmer's struggles are as fruitless as the "I's" erotic wishes, and end in the same way, in death: "Swiftly and out of sight is borne the brave swimmer." The insistent use of water imagery to suggest sexuality further links the middle-aged athlete and the protagonist: "the shadowy shore" in the scene with the expectant woman, the pier to which the boy flees, the description of orgasm in terms of "flooding" and "spilled" liquor. The death of the swimmer appears to be an elaboration of the image of the "white teeth," the emblem of destructive feminine sexuality.

If the sea, as customarily in Whitman's poetry, is the female principle — the use of the word "ruffianly" tends to make the waves human — then once again we are witnesses of a trio. This

time the helpless boy on the shore watches the destruction of man
by woman. Similarly, in the next scene he observes as the sea
destroys a ship and spews the bodies of men on the shore. The
hands which bring rest to the restless in the opening section and
which lead to autoerotic gratification in the second section are now
as impotent as the swimmer's "courageous arms": "I cannot aid
with my wringing fingers." These two scenes, then, appear to
depict the sexually aggressive woman (or mother), the destruction
of virile men by a superior force, and the "I" as a passive spectator
or helpless child — or, to put it in psychological terms, one half
of the oedipal ambivalence. At the same time the episodes suggest,
although undoubtedly their author had no such conscious intention, Whitman's fear of heterosexuality and his evasion of "manhood." Yet this is not quite the whole story, for when the body of
the swimmer is "borne" away by the sea, it disappears only to be
"born" again.

Abruptly in Section 5 the poem shifts from its sequence of
events occurring in the timeless vacuum of dreams to incidents in
historical time. At first sight the transition appears to be sudden
and perhaps even contrived, but actually the episode involving
George Washington and the tale allegedly told to the poet by his
mother are elaborations of themes present in the preceding action
of the poem. For the "I's" feeling of inadequacy as he witnesses
the deaths of the swimmer and then of the ship's crew parallels a
similar feeling on the part of General Washington, who "cannot
repress the weeping drops" when "he sees the slaughter of the
southern braves confided to him by their parents." After "the
defeat at Brooklyn" we see Washington, now about to become the
father of his country, saying farewell to his officers: "He kisses
lightly the wet cheeks one after another." Like the "fish-shaped
island" in "As I Ebb'd with the Ocean of Life," Washington is a
benevolent father-figure who can give affection and weep in pity
but who is powerless to check the slaughter of young men; and he
reappears in "The Centenarian's Story," one of the poems in
Drum-Taps:

I saw the moisture gather in drops on the face of the General;
I saw how he wrung his hands in anguish.

Interestingly, Whitman chooses, although other choices were possible, to describe "the defeat at Brooklyn," the scene of a major

historical defeat but also of a personal one. And it can scarcely be overlooked that the poem is in one sense a chronicle of the deaths of men, the husband in the coffin, the middle-aged swimmer, the sailors, and now the Revolutionary War soldiers.

The tale Whitman tells in the following section of an event in his mother's early life also centers upon loss. In her childhood a beautiful Indian squaw had come to her home one day selling "rushes for rushbottoming chairs." At once Mrs. Whitman fell in love with the Indian: "The more she looked upon her she loved her." Later in the day the Indian went on her way, but "All the week she thought of her . . . . she watched for her many a month." This tale of a young girl's infatuation with the squaw leads to an outburst of rage:

Now Lucifer was not dead . . . . or if he was I am his sorrowful terrible heir;
I have been wronged . . . . I am oppressed . . . . I hate him that oppresses me,
I will either destroy him, or he shall release me.

Damn him! how he does defile me,
How he informs against my brother and sister and takes pay for their blood,
How he laughs when I look down the bend after the steamboat that carries away my woman.

The protagonist's sudden fury is not related directly to the encounter between his mother and the Indian woman, which occurred before he was born, but to unconscious associations which, though disguised in the tale, are related to an unresolved personal conflict.

The squaw's disappearance is a betrayal and rejection of a child's love by an older woman. Like the merciless sea she is another destructive maternal figure. Unconsciously the "I" is recording a young man's feeling of maternal betrayal by projecting the betrayal upon the Indian, since he does not dare to indict the mother directly. At the same time the squaw, like his father, is his rival since she has stolen his mother's affections. Thus it is that when he is ready to "destroy" his rival, he suddenly shifts to the masculine pronoun, and at once makes clear, as Richard Chase has observed, that he is voicing his oedipal murderous tendencies. He invokes the mythic arch-traitor, Lucifer, who serves a complex function in the poem. Lucifer, of course, had rebelled against the Father, as the "I" does in his oedipal rivalry. The fallen angel had also deprived Adam and Eve of their idyllic happiness in Eden, as a father deprives the son who wants to maintain his possessive relationship with his mother. At the same time there are still traces in the passage of an earlier version in which "Black Lucifer" is an enraged slave whose master begets children by the Negro's "woman" and then sells mother and children down the river. On a mythic and social level, then, the "I" identifies himself with people as dispossessed as he is. In addition, the Indian squaw and Lucifer, both of whom are aliens, as is the Negro, are lawless and treacherous, and so too is the protagonist's frenzy for vengeance.

The journey that begins with "mirthshouting music" reaches its climax with the "I's" expression of murderous fury. But the rage is merely verbalized, not acted upon. Once more the protagonist is wringing his hands. When he exclaims, "how he does defile me," he voices his feelings of impotency, as in that fearful earlier line, "I feel ashamed to go naked about the world." The disappearance of the woman "down the bend" recalls the line in the dream sequence, "I would sound up the shadowy shore to which you [the woman] are journeying." The protagonist attributes a perhaps imaginary mirth to the man (the father) who "laughs when I look down the bend after the steamboat that carries away my woman." "My woman" is, ambiguously, a wife or, more precisely, a mother.

The verbal outburst, like the earlier orgasm, provides release for pent-up tension and anxiety. As the cyclical pattern of the poem is repeated, once again the protagonist retreats — first to the protective custody of the Dionysians, then to the "pier" after the autoerotic scene which is dominated by regressive oral imagery, and now, in a brilliant metamorphosis not without its humorous aspects, to the role of a gigantic but phlegmatic whale.

Now the vast dusk bulk that is the whale's bulk . . . . it seems mine,
Warily, sportsman! though I lie so sleepy and sluggish, my tap is death.

The whale (in color here not unreminiscent of Lucifer, or at least "Black Lucifer"), in myth and in *Moby-Dick*, plays a bisexual role not unrelated to the protagonist's confused bisexuality. The "I" momentarily fancies that "my tap is death," as he pictures himself in an aggressively masculine role. But "pennants of joy" again prove too much for him, and despite his latent power he lies "sleepy and sluggish" in the feminine sea. The final visual effect is of a fetus lying safely and securely in the womb. Again "my sinews are flaccid." The "sportsman" need not fear the child or rival: he will not — indeed, he cannot — cross the "bridge." He has returned home.

And so too, as the catalogue beginning at line 142 makes clear, the tormented, unrequited people who appear early in the poem are now sailing home. The atmosphere magically changes to reflect the "I's" new mood: there is "A show of summer softness," and the moon is no longer "floundering" because the "I" has found himself. Although there is still another trio — the light, the air, and the "I" — the eroticism is playful rather than anxiety-producing: "And have an unseen something to be in contact with them also."[5] The "tap" is now a child's harmless and innocent sexual play. Even the "myth of heaven" which "indicates the soul" is transformed, somewhat miraculously, by the childlike, narcissistic perspective from which it is viewed:

It comes from its embowered garden and looks pleasantly on itself and
    encloses the world;
Perfect and clean the genitals previously jetting, and perfect and clean
    the womb cohering,
The head wellgrown and proportioned and plumb, and the bowels and
    joints proportioned and plumb.

With this birth, "every thing is in its place." The agitated music characteristic of a young man's erotic and oedipal torment gives way to the music of the waves of the sea, not dashing white bodies against the rocks, but serene and regular and unceasing, as the sleepers, like children, "flow hand in hand over the whole earth from east to west." What an extraordinary line this is, so wondrously evocative, so natural and unobtrusive in its diction — and Whitman is alleged to be a careless artist! Almost unnoticed, the water imagery culminates in the word "flow"; "hand in hand" quietly reintroduces this pivotal motif and at the same time establishes a tactile bond where before there was only separateness; and the simple, childlike language is not only a statement of affirmation but also preparation for the completion of the circular journey.

I too pass from the night;
I stay awhile away O night, but I return to you again and love you;
Why should I be afraid to trust myself to you?
I am not afraid . . . . I have been well brought forward by you;
I love the rich running day, but I do not desert her in whom I lay so
     long:
I know not how I came of you, and I know not where I go with
     you . . . . but I know I came well and shall go well.

From what is in one sense an evasive perspective since it is a
kind of death wish for an edenic home, the final retreat, but in
another sense an acceptance of, or faith in, the meaningfulness of
life despite painful evidence to the contrary, the "I" sees himself as
part of an eternal cycle which is dominated not by a destructive
maternal figure but by a goddess of fertility:

I will duly pass the day O my mother and duly return to you;
Not you will yield forth the dawn again more surely than you will
     yield forth me again,
Not the womb yields the babe in its time more surely than I shall be
     yielded from you in my time.

How different yet similar the conclusion of *Moby-Dick* is. While
Whitman sings "a constant sacrament of praise" (to borrow Wallace Stevens' lovely phrase), and moves beyond tragedy to what,
of course, may be only illusory security, Melville records the fright-
ful destruction of the Pequod — "then all collapsed, and the great
shroud of the sea rolled on as it rolled five thousand years ago" —
only to correct this tragic perspective in an epilogue in which
Ishmael's words and invocation of the eternal mother resemble
Whitman's:

Buoyed up by that coffin, for almost one whole day and night, I floated
on a soft and dirge-like main. The unharming sharks, they glided by
as if with padlocks on their mouths; the savage sea-hawks sailed with
sheathed beaks. On the second day, a sail drew near, nearer, and
picked me up at last. It was the devious-cruising Rachel, that in her
retracing search after her missing children, only found another orphan.

⨳⨳⨳ 5 ⨳⨳⨳

"I celebrate myself"

I celebrate myself,
And what I assume you shall assume,
For every atom belonging to me as good belongs to you.

With a comic bow to Vergil and a gay farewell to Miltonic blank
verse, Whitman confidently and wittily introduces the first great
poem in American literature.[1] He frees himself and modern poetry
with a joyous yawp from its subservience to forms and techniques
appropriate to the expression of a feudalistic social order and a
unified cosmogony, but no longer viable in a democratic age, in a
fluid industrial society without a unifying principle except perhaps
the profit motive, or in a world in which flux has replaced the
harmony of the spheres. In short, Whitman severs the umbilical
cord and a truly modern poet emerges. It is at once apparent in the
lines of "Song of Myself" that this is no uncertain infant feebly
searching for poetic form, but a sophisticated, mature, complex
creator whose first book is the work of a master, as Emerson was to
recognize within one month of its publication.

"Song of Myself" is a characteristically American meditation of a solitary singer in the lonely American landscape, in a society which, despite its posturings and too extravagantly proclaimed optimism, has allowed the edenic dream to be lost in its material-istic quest. It is the reverie of the outsider, the isolate, the peren-nial American protestant, who struggles to reassert the collective dream, only to end, as Whitman does, in a retreat into the self that copes with, or, perhaps more precisely, evades, reality through imaginative transcendence into the timelessness and harmony of art. The serio-comic tone serves as a protective mechanism to dis-guise the poet's uncertainty and disenchantment from his audience and probably from himself, just as Melville's comic tactics in *Moby-Dick* are at the same time a triumphant assertion of artistic control and a concealed admission of failure and even personal cowardice. Thus despite its comic tone "Song of Myself" is self-analysis, no less so than that of the puritan clergyman who had, or at least thought that he had, the certainty of his God, his theology, and his community. Without such faith, or illusion, and without a community of adherents, which he must create in the imaginary "connections" of his vision, Whitman examines the nature of reality — "My words are words of a questioning, and to indicate reality" — with an intensity that is openly revealed in his minis-terial rhetoric and clandestinely exposed in the recurrent emotional swings from affirmation to uncertainty, as the knot that is the tormented self is untied only to be tied again until, like Natty Bumppo's majestic "Here," the final verbal assertion is made, "I stop some where waiting for you" — which is affirmation and elegy.

"Song of Myself" is, then, a meditation on the nature of the self — "What is man anyhow? What am I?" — which is the only reality left in a world overpowered by the dynamo and fragmented by the deaths of the old gods, facts of which Whitman was as keenly aware as Henry Adams or T. S. Eliot, though his answer was not to be theirs.

In the fluid and chaotic American scene at mid-century he wanted, like Emerson, to shape the American character and to reveal to the Jonathans the heroic potential residing in every man. Since he knew that the Jonathans had their hands in their (money-lined) pockets and were not listening, especially not to impractical poets who sang of themselves, Whitman tried to gain a hearing by veiling his serious purpose behind an offhand witty introduction; unfortunately, since wit demands detachment and literary sophistication, hard-headed Jonathans could hardly respond to his epic parody. In the second line Whitman employs another characteristic device when he attempts to establish a kind of amorous dialogue with his audience — "And what I assume you shall assume." The trickery of the device, however, is self-evident and reveals not only society's failure but Whitman's too: although many people appear in the poem, no one converses with the protagonist, who is, in final analysis, as thwarted as the old maid who in her fantasy caresses the bodies of twenty-eight swimmers. Only one conversation is recorded, when the poet "sarcastically" speaks to himself. For the rest there is only monologue.

The opening lines of "Song of Myself" caressingly mock a people who have taken themselves with forbidding seriousness and have shunned sensuousness from the harsh days of the colonies to the equally harsh expansion of industrialism.

I loafe and invite my soul,
I lean and loafe at my ease . . . . observing a spear of summer grass.

At once Whitman knowingly violates two rigid social conventions: one does not speak nonchalantly about a profound subject like the soul, nor in an industrial society which has flourished on the pragmatic aphorisms of Franklin does one revel in the unproductive art of loafing. At the same time the opening section violates a literary convention: Whitman does not summon the Muses or invoke God; and although "Song of Myself" presents the Dantesque moment of self-awareness in the middle of the journey (Whitman was thirty-six when he published *Leaves of Grass*), the symbols and language lack the urgency and ominous notes usually sounded when a pilgrimage to self-understanding is to be recorded. Furthermore, the depiction of the protagonist carelessly lying in the grass appears to be almost an act of flippancy or deliberately shocking showmanship: certainly no poem comparable in length and significance begins in such a casual manner. Yet, coincidentally, the opening chapter of *Moby-Dick* (1851) introduces the themes of Melville's meditation on the nature of reality in a comic context, not because

Melville was artistically unsure of himself, but, I suspect, because
from the outset he knowingly wrote a "wicked book"; and Thoreau
is deftly comic in the opening pages of *Walden* (1854).

The recumbent position of the "I" in "Song of Myself" is artistically and thematically correct, since the poem is to reject the
Western intellectual tradition and the religious emphasis upon
man's vertical relationship with the deity, as Whitman reverts to
an older, more elemental relationship. The protagonist rests upon
the bosom of Mother Earth, where he is in intimate, tactile relationship with all living things. In this position he is to ingest
experiences through all the senses, not through the mind alone.
For the Cartesian intellectualization, "I think, therefore I am,"
Whitman substitutes: I ingest and feel with all sentient matter,
therefore I exist.

The casual act of lying in the grass quietly introduces the two
major motifs in the poem — sexuality, the "procreant urge," and
death. When Whitman invites the reader to observe "a spear of
summer grass," the two motifs coalesce in one symbol, which, as
Matthiessen notes, reappears throughout the poem, until "I bequeath myself to the dirt to grow from the grass I love." This quiet
line recalls the opening lines of the poem, brings life (or love) and
death into harmony, and asserts the eternal cycle which transcends
the seeming flux and transitoriness of life, the permanence of endless renewal. This humble, insignificant particular, the grass,
miraculously — and life was always miraculous in the ever-young
eyes of Whitman — embodies universal principles, just as the
most ordinary man contains within himself the seeds of greatness.
The "spear of grass," moreover, has the appearance and the fecundating power of the phallus, which in turn is the source of life and
art, as Section 5 is to make clear, and which in the sexual act
repeats the life-death cycle.

These themes Whitman begins to orchestrate in elaborate and
subtle variations when, in Section 2, the "I" abandons the closed
order and the artificialities represented by the man-made house
and the synthetic "perfumes" for the reality of "undisguised and
naked" contact with nature. At once he sheds cultural and social
repressions or the false self, in order to discover the orgiastic self:
"I am mad for it to be in contact with me." Lovingly he observes
"the smoke of my own breath," "loveroot, silkthread, crotch and
vine," and revels in "the sniff of green leaves." Enraptured, he

listens to "the sound of the belched words of my own voice." How wonderfully right is that irreverent and ungenteel "belched"! The word itself declares the protagonist's freedom from social restrictions and decorum, and the expressive oral image, in asserting his libidinal freedom, serves at the same time as a prelude to the orality in the climax of the first movement of the poem in Section 5 — "loose the stop from your throat." The "belched words" appropriately herald the advent of the orgiastic self:

Stop this day and night with me and you shall possess the origin of all poems,
You shall possess the good of the earth and sun . . . . there are millions of suns left,
You shall no longer take things at second or third hand . . . . nor look through the eyes of the dead . . . . nor feed on the spectres in books,
You shall not look through my eyes either, nor take things from me,
You shall listen to all sides and filter them from yourself.

He rejects the exaggerated gloom and pessimism of the "No gentry" — "the talk of the beginning or the end" — and asserts the basic and eternal sexual rhythm of life:

Urge and urge and urge,
Always the procreant urge of the world.

Out of the dimness opposite equals advance . . . . Always substance and increase,
Always a knit of identity . . . . always distinction . . . . always a breed of life.

Unlike most preachers and unlike some of his solemn idolaters, Whitman sermonizes with disarming wit:

Sure as the most certain sure . . . . plumb in the uprights, well entretied, braced in the beams,
Stout as a horse, affectionate, haughty, electrical,
I and this mystery here we stand.

(That the protagonist here and elsewhere is somewhat of a stud, or stallion, is part of Whitman's wry but defensive wit, as he forces himself to laugh at a recurrent fantasy.) While others create artificial intellectual distinctions and vex themselves with seemingly important matters, "I am silent, and go bathe and admire myself," admiring "every organ and attribute of me." Like the God of Genesis, Whitman is, parodistically, "satisfied" with his self-examination, with the miracle of his own body; but unlike Jehovah he breaks forth in visceral delight:

I am satisfied . . . . I see, dance, laugh, sing;
As God comes a loving bedfellow and sleeps at my side all night and
   close on the peep of the day,
And leaves for me baskets covered with white towels bulging the house
   with their plenty. . . .

The "I" projects his hungry amorous feelings upon the environment, the landscape, and even God Himself. The reference to "baskets covered with white towels" is deceptive, for it conceals a genital association which becomes clear in the description of the white bellies of the male swimmers in Section 11, and thus plays upon the twofold significance of the staff of life, bread and the phallus. In addition, since "baskets . . . bulging" suggest impregnation, the image takes on a bisexual character not unusual in Whitman's writing, here specifically preparing for Section 5.

Momentarily the Dionysian joy subsides as the "trippers and askers" demand of the protagonist a cause-and-effect explanation of "the Me Myself." In reply to the scoffing dissonance of the crowd, the poem rises to its first crescendo, the effect much like that of Wagner's orgiastic music in, for example, the prelude to *Tristan und Isolde.* The orchestration in every detail is appropriate to the sexual union of the soul and the body which heals the cultural and religious fragmentation of man into two warring factions. Here all the motifs — the grass, the oral and bisexual images, the sexual basis of art — reappear, and the rhythm characterizes the rhythm of coitus in a brilliant but shocking marriage of sound and sense.

As in the equivalent scene in "The Sleepers," orgasmic fulfillment brings "peace" and places the protagonist in amorous contact with his fellow creatures. The music subsides into one of those delicate pianissimos in which Whitman shatters us not with his yawp but with his exquisite loveliness, again not unlike Wagner's magical effects.

Swiftly arose and spread around me the peace and joy and knowledge
    that pass all the art and argument of the earth;
And I know that the hand of God is the elderhand of my own,
And I know that the spirit of God is the eldest brother of my own,
And that all the men ever born are also my brothers . . . . and the
    women my sisters and lovers,
And that a kelson of the creation is love;
And limitless are leaves stiff or drooping in the fields,
And brown ants in the little wells beneath them,
And mossy scabs of the wormfence, and heaped stones, and elder and
    mullen and pokeweed.

Section 6, when a child asks, "What is the grass?", is a delicate
variation upon the preceding section both in subject matter and in
its emotional rhythm. The answers the "I" gives to the child's
queries, usually preceded by the words "I guess," make explicit the
phallic aspects of the grass (the "flag of my disposition"), restate
the timelessness of the natural process ("uniform hieroglyphic"),
and culminate in a lovely association of grass and death ("And now
it seems to me the beautiful uncut hair of graves"). As Kenneth
Burke rightly points out, the ensuing description of death parallels
the orality present in Section 5, in a cumulative series of associations from "curling grass" to "uttering tongues":

Tenderly will I use you curling grass,
It may be you transpire from the breasts of young men,
It may be if I had known them I would have loved them;
It may be you are from old people and from women, and from offspring
    taken soon out of their mothers' laps,
And here you are the mothers' laps.

This grass is very dark to be from the white heads of old mothers,
Darker than the colorless beards of old men,
Dark to come from under the faint red roofs of mouths.

O I perceive after all so many uttering tongues!
And I perceive they do not come from the roofs of mouths for nothing.

Obsessively Whitman regresses to the earliest childhood association
— the mother feeding the child. The emotional intensity of this
section originates not in the rational content (the questions and
answers) or in the linking of Eros and Thanatos, but in the under-

lying erotic rhythm of union, gratification, and the deathlike state
of the sexual afterglow, whether at the breast of the mother or in a
supposedly mature sexual relationship.

Although the reestablishment of the elemental mother-child
relationship in actuality provides an illusionary edenic security
for the mature man, and although sexuality is played out in infantile autoeroticism, Whitman has now stated the base not only for
"the origin of all poems," by which of course he means his poems,
but also for the specific movement of the protagonist in "Song of
Myself" from aloneness to entry into society. Slowly and artfully
Whitman begins to prepare for his next crescendo, toward the
belching out of his name in Section 24.

Convinced that he is free from the artificial self as well as artificial dichotomies, the protagonist now asserts that "[I] am not
contained between my hat and boots," for "I am the mate and
companion of people, all just as immortal and fathomless as myself." Only after candid self-examination can he generalize about
the universal human condition:

Who need be afraid of the merge?
Undrape . . . . you are not guilty to me, nor stale nor discarded,
I see through the broadcloth and gingham whether or no,
And am around, tenacious, acquisitive, tireless . . . . and can never be
    shaken away.

After noting in succeeding stanzas the life cycle — the cradle, the
lovers "up the bushy hill," and the death of the "suicide," again the
juxtaposition of sexuality and death — he listens to "the blab of
the pave," to the gaiety and groans of the city, and absorbs a wonderful resonance much as Marcel Proust was to do later from his
cork-lined room. Then, in his characteristic position, "stretched
atop of the load" of hay, the "I" wallows tactilely in rural scenes,
moves on to join hunters and fishermen, and then witnesses "the
marriage of the trapper" to a "red girl." This almost idyllic union
of two races is followed abruptly by a scene of anguish and racial
disharmony, when the protagonist befriends a "runaway slave" and
puts "plasters on the galls of his neck and ankles," a line that is
juxtaposed to the description of the Indian maiden: "her coarse
straight locks descended upon her voluptuous limbs and reached to
her feet," which, in turn, recalls an earlier line in Section 5: "And
reached till you felt my beard, and reached till you held my feet."

For a week the "I," anticipating Whitman's role during the Civil War, nurses the Negro to health as he once again plays a bisexual role: with the strength of the trapper ("One hand rested on his rifle"), he protects the fugitive, "my firelock leaned in the corner," while he duplicates the wifely ministrations of the "red girl." But this "union," like all the relationships described in Whitman's verse, ends suddenly, when the Negro flees "north."

The pain and frustration of the "I" are then transferred to the twenty-eight-year-old woman who watches, "aft the blinds of the window," twenty-eight young men "bathe by the shore." This section is occasionally termed "notorious" by commentators apparently shocked by what they consider to be the woman's (and the poet's) "abnormally acute sensitivity to touch." But to stigmatize Whitman's tactilism by the imposition of a norm is but to confirm his point: the prohibition of touch has become one of the major taboos (the eleventh commandment, according to Edward Dahlberg) of American civilization in its collective fear and hatred of the body, as man has rendered suspect one of his most natural affectional responses. Furthermore, to view the episode in terms of an irrelevant (and inhuman) moralistic pronouncement is to miss, in the words of Randall Jarrell, "such tenderness and subtlety and understanding . . . that Chekhov himself couldn't have treated . . . better."[2]

Twenty-eight young men bathe by the shore,
Twenty-eight young men, and all so friendly,
Twenty-eight years of womanly life, and all so lonesome.

She owns the fine house by the rise of the bank,
She hides handsome and richly drest aft the blinds of the window.

Which of the young men does she like the best?
Ah the homeliest of them is beautiful to her.

Where are you off to, lady? for I see you,
You splash in the water there, yet stay stock still in your room.

Dancing and laughing along the beach came the twenty-ninth bather,
The rest did not see her, but she saw them and loved them.

The beards of the young men glistened with wet, it ran from their
    long hair,
Little streams passed all over their bodies.

An unseen hand also passed over their bodies,
It descended tremblingly from their temples and ribs.

The young men float on their backs, their white bellies swell to the
     sun . . . . they do not ask who seizes fast to them,
They do not know who puffs and declines with pendant and bending
     arch,
They do not think whom they souse with spray.

Perhaps nowhere else is the pain of separateness and of unwanted
sexual chastity depicted so poignantly. And perhaps, too, nowhere
else does Whitman, though he transfers the pain to the spinster,
sketch so revealingly his own portrait.

Despite its poignancy the scene should not be treated in isolation, since it is organically related to what precedes and follows.
The woman, like the soul in Section 5, passes her hands over the
bodies of the bathers and even "declines with pendant and bending
arch" as "the young men float on their backs," an act at once suggestive of oral sexuality. Since "their white bellies swell to the sun"
("bulge to the sun" in the revised reading of 1856), not unlike the
"baskets . . . bulging the house with their plenty," the scene
culminates in a bisexual image of the impregnated womb and
sexual arousal, a bittersweet conclusion appropriate to the only
gratification fantasy permits, autoerotic release.

Seemingly unlike the hounded slave and the thwarted woman,
the "I" need not conceal himself in a room as a prisoner of society
or of his own unsatisfied desires, for Whitman allows him to roam
freely, but, it should be observed, only as an observer, not as an
active participant in the life he joyfully describes. He associates,
through the visual sense, with virile men (a butcher-boy, blacksmiths, and a Negro driver of a team of horses) and delights in
"the lithe sheer of their waists [which] plays even with their massive arms" and "the black of his [the Negro's] polish'd and perfect
limbs." From afar, like the woman, he is "the caresser of life
wherever moving." He identifies himself with the "Ya-honk!" of
the gander and with the "sharphoofed moose," for "I see in them
and myself the same old law" — the "procreant urge," as expressed
by "the litter of the grunting sows as they tug at her teats." Like
an impregnating god, "the press of my foot to the earth springs a
hundred affections."

What is commonest and cheapest and nearest and easiest is Me,
Me going in for my chances, spending for vast returns,
Adorning myself to bestow myself on the first that will take me,
Not asking the sky to come down to my goodwill,
Scattering it freely forever.

Now follows in Section 15 the first great catalogue, Whitman's eccentric and peculiarly American version of an ancient epic device. For almost seventy-five lines the protagonist ingests the heterogeneous sights and sounds of democracy with a greed not unlike that of the little boy in *The House of the Seven Gables* who cannot get enough of Hepzibah's gingerbread cookies. The ingestion is the consistent act of the self that opens the senses to every kind of experience without intellectual or social discrimination. The enumeration, without plan or order, is admittedly a hodge-podge, as diversified and disorderly as the nation it describes, but also as equalitarian in its disregard of class and social distinction, the President and his Cabinet receiving no more attention or importance than "the opium eater," "the prostitute," or the "five friendly matrons." (It is almost as though Whitman were deliberately giving the lie to writers like Cooper, Hawthorne, and James, who insisted despite their own achievements that a classless, democratic culture could not give birth to great literature.) Unlike any other American writer of the nineteenth century, Whitman bubbles over with a contagious exuberance that makes a mockery of genteel restraint and conventional artistic order and that embraces anything and everything with the uncritical eagerness of a child intent upon enjoying, not evaluating, the new world he is discovering. But Whitman's poetry plays over an emotional range that no other American writer of his time permits himself: in one way or another most authors restrict themselves to the kind of "intensity" which Henry James obsessively alludes to, the pleasures of the moral mind and the cerebral insight. This catalogue, then, consists of "the belched words" of a man proud of his humble origins and excited by the turbulent gyrations of a democracy which no doubt harmonized with his personal gyrations.

I resist anything better than my own diversity,
And breathe the air and leave plenty after me,
And am not stuck up, and am in my place.

There is a lull in the poem's progression as Whitman discusses "my place" in a rambling fashion — in its own way a justifiable artistic detour, since it affords leisurely consolidation of the experiences recorded in the catalogue. Beginning in Section 19 the poem gradually but surely rises to another crescendo, as Whitman prepares to define the self in a social context and to give the unnamed self a name. The birth of "Walt Whitman" is preluded by dazzling outbursts, as it were, from various parts of the orchestra before all the choirs merge in the triumphant sounds of Section 24.

First there is a banquet, a democratic gathering, to which are invited the kept woman, the spongers, the slave, and "the venerealee," all of whom hunger for love. At this Whitmanesque symposium (surely the Socratic parallel hovers in the background) man's sensuous needs are fulfilled.

This is the press of a bashful hand . . . . this is the float and odor of
    hair,
This is the touch of my lips to yours . . . . this is the murmur of
    yearning,
This is the far-off depth and height reflecting my own face,
This is the thoughtful merge of myself and the outlet again.

Do you guess I have some intricate purpose?
Well I have . . . . for the April rain has, and the mica on the side of
    a rock has.

The "I" rises to address the guests teasingly, comically, although what he has to say, he asserts, is no more astonishing than "the early redstart twittering through the woods."

Who goes there! hankering, gross, mystical, nude?
How is it I extract strength from the beef I eat?

Wittily (unlike a mystic) he accepts the body and reduces "inner strength" to a comic shambles; he has "found no sweeter fat than sticks to my own bones." The miracle of the self, the body, is his answer to the snivelers who say "That life is a suck and a sell, and nothing remains at the end but threadbare crape and tears."

I exist as I am, that is enough,
If no other in the world be aware I sit content,
And if each and all be aware I sit content.

One world is aware, and by far the largest to me, and that is myself,
And whether I come to my own today or in ten thousand or ten million
    years,
I can cheerfully take it now, or with equal cheerfulness I can wait.

My foothold is tenoned and mortised in granite,
I laugh at what you call dissolution,
And I know the amplitude of time.

I am the poet of the body,
And I am the poet of the soul.

In short, he is Eros, a god, or so he avers.

Because he is not afraid to accept and love his own body, he can
love the world. The excitingly erotic body is a microcosm of a
larger erotic landscape.

Press close barebosomed night! Press close magnetic nourishing night!
Night of south winds! Night of the large few stars!
Still nodding night! Mad naked summer night!

But, it must be noted, the eroticism unconsciously reverts to the
mother-child relationship, and the verbal aggression is not matched
by the protagonist's acts; even in fantasy Whitman cannot easily
assume the role of the aggressor. And so the situation described in
Section 5, as well as that in Section 11, is repeated. The "I"
undresses to accept the invitation of the "crooked inviting fingers"
of the seductive sea: "I believe you refuse to go back without feeling of me," as he passively accepts the caresses of the sea, which is
simultaneously associated with sexuality ("amorous wet"), maternity and the womb ("rock me in billowy drowse"), and death
("unshovelled and always-ready graves").

"Partaker of influx and efflux," like the sea, and "extoller of
amies and those that sleep in each others' arms," he cares not at all
for the "blurt . . . about virtue and about vice." For he has found
"a word of the faith that never balks" and "a word of reality." With
a "Hurrah for positive science!" he accepts its "facts" as "useful
and real," but "they are not my dwelling." Although Whitman
was interested in the scientific theories of the nineteenth century
and did not share Hawthorne's fear of monomaniacal scientists —
he has sometimes, dubiously, been termed a poet of the new science
— he no more revered the artificial intellectual constructs of

science than those of religion, since both degraded the body. "I,"
he says with devastating wit, "make short account of neuters and
geldings, and favor men and women fully equipped" — as rollick-
ing and rabelaisian a line as one can find in American literature.

"Fully equipped," the protagonist is about to "beat the gong of
revolt" and declare himself with exuberant and comic recklessness,
but with an artful control that only a virtuoso can achieve.

Walt Whitman, an American, one of the roughs, a kosmos,
Disorderly fleshy and sensual . . . . eating drinking and breeding,
No sentimentalist . . . . no stander above men and women or apart
    from them . . . . no more modest than immodest.

Here he affirms his bond with the land and its people, who, as his
catalogue reveals, are also "Disorderly fleshy and sensual." With a
swashbuckling comic command he clears away (again) cultural
orders and proclaims the birth of the authentic self.

Unscrew the locks from the doors!
Unscrew the doors themselves from their jambs!

He now utters "the password primeval . . . . I give the sign of
democracy," as he explicitly links his personal pilgrimage to self-
realization to the aims of a perfect (but imaginary) democracy.
The brilliant flow of words cannot conceal the fact that Whitman
has made democracy over in terms of his own needs for identity
and security. The Jonathans of his day, and later, found only
ludicrous the cries of one who refused to differentiate "fog in the
air and beetles rolling balls of dung," who seemed intent upon
finding beauty in slime, and who was willing to indulge in sexual
exhibitionism that "nice" people found childish.

I do not press my finger across my mouth,
I keep as delicate around the bowels as around the head and heart,
Copulation is no more rank to me than death is.

I believe in the flesh and the appetites,
Seeing hearing and feeling are miracles, and each part and tag of me
    is a miracle.

Divine am I inside and out, and I make holy whatever I touch or am
    touched from;

The scent of these arm-pits is aroma finer than prayer,
The head is more than churches or bibles or creeds.

Uninhibitedly, but comically too, Whitman indulges in the delights
of his "luscious" body (again the feeding motif) and makes the
physical landscape reflect his need for tactile gratification: "Winds
whose soft-tickling genitals rub against me," which also evokes
the child-mother motif.

This sensual orgy springing from autoerotic fantasies is Whitman's poetic equivalent of Wagner's Venusberg music. The erotic
outpouring is interrupted for a moment when the mind (or reality
principle) seems to silence the exuberance: "I pause to consider
if it really be"; but the discordant doubt vanishes since the protagonist desires to absorb, not to think about, his experience: "The
air tastes good to my palate." He projects upon nature his own
sexual exhilaration:

Hefts of the moving world at innocent gambols, silently rising, freshly
    exuding,
Scooting obliquely high and low.

Something I cannot see puts upward libidinous prongs,
Seas of bright juice suffuse heaven.

The earth by the sky staid with . . . . the daily close of their junction,
The heaved challenge from the east that moment over my head,
The mocking taunt, See then whether you shall be master!

Jocularly the protagonist goads himself to emulate nature's freedom
and power. As in Section 5, the poet's tongue is both tongue and
phallus, but Whitman evasively indulges in double-entendres, as
well as a pun upon the word "conceive."

My voice goes after what my eyes cannot reach,
With the twirl of my tongue I encompass worlds and volumes of worlds.

Speech is the twin of my vision . . . . it is unequal to measure itself.
It provokes me forever,
It says sarcastically, Walt, you understand enough . . . . why don't you
    let it out then?

Come now I will not be tantalized . . . . you conceive too much of
    articulation.

His "prophetical screams," he asserts, will free the silent seeds
lying in the earth — and the hidden potential of those who dare to
"undrape": "whoever hears me let him or her set out in search of
this day." But the poet-lover suddenly refuses his "final merit":
"I refuse putting from me the best I am." This is the erotic titillation — the aggression followed by withdrawal — that Whitman
invariably has recourse to whenever connections are in danger of
being formed.

Encompass worlds but never try to encompass me,
I crowd your noisiest talk by looking toward you.

In final analysis this is an Eros with marked puritanical asceticism.
    The mood alters momentarily, then, as he retreats to become
once again the recipient of sensory sensations, but this time he is
not so passive as in the section in which he listens to "the blab of
the pave." For now his body quivers as it takes in sensations:

I hear the trained soprano . . . . she convulses me like the climax of
    my love-grip;
The orchestra whirls me wider than Uranus flies,
It wrenches unnamable ardors from my breast,
It throbs me to gulps of the farthest down horror,
It sails me. . . .

The imagery in Sections 26 to 29 is primarily oral: "The orbic
flex of his [the tenor's] mouth is pouring and filling me full," "bare
feet . . . are licked by the indolent waves," "honeyed morphine,"
"my windpipe squeezed," "the udder of my heart for its withheld
drip," "pasture fields," "go and graze at the edges of me," "sharptoothed touch." Accompanying the oral images are the customary
tactile responses of a man hungering for love:

Mine is no callous shell,
I have instant conductors all over me whether I pass or stop,
They seize every object and lead it harmlessly through me.

I merely stir, press, feel with my fingers, and am happy,
To touch my person to some one else's is about as much as I can stand.

Almost at once the throbbing sexual tension finds release, in a fantasy not unlike that of the spinster in Section 11, when a gang of "prurient provokers" "encompass" (a revealing word) him in a thinly disguised homosexual interlude. The scene, however, is psychologically and artistically inevitable: sexuality must be played out on an infantile level, and the image clusters to which reference has been made prepare us for the passive or feminine role that the protagonist assumes not only here but also in Section 5 ("Unbuttoning my clothes and holding me by the bare waist"). The oral and tactile images coalesce in an evocation of the mother's breast, particularly in the elusive but significant description of the phallus: "Straining the udder of my heart for its withheld drip." Fearful but also desirous of the sexual assault, the protagonist talks "wildly" — "I have lost my wits" — until he candidly admits his own autoeroticism: "I went myself first to the headland . . . . my own hands carried me there." Then, in a characteristic shift of mood, the "I" moves from fear to the contentment of orgasmic fulfillment:

You villain touch! what are you doing? . . . . my breath is tight in its
    throat;
Unclench your floodgates! you are too much for me.

Blind loving wrestling touch! Sheathed hooded sharptoothed touch!
Did it make you ache so leaving me?

Parting tracked by arriving . . . . perpetual payment of the perpetual
    loan,
Rich showering rain, and recompense richer afterward.

Sprouts take and accumulate . . . . stand by the curb prolific and vital,
Landscapes projected masculine full-sized and golden.

As in Section 5, following sexual release he can "incorporate gneiss and coal and long-threaded moss and fruits and grains and esculent roots" — a culminative expression of the feeding imagery.[3] Now calm, sexually at peace with himself and by extension with the universe, the protagonist forms no relationship with the "provokers," who quickly vanish, but sings rather of the miracle and harmony of creation:

I believe a leaf of grass is no less than the journeywork of the stars,
And the pismire is equally perfect, and a grain of sand, and the egg of
　　the wren,
And the tree-toad is a chef-d'œuvre for the highest,
And the running blackberry would adorn the parlors of heaven,
And the narrowest hinge in my hand puts to scorn all machinery,
And the cow crunching with depressed head surpasses any statue,
And a mouse is miracle enough to stagger sextillions of infidels . . . .

"Stucco'd with quadrupeds and birds all over," emblematical perhaps of man's primitivistic origins and anticipating the appearance
of the "flowing savage" in Section 39 (and, incidentally, not unreminiscent of Queequeg's tattoos), he admires the "placid and
self-contained" animals which do not experience the agonies of
"civilized" man:

They do not sweat and whine about their condition,
They do not lie awake in the dark and weep for their sins,
They do not make me sick discussing their duty to God,
Not one is dissatisfied . . . . not one is demented with the mania of
　　owning things,
Not one kneels to another nor to his kind that lived thousands of years
　　ago,
Not one is respectable or industrious over the whole earth.

Among the animals the "I" establishes a relationship "on brotherly
terms" with "a gigantic beauty of a stallion, fresh and responsive to
my caresses," which recalls the earlier line, "Stout as a horse, affectionate, haughty, electrical." Significantly, but sadly, the protagonist's relationship with the horse is excessively ardent, virtually
orgiastic: "His nostrils dilate . . . . my heels embrace him . . . . his
well built limbs tremble with pleasure . . . . we speed around and
return," as one hears reverberating in the background words from
the crucial fifth section: "You settled your head athwart my hips
and gently turned over upon me." The protagonist uses the horse
but for "a moment," since its speed cannot emulate the motion of
man's imagination ("My Soul"): "And myself as I stand or sit pass
faster than you."
　　Up to this point in the poem Whitman has emphasized the body
almost to the exclusion of the soul after the latter's emancipatory

act in Section 5. Now he has the soul float freely through time and space, but since body and soul are not antithetical, the poem does not suddenly become a mystical experience. The soul in space assumes the same horizontal or amorous posture as the body:

My ties and ballasts leave me . . . . I travel . . . . I sail . . . . my elbows
    rest in the sea-gaps,
I skirt the sierras . . . . my palms cover continents,
I am afoot with my vision.

In the catalogue in Section 33, which parallels that in Section 15, "the fluid and swallowing soul" is essentially no different from the body as it takes in experiences: "All this I swallow and it tastes good," "tasting the sweet of the brown squash . . . . sucking the juice through a straw," "and the geese nip their food with short jerks," and "I visit the orchards of God." The landscape the soul traverses is as eroticized as that which the body discovers: "the she-whale swims with her calves and never forsakes them," "At he-festivals with blackguard jibes and ironical license and bull-dances and drinking and laughter," and "Where the bull advances to do his masculine work, and the stud to the mare, and the cock is treading the hen."

Although this second catalogue is in most respects a variation upon a theme, it also broadens Whitman's canvas, since the "soul" is not confined to the contemporary American terrain but wanders in a universal, timeless landscape. At one moment the "I" presses "the flesh of my nose to the thick plate-glass" of "shop-windows in Broadway": "My right and left arms round the sides of two friends and I in the middle" (once again Whitman's familiar trio). In successive lines he is in settlements with a "bush-boy," handing lemonade to a hospital patient, observing a "coffined corpse when all is still, examining with a candle," dickering in a port, and "Hurrying with the modern crowd . . . / Hot toward one I hate, ready in my madness to knife him." Abruptly, as in "The Sleepers," the mood alters from murderous rage to love, from violent involvement to lonely meditation:

Solitary at midnight in my back yard, my thoughts gone from me a
    long while,

Walking the old hills of Judea with the beautiful gentle god by my
side. . . . .

Is this a picture of Jesus or of Eros ambiguously transplanted to
Judea or a reappearance of the god who is "a loving bedfellow" —
or a veiled "Calamus" association?

Sensually stretching "around on the wonderful beauty," the self
(the soul) asserts: "I am a free companion" — and without guilt
turns "the bridegroom out of bed" and tightens the bride "all night
to my thighs and lips." Consistency perhaps demands that the
soul continue in the aggressively sexual role defined in Section 5,
yet such is Whitman's innate fear of assertiveness, or maleness,
that the self is immediately transformed into a wife who bewails
the loss of her husband:

My voice is the wife's voice, the screech by the rail of the stairs,
They fetch my man's body up dripping and drowned.

Next the protagonist identifies himself with the brutally beaten
slave, "the mashed fireman with breastbone broken," and with
other wounded and dying men. Sexuality and pain, life and death
— the pendulum swings with Whitman's characteristic oscilla-
tions: "Agonies are one of my changes of garments." Verbal and
emotional parallels between these scenes of physical pain and the
earlier scenes of physical joy are striking. "As I lean on a cane and
observe [the wounded]" refers back to the fifth line of the poem:
"I lean and loafe at my ease . . . . observing a spear of summer
grass." "My hurt turns livid upon me" evokes "You settled your
head athwart my hips and gently turned over upon me" (Section
5). In the episode of the tormented slave, "I wince at the bite
of the dogs" conjures up the sexual assault in Sections 28 and 29,
"Sheathed hooded sharptoothed touch." Similarly, the protagonist's outburst in his identification with the slave, "Hell and
despair are upon me . . . . crack and again crack the marksmen,"
repeats his emotional turbulence in the scene with the "provokers,"
"I am given up by traitors; / I talk wildly . . . . I have lost my
wits." The description of the fireman after his body is removed
from the debris, "I lie in the night air in my red shirt," also recalls
Section 28, "They have left me helpless to a red marauder."

In Whitman's consistently undifferentiated universe his protagonists are eager recipients, ingesters, of all experience.

All this I swallow and it tastes good . . . . I like it well, and it becomes mine,
I am the man . . . . I suffered . . . . I was there.

Which is scarcely a messianic statement of compassion so much as it is the candid, perhaps somewhat desperate, cry of a man who wants to justify and to dignify his (and man's) existence. Despite the assertions of those who damn Whitman's affirmations without troubling to study the means by which he arrives at his conclusions, he, like Emerson, never skirts harsh realities; he refuses, however, to be overwhelmed by evil or innate depravity. One sees more or less what one wants to see: Whitman sees the cycle of existence not in the negative terms of Ecclesiastes or of Melville, but in the positive terms of the eternal potentialities open to man if he is willing to grasp them:

Distant and dead resuscitate,
They show as the dial or move as the hands of me . . . . and I am the clock myself.

The "clock" serves as a transitional device from deaths in the present to three elegiac sections (34–36) relating the deaths of soldiers in "a jetblack sunrise" at Alamo, of sailors lost in a "frigate-fight," and of a ship's crew. These disasters duplicate the death scenes in "The Sleepers" (the swimmer, the passengers aboard a ship, and Washington's soldiers in the Revolutionary War), as both poems pass through "hell and despair" or the Everlasting No. Both protagonists are momentarily overcome with rage and perhaps feelings of helplessness. "O Christ! My fit is mastering me!" the protagonist in "Song of Myself" cries. The emotional swings are especially turbulent here and in the following section — from the "fit" to "the rebel . . . gaily adjusting his throat to the rope-noose," from the weary beggar sitting with hat outstretched to "I rise extatic through all, and sweep with the true gravitation." And then at once from ecstasy to

Somehow I have been stunned. Stand back!
Give me a little time beyond my cuffed head and slumbers and dreams
    and gaping,
I discover myself on a verge of the usual mistake.

That I could forget the mockers and insults!
That I could forget the trickling tears and the blows of the bludgeons
    and hammers!
That I could look with a separate look on my own crucifixion and
    bloody crowning!

I remember . . . . I resume the overstaid fraction. . . .

When he resumes "the overstaid fraction" he is ready to "troop
forth replenished with supreme power, one of an average unending
procession": he has been preoccupied with pain, which excludes
or minimizes joy; he has been preoccupied with defeat, which
excludes victory; tragedy, or "my own crucifixion," has absorbed
him in the separateness of pain and self-pity and has momentarily
eclipsed the comic vision of men united in joy.

In the cyclical fashion characteristic of the poem and of the
sexual rhythm upon which it is based, "crucifixion" is (once more)
followed by resurrection, doubt and vacillation (the Everlasting
No) give way to affirmation (the Everlasting Yea), and death
culminates in the birth (or rebirth) of the "friendly and flowing
savage" in the thirty-ninth section (or week). The final movement
of the poem is Whitman's "Ode to Joy." The "savage" is the culmination of the birth imagery that sees the emergence of the
sensuous body in Section 5, of "Walt Whitman" in Section 24,
and of sexual man in Sections 28 and 29. Coincidentally, Whitman's "friendly and flowing savage" marks his departure from
Emerson, who confided to his Journal in 1842 that he "could not
stand the dissipation of a flowing and friendly life." Whitman
wallows joyfully in the "dissipation" as he marries sound and sense
in a crescendo which is a kind of epithalamion.

Earlier motifs are repeated, for the words of the savage are
"simple as grass," and he too sends forth emanations from all the
senses — "the tips of his fingers," "the odor of his body," and "the
glance of his eyes." He is a comic impregnator, a fertility god:

On women fit for conception I start bigger and nimbler babes,
This day I am jetting the stuff of far more arrogant republics.

To the impotent, "I blow grit within you" and "lift the flaps of
your pockets." To "a drudge of the cottonfields . . . I put the
family kiss." To the dying, "I dilate you with tremendous breath."
The oral images evoke the womb and birth, as the overlord of
creation fills all the bodily openings and proclaims the powers of
the democratic artist: "I do not ask who you are . . . . that is not
important to me." Never before in literary history had an artist so
passionately (almost stridently) "embraced" the common man,
even the "emptier of privies."

Whitman's savage is a man-god gleefully asserting his creative
powers and gaily toppling the idols of the past. With witty arrogance the savage takes on the cosmos:

Flaunt of the sunshine I need not your bask . . . . lie over,
You light surfaces only . . . . I force the surfaces and the depths also.

Earth! you seem to look for something at my hands,
Say old topknot! what do you want?

With gusto he goes into the marketplace, "Outbidding at the start
the old cautious hucksters, from "Jehovah" to "hideous-faced
Mexitli": "Honestly taking them all for what they are worth, and
not a cent more." The "cautious hucksters" through the ages have
sold food for the soul only, offering limited and limiting concep-
tions of man. The man-god dismisses them with one of the most
brazen and outrageously comic lines in literature: "The most they
offer for mankind and eternity less than a spirt of my own seminal
wet." The hucksters, Whitman admits, "did the work of their
day," but they no longer speak to democratic Americans: "Accepting the rough deific sketches to fill out better in myself . . . .
bestowing them freely on each man and woman I see." (Whitman
throughout this passage plays upon economic imagery like a
metaphysical poet.) The new man has new "revelations" of his
time and his place: "considering a curl of smoke or a hair on the
back of my hand as curious as any revelation." He does not have
to conjure up the Trojan War to observe heroism: "Those ahold of

fire-engines and hook-and-ladder ropes more to me than the gods
of the antique wars." (The death of the fireman in Section 33 has
the heroic beauty of an Homeric death scene.) Nor does he have
to turn to the Virgin or the glories of Renaissance art to discover
beauty:

By the mechanic's wife with her babe at her nipple interceding for
    every person born;
Three scythes at harvest whizzing in a row from three lusty angels
    with shirts bagged out at their waists. . . .

For beauty has not vanished with the collapse of the Mediterranean
norms or the death of the old gods; it emerges everywhere in the
most unlikely places.

The bull and the bug never worshipped half enough,
Dung and dirt more admirable than was dreamed,
The supernatural of no account. . . .

This marvelously witty section, one of the finest in the poem, concludes with two incomparable lines which are a comic and sexual
climax as well as a statement of faith, self-mockery which makes
the savage's aggressiveness tolerable as well as satire upon the
"science" of phrenology, a ribald statement of the source of
artistic creativity as well as a lovely birth image.

By my life-lumps! becoming already a creator!
Putting myself here and now to the ambushed womb of the shadows!

With comic exuberance Whitman thus spells out a modern artistic
credo of the sublime and in his portrait of the artist adumbrates the
esthetic epiphanies of a secular, democratic age.

   And so "My own voice, orotund sweeping and final," sounds to
the crowd:

Come my children,
Come my boys and girls, and my women and household and intimates,
Now the performer launches his nerve . . . . he has passed his prelude
    on the reeds within.

The musical analogy is apt: music suggests "the flowing savage" or the authentic, primeval self; the fluid quality of continuity; and the orgiastic nature of love ("Ever love . . . . ever the sobbing liquid of life"). Music represents the taking in and giving out of the sensuous experiences necessary for the Whitmanesque whole self, for his banquet or "feast" which the dire, sense-denying words of the "cautious hucksters" spoil: "Easily written loosefingered chords! I feel the thrum of their climax and close." Music, in short, leads to the "omnivorous words" which "indicate reality," the reality beyond that of "this printed and bound book," "saints and sages in history," and "sermons and creeds and theology" — the reality of the sentient, democratic self.

At last the "I" will make explicit what has been implicit, as he dramatically rises from the earth, from his meditative survey of a "spear of summer grass."

It is time to explain myself . . . . let us stand up.

What is known I strip away . . . . I launch all men and women forward with me into the unknown.

The clock indicates the moment . . . . but what does eternity indicate?

Keeping "no account with lamentation," he is not afraid to face "the huge first Nothing, the vapor from the nostrils of death"; for the cradle endlessly rocks:

Long I was hugged close . . . . long and long.
Immense have been the preparations for me,
Faithful and friendly the arms that have helped me.

Cycles ferried my cradle, rowing and rowing like cheerful boatmen;
For room to me stars kept aside in their own rings,
They sent influences to look after what was to hold me.

The verbal expansiveness of the savage-poet, like Ahab's "crazy" proposals to his crew, exerts such hypnotic power that one does not recognize immediately the regressive imagery upon which it is predicated. Not only does the "cradle" evoke the sheltered mother-child relationship so omnipresent in Whitman's poetry, but his description of the life cycle — "youth," "manhood balanced and florid and full!" and "old age superbly rising!" — significantly depicts "manhood" as a state in which his lovers "suffocate" him, "bussing my body with soft and balsamic busses." In short, the important middle part of man's life is described in arrested infantile terms, those of a Rip Van Winkle rather than of the self-reliant "manly" man of Emerson.

There is another unresolved conflict, since Whitman's awareness of man's solitary lot clashes with his fantasy of the poet-savior. At one moment he consigns man to the lonely protestant quest —

Not I, not any one else can travel that road for you,
You must travel it for yourself . . .
. . . .
You are also asking me questions, and I hear you;
I answer that I cannot answer . . . . you must find out for yourself —

only to assume almost immediately a parental relationship with the disciple when he offers the pilgrim biscuits, milk, and a "goodbye kiss" — a kind of parody of the Last Supper and a witty rebuttal to the puritanical fear of emotions; Whitman, significantly, is both father and mother:

Long enough have you dreamed contemptible dreams,
Now I wash the gum from your eyes,
You must habit yourself to the dazzle of the light and of every moment
    of your life.

Long have you timidly waded, holding a plank by the shore,
Now I will you to be a bold swimmer,
To jump off in the midst of the sea, and rise again and nod to me and
    shout, and laughingly dash with your hair.

Then the teacher, like his master Emerson, reminds his readers: "He most honors my style who learns under it to destroy the teacher." But a few lines later the self-confident artist contradicts himself:

I teach straying from me, yet who can stray from me?
I follow you whoever you are from the present hour;
My words itch at your ears till you understand them.

And in one sense Whitman is right, since his verses "itch" at our ears seductively and lead us to the aural delights of his delightfully unreal universe; yet our minds, those perennial deflators of our hearts and those servants of rationalism and of the reality principle, note, as the sounds fade away, that the overman's credo proposes an independence not only unattainable in a peopled world but also predicated upon childlike dependency.

But such logical matters are of little consequence in evaluating the artistic unity or in experiencing the emotional impact of this incomparable poem. "Song of Myself," structurally, reflects the natural and human cycles that are its subject matter; the motifs coil and uncoil like the waves of the sea, to use Whitman's figure of speech, or more precisely and humanly, like "the procreant urge," the sonorous images coming and receding like birth and death. The poet-overman assures the solitary wanderer (the reader):

It is you talking just as much as myself . . . . I act as the tongue of you,
I was tied in your mouth . . . . in mine it begins to be loosened —

lines which are reminiscent of those in Section 5:

Loafe with me on the grass . . . . loose the stop from your throat,
Not words, not music or rhyme I want . . . . not custom or lecture, not even the best,
Only the lull I like, the hum of your valved voice.

"In the open air," not in a "shuttered room or school," and for "roughs and little children," not for the followers of the "hucksters," the protagonist summarizes his vision:

I have said that the soul is not more than the body,
And I have said that the body is not more than the soul,
And nothing, not God, is greater to one than one's-self is. . . .
. . . .
I hear and behold God in every object, yet I understand God not in the least,
Nor do I understand who there can be more wonderful than myself.

Section 49 reiterates that death does not "alarm" him, since it is part of the cycle: "I recline by the sills of the exquisite flexible doors . . . . and mark the outlet, and mark the relief and escape." (Quietly the line recalls the comic exhilaration of an earlier one: "Unscrew the locks from the doors!") Even corpses are not offensive — "you are good manure" —

I smell the white roses sweetscented and growing,
I reach to the leafy lips . . . . I reach to the polished breasts of
    melons. . . .

This evocation of the child at the breast of the eternal mother brings to our eyes and ears once more a line in Section 5: "And reached till you felt my beard, and reached till you held my feet." The birth motif is further developed in an exquisite passage:

Of the turbid pool that lies in the autumn forest,
Of the moon that descends the steeps of the soughing twilight,
Toss, sparkles of day and dusk . . . . toss on the black stems that decay
    in the muck,
Toss to the moaning gibberish of the dry limbs.

I ascend from the moon . . . . I ascend from the night,
And perceive of the ghastly glitter the sunbeams reflected,
And debouch to the steady and central from the offspring great or
    small.

The sexual rhythm, unlike that in Sections 5 and 29, is quieter, less physical, appropriately so at this juncture as Whitman generalizes his theme and prepares for the quiet conclusion of the poem. "Debouch," rather than being an affected usage of a French word such as sometimes occurs in Whitman's verse, is carefully chosen and suggestive on at least three levels: literally it means to emerge from the mouth or an opening, thus referring to the birth of the "offspring" as well as to the creative act and utterance of the artist himself; in its military sense it recalls the "sentries" guarding the sexual passageways in Section 28; and again in a military sense it means to come forth from a shut-in place into open country — all of which meanings parallel the birth throes recorded in this poem and the journey from personal and cultural repressions to freedom and affirmation:

It is not chaos or death . . . . it is form and union and plan . . . .
it is eternal life . . . . it is happiness.

The word "happiness" leads Whitman in Section 51 into a virtuoso performance without parallel in American literature, except perhaps in Ishmael's tragicomic "unbuttoning" in *Moby-Dick* ("A Bower in the Arsacides"), the contemporary work with which "Song of Myself" has most artistic affinities. With immodest ribaldry Whitman proclaims his prophetic role:

The past and present wilt . . . . I have filled them and emptied them,
And proceed to fill my next fold of the future.

For a moment he sounds like "crazy" Ahab except that his mockery is reverent of self and otherness and is devoid of gnawing self-hatred:

Listener up there! Here you . . . . what have you to confide in me?
Look in my face while I snuff the sidle of evening,
Talk honestly, for no one else hears you, and I stay only a minute
    longer.

Though he good-naturedly flaunts his equality with the "Listener" and once again attacks the dogmas of the "cautious hucksters" ("Talk honestly"), the middle line is a brilliant inversion of the mother-child motif, as Burke suggests. The protagonist, who is as certain of himself as Whitman is of his art, honestly avows his lack of logic and his inconsistency, as do Emerson and Montaigne.

Do I contradict myself?
Very well then . . . . I contradict myself;
I am large . . . . I contain multitudes.

He informs us: "I wait on the door-slab" for the companion who "will soonest be through with his supper." The door is open, the feast is ended.

In the awesome conclusion of *Moby-Dick* the predatory bird seems to be part of a diabolic plan to topple Ahab from his "top-most greatness," but in Whitman's finale the hawk is amused by the "gab" since everything is part of a beneficent plan. At this

climactic moment Whitman dares, such is his masterful control, to
deflate the greatness of his protagonist (Walt Whitman) without
loss of dignity or grandeur. The "yawp" becomes a pianissimo in
which the orgiastic note is present but muted. The protagonist
permits himself to be coaxed amorously as, in effect, the runaway
slave is accepted by the "runaway sun," and the frustration of the
chaste woman in Section 11 disappears in the "merge" with death.
The "I" who is "observing a spear of summer grass" at the beginning of the poem is now beneath the earth, and for the last time
(which is for all time) addresses "you" seductively.

The spotted hawk swoops by and accuses me . . . . he complains of my
    gab and my loitering.

I too am not a bit tamed . . . . I too am untranslatable,
I sound my barbaric yawp over the roofs of the world.

The last scud of day holds back for me,
It flings my likeness after the rest and true as any on the shadowed
    wilds,
It coaxes me to the vapor and the dusk.

I depart as air . . . . I shake my white locks at the runaway sun,
I effuse my flesh in eddies and drift it in lacy jags.

I bequeath myself to the dirt to grow from the grass I love,
If you want me again look for me under your bootsoles.

You will hardly know who I am or what I mean,
But I shall be good health to you nevertheless,
And filter and fibre your blood.

Failing to fetch me at first keep encouraged,
Missing me one place search another,
I stop some where waiting for you

6

"singing the phallus"

In his old age, in 1889, Whitman observed to Horace Traubel that Natty Bumppo was "peculiarly a Leaves of Grass man." Of Cooper he said: "There were reasons why he and I should have fraternized: I look upon Cooper as new rather than old — as belonging to our era, as cultivating our graces."[1] As usual, Whitman gave no "reasons": in prose and in conversation he preferred to hint; but his "indirections" cannot be dismissed lightly. For Whitman was making an astute comparison without the explicitness of Edwin Fussell's well-taken point: "The Leatherstocking Tales are not in any ordinary sense great art; but the rest of American writing through Whitman is a series of footnotes on them."[2]

Whitman's hero is in many respects an elaboration of Cooper's — this despite the fact that Natty Bumppo is a saint who successfully defends his purity against the aggressive designs of women, while Whitman's overman, with comic hyperbole, prides himself on his power to impregnate the cosmos, but, significantly, forms no permanent relationships with the opposite sex. Like Natty, Whitman's savage is always in motion, which may be but another way to say, in flight. The overt and almost exhibitionistic phallicism in Whitman has its counterpart in Cooper's reverence for Natty's prowess as a hunter and for the magical (religious) powers of his rifle, which wards off all evil, including women. What else is the following account of Natty's rifle in Chapter XXV of *The Deerslayer* but an instance of disguise and displacement?

The Mingos [the evil Indians] will turn green with envy; and, what is more, they will not ventur' heedlessly near a village where it is known to be kept. So look well to it, Delaware, and remember that you've now to watch over a thing that has all the valie of a creatur', without its failin's. Hist [Delaware's sweetheart] may be and should be precious to you, but Killdeer will have the love and veneration of your whole people.

Like the savage, who appears full-grown out of the endless space of fantasy, Natty Bumppo is an orphan who owes nothing at all to his parents, whom apparently at an early age he leaves behind in the settlement as he takes himself off to the frontier to live with the "good" Indians, where he matures in an environment uncorrupted by civilized destructiveness (or cultural repressions). So, too, Whitman's characteristic protagonist abandons home, family, and civilized institutions in order to become a "rowdy"; or, as he puts it in "Song of Myself," the savage's "Behaviour [is] lawless as snowflakes" — a lovely justification of amorality and rugged individualism. Natty, too, is a law unto himself, although he never abandons his Anglo-Saxon virtues and racial theories, but at the same time he has messianic pretensions, for his "Here!" in effect makes him the son of the protestant deity. Similarly, Whitman's savage is a teacher or a poet of the body rather than a Don Juan. Deadly with his trusted rifle — Natty is the antithesis of the effeminate Christ of Renaissance art — he is, however, dead instinctually. Balzac justifiably termed Natty "a magnificent moral hermaphrodite, born between the savage and the civilized worlds." For Cooper's hero is a saint American-style. His manly asceticism, or athletic saintliness, reappears triumphantly, and insistently, in the pages of *Walden, Adventures of Huckleberry Finn, The American, The Sun Also Rises,* and *The Great Gatsby.* The alleged sexual exploits of Whitman's creation, we feel, are but wish fulfillment: the chastity of the conception is inescapable.

Throughout his five tales relating the life of Natty Bumppo, Cooper toys, fearfully, with the union of the red man and the white trapper: Natty, we are told, "consorts" not with women but with Chingachgook, and the only genuine affectional scenes involve Natty's relationships with Indians like Uncas and Hard-Heart. Death occasionally has to intervene to protect Natty's purity and Cooper's beliefs in white supremacy. The union that Cooper unconsciously craves while he fears its social and moral consequences is clearly revealed in Chapter VI of *The Last of the Mohicans*. The scene is a pictorial tableau which becomes a revelation of the unconscious: the setting, "a narrow, deep cavern in the rock," has the womblike characteristics of similar settings in Poe, Hawthorne, and Melville; and the light and shadows cast by "a blazing knot of pine," held by Natty himself, have qualities not only of a dream but also of Plato's cave:

The strong glare of the fire fell full upon his sturdy, weather-beaten countenance and forest attire, lending an air of romantic wildness to the aspect of an individual who, seen by the sober light of day, would have exhibited the peculiarities of a man remarkable for the strangeness of his dress, the iron-like inflexibility of his frame, and the singular compound of quick, vigilant sagacity, and of exquisite simplicity, that by turns usurped the possession of his muscular features.

The romantic but intellectual (or moralized) idealization of the whiteness of Natty and his virtues is eclipsed by the fuller and more emotional depiction of the redness of the noble Uncas,

his whole person thrown powerfully into view. The travellers anxiously regarded the upright, flexible figure of the young Mohican, graceful and unrestrained in the attitudes and movements of nature. Though his person was more than usually screened by a green and fringed hunting-shirt, like that of the white man, there was no concealment to his dark, glancing, fearless eye, alike terrible and calm; the bold outline of his high, haughty features, pure in their native red; or to the dignified elevation of his receding forehead, together with all the finest proportions of a noble head, bared to the generous scalping tuft . . . . The ingenuous Alice gazed at his free air and proud carriage, as she would have looked upon some precious relic of the Grecian chisel, to which life had been imparted by the intervention of a miracle; while Heyward . . . . openly expressed his admiration at such an unblemished specimen of the noblest proportions of men.

His morality momentarily subordinated to what he would term his poetic sense, Cooper reveals regret that despite his moral grandeur his Yankee leatherstocking lacks the physical beauty and non-rational power of the transplanted classical hero — an inadvertent admission of a failure both of Christianity and of American democracy. Even in *The Prairie,* where Natty is established as the first of the American saints, Cooper complements the waning strength of the eighty-year-old trapper with the "Apollo-like person of Hard-Heart," who becomes what no white man becomes in the tales, Natty's son.

The savage in "Song of Myself" fuses Natty and Uncas, the frontiersman and the classical hero.

The friendly and flowing savage . . . . Who is he?
Is he waiting for civilization or past it and mastering it?

Is he some southwesterner raised outdoors? Is he Canadian?
Is he from the Mississippi country? or from Iowa, Oregon or California? or from the mountain? or prairie life or bush-life? or from the sea?

Wherever he goes men and women accept and desire him,
They desire he should like them and touch them and speak to them and stay with them.

Behaviour lawless as snow-flakes . . . . words simple as grass . . . . uncombed head and laughter and naivete;
Slowstepping feet and the common features, and the common modes and emanations,
They descend in new forms from the tips of his fingers,
They are wafted with the odor of his body or breath . . . . they fly out of the glance of his eyes.

Like Cooper's, Whitman's figment is a man-god in Western (almost cowboy) attire, an Adam of the New World (without an Eve), and a poet.

The American hero, or representative man of the collective fantasy, differs fundamentally from his European counterpart in a "century of hero-worship" and from Emerson's "representative men." He is a New World phenomenon, an "original," a typically idiosyncratic offshoot of our unphilosophical adaptation of Lockean philosophy, of our classless and mobile society, and of the resultant loneliness and isolation which characterize our literature and life. The American hero, of humble, democratic origins, is more muscular than intellectual, more moralistic (or addicted to Ben Franklinisms) than philosophical, and perhaps more comic than tragic, since he never completely outgrows the whoppers of a Paul Bunyan or a culturally decreed optimism. He is the very model of a self-made man, or of self-reliance, which makes him, unwittingly, into an asocial creature always in flight from entangling emotional and familial involvements. He manages somehow, perhaps because there is no denying his puritanical heritage, to maintain his peculiarly American muscular protestantism that professes to scorn the "effeminate" worship of the Virgin in its "manly" relationship with a deity created in its own image. In short, the American hero is an outrageous but lovable hybrid, but so, too, are artistic masterpieces like *The Scarlet Letter, Moby-Dick, Walden,* and "Song of Myself."

Characteristically, despite the unending but vain search for an epic that will subsume the vast, heterogeneous American landscape and amorphous American society, this hero is lyrical and elegiac rather than epic. The conception rests not so much upon nostalgia for what was, as upon a longing for what will be if artist-gods fashion the future. In other words, the hero, despite his (exaggerated) brawn and his (comic) exploits, reflects the personal and collective anguish of writers and of a people who conceal their uncertainties and anxieties behind heroic posturing. The hero, born at a time when civilization was at what later is called the abyss, was expected to perform unperformable miracles — to fill the void of a waning protestantism and a declining patriarchy, both religious and social, to restore manliness to a society obsessively afraid of the Dame Van Winkles, to come to terms with the hated but covertly admired Indians, to maintain heroic ideals against the leveling tendencies of Jacksonian democracy, to supply emotional and affectional gratification in the age of capitalism and the dynamo. Under such circumstances the hero could be but a lovely abstraction, the utterer of beautifully futile words to the winds of change. (Rightly, the "spotted hawk . . . complains of my gab and my loitering.") The crowning irony of the conception — and an unconscious admission of despair — is the fact that these heroes found no race, leave no offspring. At the moment of his apotheosis, Natty Bumppo says, "Here!" but the reality and biological principle must say in turn, "Where?" And Whitman is forced to say at the conclusion of "Song of Myself," "If you want me again look for me under your bootsoles."

The stridently virile American hero is the creation, not only of disaffected and isolated artists, but also of a society which feared attacks upon its manliness, presumably by women, and particularly by mothers, who were, ambivalently, raised to heights reserved only for (nonexistent) angels. Manliness was insisted upon in attire, deportment, prose style, and moral sentiments. Wrestlers were, in the journalistic jargon of the day, exemplars of "muscular Christianity." The pervasiveness of the cultural ideal (and fear) is evident in an anecdote which Captain Frederick Marryat records in *Diary in America:* (1839):

I recollect a gentleman introducing me to the son of another gentleman who was present. The lad, who was about fourteen, . . . shortly after left the room; and then the gentleman told me, before the boy's father, that the lad was one of the right sort, having already fought, and wounded his man; and the father smiled complacently at this tribute to the character of his son.[3]

The gentleman's reaction is scarcely different, except for the significant absence of sadism and of boastfulness, from Natty's reaction when in *The Deerslayer* he is compelled to kill his first "bad" Indian, or from Whitman's famous outburst, the childish aggressiveness of which the comic context cannot wholly disguise:

Walt Whitman, an American, one of the roughs, a kosmos,
Disorderly fleshy and sensual . . . . eating drinking and breeding. . . .

Edward Carpenter asserts that "Whitman's full-blooded, co-pious, rank, masculine style must always make him one of the world's great originals" — a dubious esthetic claim, but a characteristic nineteenth-century reaction based on an assumed sexual distinction in poetic and prose styles. When Whitman's poetry was attacked by Bayard Taylor and others in 1876, John Burroughs wrote to the *New-York Tribune:*

The trouble with Whitman is, he gives us something more and better than mere literature or art, and the main influence of his poems is in the direction of health, character, and manly activity . . . . What he gives us is well oxygenated; it is red, arterial blood, and has in it the making of virile, robust men.[4]

Whitman's gratification over Burroughs' "red-blooded espousal of the book — of my code" reminds us again of Marryat's gentleman as well as of Hemingway's hirsute pride.

With that remarkable intuition that makes him the spokesman of his age, Emerson observes in one of his most famous sentences in "Self-Reliance": "Society everywhere is in conspiracy against the manhood of every one of its members" — a statement which succinctly sums up "civilization and its discontents" in a singularly appropriate castration analogy. Whitman concurs with witty crudity in "Song of Myself": "And make short account of neuters and geldings, and favor men and women fully equipped." Emerson goes on in the same essay to assail "parlor soldiers" and "city dolls" — startlingly virile and ugly epithets on the part of the gentle sage to characterize the Adams of the New World, until we recall the concealed anguish in an entry in his *Journals* about 1841: "Give me initiative, spermatic, prophesying, man-making words." Emerson is quite clear in his noble words about conformity and independence, or self-reliance; but fear, presumably stemming from his ministerial heritage, from his public role as a preacher-lecturer, and from personal inhibitions, forces him to verbally effective but vague conclusions. In place of "Christianity, entrenched in establishments and forms," he proposes "some vigor of wild virtue," and he urges men to "enter into the state of war and wake Thor and Woden, courage and constancy, in our Saxon breasts." (Curiously, Washington Irving introduces the same Norse deities in the preface to his tale of the evasive tactics of Rip Van Winkle, who conveniently sleeps through the troubling years of his maturity.) Ambiguously but repeatedly Emerson implores men to seek "that source, at once the essence of genius, of virtue, and of life, which we call Spontaneity or Instinct." Thus the intuition of his lovely mind does not lead to explicit definition or concrete formulation, but Whitman is soon to fill the void.

In "The Maypole of Merry Mount," composed in the same decade as "Self-Reliance," Hawthorne depicts in miniature the historical and cultural crucifixion of the American "passional self." "Bright were the days at Merry Mount, when the Maypole was the banner staff of that gay colony!" It is a glorious spring day — the kind that gladdened the heart of Geoffrey Chaucer and saddened that of the latter-day puritan, T. S. Eliot — redolent with flowers, stained with brilliant colors. Around the "gayly decked" maypole

the Merry Mounters gyrate in elemental dance rhythms and flaunt
their animalistic natures in attire borrowed from the wolf, the he-
goat, and the bear. The setting and imagery are orgiastic; the phallic symbol dominates a landscape which can perhaps be best
described by a line from "Song of Myself": "Landscapes projected
masculine full-sized and golden." Suddenly appear the puritans,
led by the black figure of Endicott, with his "keen sword." They
cut down the Maypole and erect in its place the whipping post, the
symbol of cultural repression. The Lord and Lady of May — he
"with a scarf of the rainbow pattern crosswise on his breast" and
she "not less gayly decorated" — meekly accept the puritan dis-
pensation and "garments of a more decent fashion." The young
man submits to the ultimate humiliation, voluntary surrender of
his individuality, when his hair is cropped "in the true pumpkin-
shell fashion." The final line of the story — "They went heaven-
ward, supporting each other along the difficult path which it was
their lot to tread, and never wasted one regretful thought on the
vanities of Merry Mount" — is Hawthorne's prim but somewhat
grim rationalization of the coming-of-age in America, but sounds,
with no doubt unintentional irony, like a joyless echo of the conclusion to *Paradise Lost.*

A joyless echo it is, since Hawthorne in effect justifies the
destruction of "the essence of genius, of virtue, and of life, which
we call Spontaneity or Instinct." But the rigorous control of the
tale — the too-careful balancing of the orgiastic excesses of the
Merry Mounters and the religious excesses of the puritans —
makes the resignation of the conclusion suspect: Hawthorne does
not resolve the human and cultural conflict, he manipulates it for
his artistic purposes. The conflict reasserts itself in later tales and
romances in his almost obsessive consideration of the hostility
between orgiastic life and repressive civilization, and in his later
creations, the only erotic women in nineteenth-century American
literature, Beatrice Rappaccini, Georgiana, Hester Prynne, and
Zenobia, who, unfortunately, love men that have bowed before the
authority of Endicott, governor and castrator. Despite this lack of
fulfillment, these women remain triumphant in our memories, just
as the scene in the forest in which Hester releases her beautiful
tresses and unveils her erotic glory eclipses the fate of the pathetically weak and vacillating Arthur Dimmesdale.

Like Emerson and Hawthorne, Herman Melville testifies to the "conspiracy against the manhood of every one of its members," since from the beginning of his career to *Billy Budd* he records the fates of his orphans in the framework of a castration metaphor. Disillusioned by "snivelization," Tommo in *Typee* seeks Eden among the natives, far away from the hypocritical tyranny of Christian missionaries and from the brutal regimen of ship captains, the latter-day Endicotts. Both his body and his mind, however, deny his heart, the body producing an incapacitating injury (a symbolic emasculation) which protects his virtue from Fayaway's too freely offered affections, and the mind so preoccupied with self-generated fantasies of cannibalism that the Pacific Merry Mount takes on the characteristics of one of Poe's nightmares. Although Tommo eventually resorts to murder in order to escape from the cannibals, the savage reappears, as does the unresolved conflict, in the character of colorfully tattooed Queequeg. For Queequeg, with markings on his body as elaborate as those on Achilles' shield and with a comic phallic idol, dominates the early pages of *Moby-Dick,* and Ishmael's marriage to the native is the most affective depiction of personal relationships in Melville's writings: "Thus, then, in our hearts' honeymoon, lay I and Queequeg — a cosy, loving pair." Although Melville endeavors to minimize the emotional attachment by recourse to parody — "Queequeg was George Washington cannibalistically developed" — the tender description of the savage is in conflict with the destructive intellectual device. In the fashion of Hawthorne, he has the savage Eros join the other members of the *Pequod* at the bottom of the sea, only, ambivalently, to have Queequeg's heraldic coffin become the cradle for Ishmael's survival.

The Endicott of the *Pequod,* the mad Ahab, who easily seduces his crew to pursue the perverted course of seeking the white whale, is emotionally and physically castrated, having experienced a threefold emasculation before his "topmost greatness" is toppled into the sea when the mast of the *Pequod,* like the Maypole, is destroyed. Only the orphan-son survives; unlike his biblical counterpart, he is to establish no race: in his lovely, beautifully modulated meditation, he is to impose artistic order upon chaos and to achieve the only catharsis permitted in Melville's bleak universe — the catharsis of art. Not coincidentally, Melville likens Billy Budd to Haw-

thorne's Georgiana, whose erotic power, symbolized by the hand
in the birthmark on her cheek, Aylmer destroys with his "love"
potion, just as Billy's father surrogate, Captain Vere, destroys the
erotic power which lures Claggart to the lad. Poor, stuttering,
sterile Billy, whose overdescribed Greek beauty is not unlike that
of the Lord of the May, receives for unspecified "reasons" heroic,
but parodistic, treatment in the death scene: "In the present instance, for special reasons, the mainyard was assigned" — for an
hermaphroditic apotheosis and evasion of the "muscular spasm."

Billy's crucifixion is but another version of Natty's "Here!" as
is James's "Live," which becomes a kind of narcissistic moral self-
apotheosis when Lambert Strether at the conclusion of *The Am-
bassadors* returns to America to live out his barren life without
mate or heirs. The lonely grandeur of these heroes, with thinly
concealed messianic undertones, concedes the triumph of civilization over the instinctual life, as in "The Maypole of Merry Mount,"
as well as the failure of their creators to offer a meaningful alterna-
tive to the social conditions that compel Thoreau to say in the early
pages of *Walden:* "The mass of men lead lives of quiet desperation." The same conflict evident in the writings of Hawthorne and
Melville appears in Thoreau, for the "bachelor of thought and
nature," to use Emerson's words, expatiates on "higher laws" in
Walden but attempts in *A Week on the Concord and Merrimack
Rivers* to transplant hedonistic Greece to his chaste New England
environment:

In my Pantheon, Pan still reigns in his pristine glory, with his ruddy
face, his flowing beard, and his shaggy body, his pipe and his crook,
his nymph Echo, and his chosen daughter Iambe; for the great god
Pan is not dead, as was rumored. No god ever dies. Perhaps of all the
gods of New England and of ancient Greece, I am most constant at
his shrine.

A man who was shocked to discover a fungus labeled *"Phallus
impudicus"* is a strange worshiper of a phallic deity.

The subterranean phallicism in nineteenth-century American
literature — the puberty rite in *The Deerslayer* when Natty reluctantly but not without pride kills his first Indian, the initiation of
Robin in Hawthorne's "My Kinsman, Major Molineux," the phallic farce in *Moby-Dick* — is brought to the surface in Whitman's

conception of an ithyphallic overman, a frankly genital Adam. To assert, however, as Henry Adams does, that Whitman was the only writer in the century to recognize the power of the libido is to overvalue Whitman's frankness and to slight the latent content in Cooper, Hawthorne, Melville, and others. Whitman undrapes the "body electric" in one way, Hawthorne and Melville in another, less explicit fashion. The devil in "Young Goodman Brown," for instance, is riotously bawdy and exhibitionistic, deserving of a place in Restoration comedy; and the chapter entitled "The Cassock" in *Moby-Dick* is one of the most rabelaisian passages in American literature, although Melville's comic detachment disguises and distances the phallicism. Whitman differs from his contemporaries only in that he capitulates less to the whipping posts of the Endicotts: although he does not hesitate to flaunt anatomical details and to insist that the body is no less to be admired than the soul, the verbalized hedonism is frequently in conflict with the regressiveness of his protagonists and the consistent evasion of "the bridge" by means of a verbal leap to affirmation of what sometimes is a protective infantile state. Furthermore, Whitman is most successful in resurrecting the body in the first two editions, even though his "indirections," or concealments, are protected by ambiguous phraseology and comic evasiveness. In 1860 and later, particularly in the "Calamus" sequence, the tone is more elegiac than hedonist. But at the same time, despite the wits who aver that *Leaves of Grass* "contains all leaves except figleaves," or (like Wyndham Lewis) call Whitman the "American baby" who "rolled about naked in the American surf, uttering 'barbaric yawps,' " he dared to depict Everyman's journey to selfawareness not in terms of a developing moral sense but in a young man's awakening sexuality, and to recognize the sexual basis of art as well as the powers and limitations of his poetry and of art in general, when he freely concedes in "Calamus" that artistic sublimation is but another form of repression.

One of Whitman's most original and striking (prudes would say, shocking) poems was called on its appearance in 1856 "Bunch Poem," appropriately in view of its genital imagery; in 1867 "the good gray poet" misleadingly gave it the Emersonian title "Spontaneous Me." Audaciously and wittily, Whitman discusses the sexual origins of poetry:

The real poems, (what we call poems being merely pictures,)
The poems of the privacy of the night, and of men like me,
This poem, drooping shy and unseen, that I always carry, and that
    all men carry,
(Know, once for all, avowed on purpose, wherever are men like me,
    are our lusty, lurking, masculine, poems,) . . .

Which, of course, is also a delightful and earthy extension of the
transcendentalist's faith in the dignity and potentiality of democratic man! Whitman was willing to cut through the cant by
which man lives, and was able to keep his faith while recognizing
the orgiastic sources of art and life.

The poem begins prosaically with a conventional, pastoral description of the "I" and "the friend I am happy with" as they
walk "late in autumn." The poet observes the "gorgeous" natural
scenes, but these are only "beautiful dripping fragments," incomplete "pictures," the subject matter of those who refuse to write
"real poems" of human longing and love. These evaders ignore

Arms and hands of love — lips of love — phallic thumb of love —
    breasts of love — bellies pressed and glued together with love,
Earth of chaste love — life that is only life after love. . . .

The evaders find nature virginal, but to Whitman "the body of
the earth" is suffused with his own erotic need:

The hairy wild-bee that murmurs and hankers up and down — that
    gripes the full-grown lady-flower, curves upon her with amorous
    firm legs, takes his will of her, and holds himself tremulous and
    tight upon her till he is satisfied. . . .

(Similarly, since the differences between the two writers are almost
invariably exaggerated, Melville's sea is suffused with his own
erotic despair.)

The following line, "The wet of woods through the early hours,"
at first sight seems to be only a description of the environment but
actually anticipates the later ejaculatory passages. For immediately
we discover "Two sleepers at night lying close together as they
sleep, one with an arm slanting down across and below the waist
of the other" — the "I," apparently an older man, and a boy, who

confides to the other an almost classic masturbatory dream: "The dead leaf whirling its spiral whirl, and falling still and content to the ground." Both are consumed with the "torment" of sexual desire, particularly the narrator who, unlike the "hairy wild-bee," has been unable to obtain gratification:

The no-formed stings that sights, people, objects, sting me with,
The hubbed sting of myself, stinging me as much as it ever can any one,
The sensitive, orbic, underlapped brothers, that only privileged feelers
    may be intimate where they are. . . .

This scene ends without consummation. The "I" records the frustration of a "young woman that flushes and flushes," of an "angry" youth, like the protagonist in "The Sleepers," who wakens at night "seeking to repress what would master him," and of the narrator himself who, in a typical Whitmanesque transformation, suddenly ceases to be an older male and becomes the autoerotic youth: "The souse upon me of my lover the sea, as I lie willing and naked." Once again the "I" is both subject and object of his frustrated drives.

Abruptly and not inappropriately, since the "I" is now a passive youth, there appears, seemingly from nowhere, a mother who keeps "her vigilant eyes" fixed on "the twin-babes that crawl over the grass in the sun." Unlike the thwarted lovers described earlier, the "twin-babes" are enjoying themselves in the shelter of the mother's kindness, but in view of what appears to be an unconscious parallel between the two children and the lovers, as well as the earlier genital allusion ("orbic, underlapped brothers"), the mother's appearance is mandatory since she serves as a cultural and instinctual censor inhibiting sexuality. (Thus the poem is one more instance of Whitman's subservience to the maternal figure.) The "I" rationalizes that he must not "skulk or find myself indecent, while birds and animals never once skulk or find themselves indecent" — an assertion which is immediately qualified when he alludes to "The great chastity of paternity, to match the great chastity of maternity," which is the sentiment not of a hedonist but of a child who does not dare to attribute the "honey of generation" to his parents. It is hardly, then, surprising that his Adamic oath does not conceal the "gnaw" beneath the verbalization.

The oath of procreation I have sworn — my Adamic and fresh daughters,
The greed that eats me day and night with hungry gnaw, till I saturate
what shall produce boys to fill my place when I am through. . . .

Even more significant is the fact that impregnation becomes in the
closing lines an autoerotic image:

The wholesome relief, repose, content,
And this bunch plucked at random from myself,
It has done its work — I toss it carelessly to fall where it may.

(The poem is almost a perfect example of the orgasmic rhythm
underlying Whitman's art: the restless, anxious movement of the
verse and of the protagonist reflect the anguish of passionate but
unfulfilled desire — "the irritable tide that will not be at rest" —
until the peace that comes with sexual release and artistic expression, which are autoerotic.)
    What makes these lines startling is Whitman's audacious refuta-
tion of the biblical taboo: the poet, turned in upon himself, is an
onanist. The "anger" of the frustrated boy-man is assuaged when
the infertility of the masturbatory dream is transformed into the
fertility of art — a point made clear by the similarities between
the last line, "I toss it carelessly to fall where it may," and the
earlier one, "The dead leaf whirling its spiral whirl, and falling still
and content to the ground." And the apparent pun upon "content"
— pleasure and sperm — is consistent with the sexual and artistic
meanings.
    Perhaps no arist has ever so explicitly specified the sexual source
of his art, his "sacred fount." "Trickle Drops," one of the
"Calamus" poems, is, as Kenneth Burke points out, developed
"after the analogy of violence done upon the self."[5]

O drops of me! trickle, slow drops,
Candid, from me falling — drip, bleeding drops,
From wounds made to free you whence you were prisoned,
From my face — from my forehead and lips,
From my breast — from within where I was concealed — Press forth, ·
red drops — confession drops,
Stain every page — stain every song I sing, every word I say, bloody
drops,

Let them know your scarlet heat — let them glisten,
Saturate them with yourself, all ashamed and wet,
Glow upon all I have written or shall write, bleeding drops,
Let it all be seen in your light, blushing drops.

In 1867 Whitman altered the first line to read: "Trickle drops! my blue veins leaving" — a seemingly insignificant and clarifying change until one realizes that he is deleting the onanistic metaphor.

As indicated earlier, Whitman for over twenty years wrote anonymous reviews of *Leaves of Grass,* on the egomaniacal but indisputable premise that he understood his own poetry better than anyone else. Actually, however, his reviews were a concession to public taste, filled with chitchat that conforms to journalistic "human interest," and are less useful than the following lines in "From Pent-up Aching Rivers":

From that of myself, without which I were nothing,
From what I am determined to make illustrious, even if I stand sole
    among men,
From my own voice resonant — singing the phallus. . . .

In prose — in the bombastic preface to the first edition of *Leaves of Grass,* in *Specimen Days,* and in later scribblings — Whitman almost always assumes the public mask of the journalist, and although he is not dishonest, he reveals the limitations of the journalistic mentality that make him nothing more than a mediocre newspaperman in his early days and a garrulous writer of chatter in his declining years. Interestingly, he never found an authentic voice in his prose: his early writings are indistinguishable from those of countless hacks, and his solemn pronouncements about the inadequacies of the United States in *Democratic Vistas* are stilted and tortuous. The authenticity of the poetry is established by the unique verse and personal rhythm which make his lines distinctive and inimitable. When he becomes the unabashed preacher in poetry, as he assumes the mantle of the bard and mutes the sexual imagery — and the admitted basis of his art — he sounds like one of the fashionable preachers of the day. As Emerson's example proved, the lecture platform was the nineteenth-century equivalent of the puritanical whipping post.

As long as the body is "electric" — orgiastic red is the characteristic color in Whitman's poetry — his poetry evokes a primordial world which is peculiarly Whitmanesque. "I Sing the Body Electric," which in 1860 was placed among the "Children of Adam" poems, is his version of "The Maypole of Merry Mount." Even in its first version, when it opens with more erotic fervor than in its revisions,

The bodies of men and women engirth me, and I engirth them,
They will not let me off nor I them till I go with them and respond
    to them and love them . . . ,

it is a kind of sermon addressed to the life-deniers, the defilers of the body. The orthodox and the traditionalists delight only in a "beautiful" anatomy of the soul, but Whitman takes "account" of the beauty of every part of the physical anatomy. The body becomes a vibrant terrain of "circling rivers," a "wonder" — a miraculous personal landscape. Nature in Whitman's poetry never overpowers the self; in fact, nature exists usually only as a projection of the "I's" emotional state of elation or despair. Unlike those who describe the journey of the soul in abstract, nonphysical formulations, he lovingly and caressingly journeys into every recess of the breathing human body as it undulates during impregnation, emerges from the gates of the womb into the mysteries of the world, and then moves uncertainly through a world intent upon denying its existence and even misusing it as merchandise, until it passes through the gates into the womb of death. In his version of the puritan's spiritual pilgrimages he banishes the myths of heaven and hell in order to sing of the joys of a terrestrial and physical Eden:

Whatever the survey, whatever the sea and the sail, he strikes soundings at last only here,
Where else does he strike soundings, except here?

Ignoring the saints and "representative men," the poet singles out democratic men and women engaged in prosaic activities, and he neglects their faces (their rational or spiritual natures) to focus upon the "limbs and joints," the waist, the back of the neck.

The young fellow hoeing corn — the sleigh-driver guiding his six
horses through the crowd,
The wrestle of wrestlers, two apprentice-boys, quite grown, lusty, good-
natured, native-born, out on the vacant lot at sun-down, after work,
The coats and caps thrown down, the embrace of love and resistance,
The upper-hold and under-hold, the hair rumpled over and blinding
the eyes;
The march of firemen in their own costumes, the play of masculine
muscle through clean-setting trousers and waist-straps,
The slow return from the fire, the pause when the bell strikes suddenly
again, and the listening on the alert,
The natural, perfect, varied attitudes — the bent head, the curved
neck, and the counting,
Such-like I love. . . .

Here and elsewhere, Whitman idealizes the body, not unlike the
painters and sculptors of the era, except that his delight in the
sensuous play of muscles and in nudity, particularly of his athletic
males, is relatively unchecked by social constraints. His American
subject matter was to appear, without idealization, in the paintings
of his friend Thomas Eakins, who discovered similar visual excitement and the beauty of muscular power in wrestlers and boxers,
rowers on the Schuylkill River, and surgeons who wield their
knives with awesome control. A few years before the appearance
of *Leaves of Grass,* in 1852, Horatio Greenough had anticipated
Whitman, although he sought to incorporate a biblical justification:

In nakedness I behold the majesty of the essential, instead of the trappings of pretension. The agendum is not diminished; it is infinitely
extended. We shall have grasped with tiny hands the standard of
Christ, and borne it into the academy, when we shall call upon the
architect and sculptor and painter, to seek to be perfect even as our
father is perfect. The assertion that the human body is other than a
fit exponent and symbol of the human being, is a falsehood, I believe.
I believe it to be false on account of the numerous palpable falsehoods
which have been necessary in order to clinch it.[6]

"Such-like I love — I loosen myself, pass freely," Whitman
exclaims at this point in "I Sing the Body Electric," but the statement is not quite accurate, since the "I" must undergo a ritual

necessitated by the psychological continuum. At first sight the account of a venerable eighty-year-old man, a "gunner and fisher," the father and grandfather of handsome children and grandchildren, seems to be a digression; but before the young man (the son) can enter man's estate, he must have the blessing, or permission, of a paternal surrogate: "You would wish to sit by him in the boat, that you and he might touch each other." With this "touch" or gesture of approval, as in "The Sleepers," the "I" is permitted to surround himself with "beautiful, curious, breathing, laughing flesh," to "touch any one." (It may be noteworthy, in view of his ambivalence toward his own father, that Whitman retreats a generation to the grandfather figure.) The "I" exclaims: "I do not ask any more delight — I swim in it, as in a sea." This water imagery introduces the orgiastic note which will culminate in scenes of bodily intoxication.

Dramatically Whitman states:

This is the female form,
A divine nimbus exhales from it from head to foot.

Despite the "nimbus" this is not Beatrice or a platonic abstraction. It is another kind of abstraction: an electrical force with "mad filaments" and "ungovernable shoots," it is the naked energy of the libido that exerts a "fierce undeniable attraction." Or perhaps it is more accurate to say that this is the "virgin" of the erotic imagination, the American Aphrodite ill at ease in an environment chilled by the whipping post of the puritans and of their successors, the merchants. Unlike the Lord and Lady of May, the "I" and the female do not conceal their need or consult their consciences; deliriously they fuse in the timeless, orgasmic motions of the fertile earth:

Ebb stung by the flow, and flow stung by the ebb — love-flesh swelling
    and deliciously aching,
Limitless limpid jets of love hot and enormous, quivering jelly of love,
    white-blow and delirious juice,
Bridegroom-night of love, working surely and softly into the prostrate
    dawn,
Undulating into the willing and yielding day,
Lost in the cleave of the clasping and sweet-fleshed day.

What an extraordinary passage this is! Aurally and visually it recaptures the muscular strain and release of coitus, the irresistible motion and relaxation, without detracting from the beauty of the fusion.

From "the bath of birth" a child is born. Biblical diction aptly describes the miracle, since to Whitman every "nucleus" is godlike, a part of the "divine average," a part of the mystery, fascinating to him, for obvious reasons, that heroes and geniuses spring from families unblessed and undistinguished. When woman fulfills her role ("You are the gates of the body, and you are the gates of the Soul") and when man fulfills his role — and neither succumbs to the fallacious separation of the body and the soul —

All is a procession,
The universe is a procession, with measured and beautiful motion.

And so, structurally, the beautiful motions of the men and women described in the poem culminate in this orgiastic scene, which, in turn, leads in usual Whitmanesque fashion to a vision of tranquillity and order.

Since he is celebrating the divinity of the body, he becomes forthrightly satirical in two auction scenes in which an indifferent auctioneer is selling a man and a woman. The poet pushes aside the "sloven" who "does not half know his business," and reveals to the money-eyed purchasers "this wonder," for whom "the globe lay preparing quintillions of years." The poet strips off the clothes to expose the "exquisite senses" of "the father of those who shall be fathers in their turns" and of "the teeming mother of mothers." This is the preacher's lesson to the corrupters of the human body: "If any thing is sacred, the human body is sacred."

The sermon, however, is not over, for he must reinforce his democratic and Emersonian moral. The soul and the body are one, and all men share the same body. In an intoxicated rhapsody (not, however, without Apollonian control) he itemizes the parts of the body. He is saying in effect that all love begins with self-love, that the first love object of the child is his own body, particularly the genitals, and that those who cannot love their own bodies cannot experience love. The rhapsody moves from narcissism to love of another, as the poet touches and gazes upon another body: "The

circling rivers, the breath, and breathing it in and out." This is the
lovely, particularized imagery that Whitman invariably achieves in
those exquisite moments when he rediscovers the hidden beauty
that his age and our tradition deny.

O I say now these are not the parts and poems of the body only, but of
   the Soul,
O I say these are the Soul!

And yet there is something lacking. The female with her "divine
nimbus" is nameless, and the male whose body delights the poet is
faceless and anonymous. Surely the individual cannot assert his
worth or even his dignity until he is blessed and particularized by
means of a name. The ritual, in other words, is not completed in a
meaningful social context, but in a verbal context of abstractions
— the electrical body, the soul, "the divine average" — which,
however beautiful, are evasions.

The 1860 edition of *Leaves of Grass* in many respects marks
the culmination of Whitman's poetic career. Although the 1855
edition has a unity which makes it in this respect the most satisfying of all editions, it does not include such superb later poems as
"Crossing Brooklyn Ferry," "Out of the Cradle Endlessly Rocking,"
"As I Ebb'd with the Ocean of Life," and the "Calamus" sequence.
The rearrangements and additions after 1860, with but a few
notable exceptions, as well as the generally misguided deletions
and verbal tamperings, contribute little to Whitman's stature or for
that matter to the unity of *Leaves of Grass*. The groupings in the
1860 edition are, rightly, inexact and elastic but consonant with
the depiction of the self: the later order is that of an older man
who has lost touch with his youthful enthusiasms, and Whitman
is not impressive in the editorial role of "man thinking." The third
edition, which appeared just before Whitman's beloved Union was
to undergo a blood bath rarely equaled in previous history, is
crucial in two other ways. The Adamic hero, the ithyphallic poet-
god, was making his last stand, as it were, since he, like the poet,
was aging and thus yielding to middle-aged realism. In addition,
there appear for the first time poems which reveal another, and no
doubt truer, picture of their creator, who was not "lawless" but
often fearful and timid.

The volume opens with a new poem, later to be entitled "Starting from Paumanok," which strains to perpetuate the picture of the "rowdy" in its overassertive beginning:

Free, fresh, savage,
Fluent, luxuriant, self-content, fond of persons and places,
Fond of fish-shape Paumanok, where I was born,
Fond of the sea — lusty-begotten and various,
Boy of the Mannahatta, the city of ships, my city. . . .

Later there is a passage precious and funny in a way Whitman no doubt did not intend:

No dainty dolce affettuoso I;
Bearded, sunburnt, gray-necked, forbidding, I have arrived,
To be wrestled with as I pass, for the solid prizes of the universe,
For such I afford whoever can persevere to win them.

This is a far cry from the quiet and comic majesty of the opening line in the first edition: "I celebrate myself." But even the aggressiveness of the 1860 edition is better (and truer to his poetic inspiration) than the prosiness of the poem which was placed first in 1867 and in every subsequent edition:

One's-Self I sing, a simple separate person,
Yet utter the word Democratic, the word En-Masse.

Of physiology from top to toe I sing,
Not physiognomy alone nor brain alone is worthy for the Muse, I say
   the Form complete is worthier far,
The Female equally with the Male I sing.

Of Life immense in passion, pulse, and power,
Cheerful, for freest action form'd under the laws divine,
The Modern Man I sing.

Here "the good gray poet" takes over, as Whitman mistakenly attempts to clarify and to modify for the sake of popularity among the democratic masses, which he should have known (as he no doubt did know) that he was not destined to obtain, and for the sake of establishing a public image which conflicts with his subjec-

tive art and his depiction of himself as a "rowdy." Perhaps he was
more frightened than he cared to admit when he lost his governmental post in 1865 because of the indecencies of his poetry. At
any rate he consented to William Michael Rossetti's proposals for a
bowdlerized English edition of selections from *Leaves of Grass*;
and in a preface for this publication, which, although written completely by the poet, was to appear under William D. O'Connor's
signature, his first point was: "That personally the author of
Leaves of Grass is in no sense or sort whatever the 'rough,' 'the
eccentric,' 'vagabond' or queer person, that the commentators,
(always bound for the intensest possible sensational statement,)
persist in making him."[7] When one of the world's great eccentrics
disavows his eccentricity, we justifiably suspect his motives and
his honesty, but the statement is not without honesty in its implied
acknowledgment of the poet's delicate, shrinking, and at times
conventional temperament.

Although many critics refer to Whitman's *personae,* they attempt to make a distinction between the poetic figment and the real
Whitman which the idolaters, understandably, do not make —
understandably, because Whitman himself does not always differentiate. Thus the detailed depiction of the heroic impregnator in
"A Woman Waits for Me" (entitled "Poem of Procreation" on its
appearance in 1856) is both personal and fictional:

It is I, you women — I make my way,
I am stern, acrid, large, undissuadable — but I love you,
I do not hurt you any more than is necessary for you,
I pour the stuff to start sons and daughters fit for These States — I
    press with slow rude muscle,
I brace myself effectually — I listen to no entreaties,
I dare not withdraw till I deposit what has so long accumulated within
    me.

Through you I drain the pent-up rivers of myself,
In you I wrap a thousand onward years,
On you I graft the grafts of the best-beloved of me and of America,
The drops I distil upon you shall grow fierce and athletic girls, new
    artists, musicians, and singers,
The babes I beget upon you are to beget babes in their turn,
I shall demand perfect men and women out of my love-spendings,
I shall expect them to interpenetrate with others, as I and you inter-
    penetrate now,

I shall count on the fruits of the gushing showers of them, as I count on
   the fruits of the gushing showers I give now,
I shall look for loving crops from the birth, life, death, immortality,
   I plant so lovingly now.

For although it may be plausibly argued that in these lines Whitman speaks metaphorically of the creative powers of poetry, specifically of his own art, the underlying fantasy resembles a masturbatory rape dream; the fixation upon power over a reluctant victim is disturbingly regressive, even though it may be intricately related to Whitman's sublimations in verse and to his artistic fount, or, for that matter, to what may be called artistic paranoia.

And it must also be acknowledged, since nothing about Whitman's person or poetry is simple, that the wit in "Song of Myself," particularly in his jocular announcement of his own identity in Section 24 — "an American, one of the roughs, a kosmos" — and in the description of the "flowing savage" later, permits Whitman to avail himself of the duplicity of comedy, the satisfaction of his aggressiveness in a self-protective comic context. For wit disguises the evasiveness and radical alienation, and even hostility, of Whitman's protagonist, just as the brilliant literary wit of Ishmael, which ranges destructively over man's philosophical assumptions and societal ties, conceals the fact that Ishmael's monomaniacal art, like Ahab's monomaniacal pursuit of a white whale, "unbuttons" the infinitely fragile man and leaves him an orphan on an endless pilgrimage.

In Whitman's longest self-portrait in his poetry, in "Song of the Broad-Axe," there is, unless my ears deceive me, self-mockery which militates against the self-aggrandizement while establishing it with cosmic overexuberance:

His shape arises,
Arrogant, masculine, näive, rowdyish,
Laugher, weeper, worker, idler, citizen, countryman,
Saunterer of woods, stander upon hills, summer swimmer in rivers or
   by the sea,
Of pure American breed, of reckless health, his body perfect, free from
   taint from top to toe, free forever from headache and dyspepsia,
   clean-breathed,
Ample-limbed, a good feeder, weight a hundred and eighty pounds,
   full-blooded, six feet high, forty inches round the breast and back,

Countenance sun-burnt, bearded, calm, unrefined,
. . . .
Attitudes lithe and erect, costume free, neck gray and open, of slow
    movement on foot,
Passer of his right arm round the shoulders of his friends, companion
    of the street,
. . . .
A Manhattanese bred, fond of Brooklyn, fond of Broadway, fond of the
    life of the wharves and the great ferries. . . .

This passage disappeared in the next edition of *Leaves of Grass,*
in 1867. Serious readers — and Whitman's readers for the most
part have been plagued by their messianic desires — had not been
amused by the humorous egomania of the description; more important, Whitman, now desirous of fame as a democratic and "religious" bard, was no longer as artistically certain of his goal as in
the years between 1855 and 1860. Furthermore, the intervening
war left all kinds of casualties, including the premature death, or
at least attenuation, of "the rough." Whitman and the land returned to normalcy at the dawn of the "gilded age."

And yet this is too neat an explanation. "As I Ebb'd with the
Ocean of Life," which appeared for the first time in the 1860
edition, is a poignant admission of defeat and retreat: "before all
my insolent poems the real ME still stands untouched, untold,
altogether unreached" — which, of course, is but a boldly candid
half-truth. But the poem reveals that Whitman from almost the
beginning of his career was aware that his ithyphallic man-poet
was born out of fantasy, and that his poetry compensated for
almost intolerable personal frustration. This kind of self-awareness, which a man with bardic aspirations or political motivations
seldom acknowledges in public, establishes Whitman's human
greatness: unlike his idolaters and detractors, he fumbled and
stumbled into the hearts of his all-too-human readers, who in turn
befriended him as no other poet has been befriended — by calling
him Walt.

Thus it is no lessening of his achievement to state, as he admits
in his indirections, that the Adamic hero is imprisoned in and
checked, first, by the creator's psyche and, second, by cultural
taboos: the personal censor is as important as the Victorian censor.
(It is not without significance that some of his most dedicated

followers, including William D. O'Connor and Mrs. Anne Gilchrist, protested the excisions and revisions in later editions to no avail.) The "savage" in "Song of Myself," the most fully delineated overman, verbalizes his potency brilliantly and often wittily, but there is something resembling sexual titillation in a seductiveness which ends in his refusal to answer the questions of his followers ("My words itch at your ears till you understand them") or in a caress that does not lead to sexual union but to an injunction that each man must travel alone. The "savage" is at once an overman and a hedonistic puritan or puritanical hedonist. For a moment, as we have noted, the "I" in "The Sleepers" leads the "journeymen divine," those Americanized (and thus puritanical) Dionysians engaged in a phallic rite, only to retreat quickly into a passive, infantile role. Even the "I" in "A Woman Waits for Me" sounds somewhat apologetic and certainly something less than a Don Juan when he says: "I dare not withdraw till I deposit what has so long accumulated within me." This semidivine impregnator receives little gratification from sexual union, and even in fantasy Whitman limits coitus to propagation — even if it is the propagation of an imaginary new American race. In fact, all the overmen seem more at ease in a masculine environment where they observe with untroubled delight the heroism of firemen, swimmers, wrestlers, sailors, and soldiers, who flirt, not with women, but with death. However greatly Whitman professes to admire women, in his poetry they are almost without exception chaste mothers of the race. Though Whitman dares to sing of male love and to express it, even though somewhat obliquely, in startlingly frank scenes, almost everywhere, as in "Spontaneous Me," these episodes conclude without consummation, except in those passages where he partially (some would say, completely) disguises the physical aspects, as in the fifth section of "Song of Myself," by allegorizing union in terms of the body and the soul.

The words, as it were, take on an independent existence as the poet proclaims the joys of sexuality and sings of the phallus, but behind the verbal façade the reality of the man's frustration and terrible loneliness cannot be hidden. Indeed, in the "Calamus" poems Whitman himself discloses the truth.

7

"the tenderest lover"

> Publish my name and hang up my picture as that of the
>   tenderest lover,
> The friend, the lover's portrait, of whom his friend, his
>   lover, was fondest,
> Who was not proud of his songs, but of the measureless
>   ocean of love within him — and freely poured it
>   forth. . . .
>
> — "Recorders Ages Hence"

During a famous walk on the Boston Common in 1860, Ralph Waldo Emerson, who had impulsively greeted Whitman "at the beginning of a great career," urged the poet to exclude or to modify his sexual poems. Not only did Whitman deny the aging sage's request but also undoubtedly "forgot" to tell him, since the poet's was not an open nature, that the third edition of *Leaves of Grass*, which he was seeing through the press at the time, contained a greatly expanded treatment of sexuality, "Children of Adam," as well as a venture "In paths untrodden" in order to celebrate male friendship. With his usual studied artfulness Whitman appeared to balance his celebration of comradeship with chants of heterosexual passion. But the balance was deceptive: some of the finest poems in the "Children of Adam" section celebrate manly attachments ("Spontaneous Me" and "We Two, How Long We Were

140

Fool'd"); and there can be no doubt — we do not need the poet's admission that "they expose me more than all my other poems" — that the "Calamus" songs spring from Whitman's longing for a male lover. "Children of Adam" expresses the public image of the singer of sexuality; "Calamus" exposes the private man and his personal hunger.

In the eighth "Calamus" poem, so autobiographical that he did not reprint it after 1860, Whitman recapitulates his intellectual and emotional development.

Long I thought that knowledge alone would suffice me — O if I could but obtain knowledge!
Thou my lands engrossed me — Lands of the prairies, Ohio's land, the southern savannas, engrossed me — For them I would live — I would be their orator;
Then I met the examples of old and new heroes . . . . And it seemed to me that I too had it in me to be as dauntless as any — and would be so;
And then, to enclose all, it came to me to strike up the songs of the New World — And then I believed my life must be spent in singing. . . .

Such dreams of power and fame, like most youthful fantasies, omit human relationships and involvements, and so in maturity the poet weighs the cost and the loss, and is no longer enamored of his prophetic role: "it is now empty and tasteless to me."

I heed knowledge, and the grandeur of The States, and the example of heroes, no more,
I am indifferent to my own songs — I will go with him I love,
It is to be enough for us that we are together — We never separate again.

Thus in those moments of truth which "the solitary singer" was given to in 1859 and 1860 he saw himself not in the heroic mold of his own cosmic impregnator but in a role which he was shortly to satisfy in his ardent involvement with wounded and dying soldiers, Peter Doyle, and then Harry Stafford — as an older mother-father to youths who were as emotionally insecure as the young Walter Whitman. The poet could not chant of the heterosexual love which he apparently had never experienced and which, despite his brave words about sexuality, he no doubt feared. As

Frank Harris observes, "He is frank, indeed, outspoken even, but astoundingly superficial — the heights and depths of passion have not been plumbed by him. Turn to 'Solomon's Song,' . . . and you will find the Jewish singer is infinitely Whitman's superior."[1] But his unfulfilled love of young men and his vision of a democracy in which male camaraderie is to reign (a mother surrounded by her loving boys) Whitman turned into moving poetry. Personally and culturally it was perhaps inevitable that the greatest body of love poetry in American literature should celebrate male love, and that "Calamus" resembles Shakespeare's sonnets rather than *The Song of Solomon*.

In the "Calamus" poems Whitman claims that he walks "In paths untrodden," but this is a poetic falsehood. He explores no new "paths" in "Calamus"; he merely uncovers with fewer indirections the narcissistic and homosexual bases of his art. From the beginning of his career, passion involved almost exclusively male relationships. "The Child and the Profligate," a tale published in 1841, almost twenty years before the appearance of "Calamus," reveals the themes of the later poetry. A fatherless boy, apprenticed to a cruel taskmaster, seeks escape from the tyrant in the male society of a barroom. An ugly brawl erupts when a drunken sailor makes Claggart-like advances to the lad, who is saved from harm or worse by the intervention of a stranger, a handsome profligate named Langston. In revealing Langston's consciousness, Whitman lays bare his own "wondrous" search for love which, significantly, can only be satisfied by "strangers":

Why was it that from the first moment of seeing him, the young man's heart had moved with a strange feeling of kindness toward the boy? He felt anxious to know more of him — he felt that he should love him. O, it is passing wondrous, how in the hurried walks of life and business, we meet with young beings, strangers, who seem to touch the fountains of our love, and draw forth their swelling waters. The wish to love and to be loved . . . will burn with a lovely and pure brightness.[2]

The two young men spend the night together — in separate beds, according to a later version! "The Madman," a fragment printed in 1843, also records a sudden but ardent friendship between two youths.

Like the later poems, the prose is based on the unrealities of fantasy: strangers are filled with transforming love; the younger boys, homeless and parentless, are without filial conflicts or attachments; the older ones are not only social outcasts (a profligate in the first story and an infidel in the second) but also beyond good and evil. Reality breaks through, however, when, as in "The Child and the Profligate," death puts an end to the dubious passion, and when, as in the "Calamus" poem "We Two Boys Together Clinging" (the title itself reveals desperation and regressiveness), the youths briefly defy the social code ("No law less than ourselves owning"), only to vanish into the ambiguous geography that is fantasy. For Whitman perceives all too clearly, and perhaps bitterly, the transience of this kind of love.

One of the interesting differences in his depiction of adhesive relationships is that the lads in the prose have a hermaphroditic beauty, not unlike Billy Budd's or that of the recurrent Apollos one encounters in nineteenth-century literature, as in this passage from "A Legend of Life and Love" (1842):

Nathan, the elder, had hardly seen his twentieth summer. He was a beautiful youth. Glossy hair clustered upon his head, and his cheeks were very brown from sunshine and the air. Though the eyes of Nathan were soft and liquid, like a girl's, and his lips curled with a voluptuous swell, exercise and labor had developed his limbs into noble and manly proportions.

(No maiden in the prose or the poetry is depicted with such loving care; for that matter, neither in the tales written when Whitman was in his twenties nor in the poetry of his maturity does a youth simply fall in love with a maiden.) In the poetry, on the other hand, the admired young men are usually muscular "rowdies," or athletic abstractions, who come from the working classes and who are as semiliterate as the members of Whitman's own family. In other words, the poetic figments resemble those lengthy lists of young men which appear in his notebooks and diaries throughout his life. In "Miracles" he writes, "Or whether I go among those I like best, and that like me best — mechanics, boatmen, farmers," a passage which he omitted in the 1881 revision. In "By Blue Ontario's Shore," he admits, "I have gone freely with powerful uneducated persons, and with the young, and with the mothers of families." (Surely the omissions here are significant.) In "City of Orgies" he will not "converse with learned persons, or bear my share in the soiree or feast." But in "Native Moments,"

        I pick out some low person for my dearest friend,
He shall be lawless, rude, illiterate . . .

          . . . Why should I exile myself from my companions?

For, he adds, "I will play a part no longer." These poetic statements can be matched by the ardent expressions in his letters to young men and the coolness and distance maintained in communications with his intellectual equals. But it is equally obvious that Whitman was not quite so much at ease among the common people as he claims in his verse. His poetry from beginning to end is a lonely landscape of a solitary singer, a fact again confirmed by the "Calamus" chants. And so the pattern was in life. If for a moment we glance at the years in which we can follow his day-by-day living arrangements, we cannot but be struck by the fact that from 1863 until his stroke in 1873 he lived alone in Washington, despite his mother's desire to join him there and despite his toying with the idea of living with Peter Doyle and some of the veterans; that from 1873 to 1884 he lived, not happily, he informed his nieces, with his brother in Camden, and then in an attic room; and that from 1884 until his death he stayed alone in his "shanty" on Mickle Street except for the presence of a housekeeper and a succession of male nurses toward the end. Even *Specimen Days,* in which much space is devoted to the period in the late 1870s when he recovered his health, is more preoccupied with Whitman's solitary activities at the "pond" than with the Stafford family who befriended him at the time. As is often the case in his poetry, Whitman candidly, if briefly, acknowledges his dilemma in "Myself and Mine," where, before the revision of 1867, appear these revealing lines:

It is ended — I dally no more,
After to-day I inure myself to run, leap, swim, wrestle, fight,

. . . .

To speak readily and clearly — to feel at home among common people. . . .

As noted in an earlier chapter, it was not until 1856, a year after his father's death, that Whitman was prepared to say, "I announce adhesiveness," and only then with recourse to phrenological jargon, in itself an evasive act, since only initiates could fully understand the implications. However, passion for the most part has a homosexual cast in the first edition of *Leaves of Grass*, not only in the account of the Dionysian "journeymen" in "The Sleepers" but also in the worship of the phallus in many other poems. The first great climax in "Song of Myself," the union of the body and the soul in the fifth section, is thinly veiled oral sexuality. Before the soul is free for its journey, the protagonist, in Sections 28 and 29, is sexually assaulted and degraded by "prurient provokers" — a state which he fears as he welcomes it. The homosexual cast of the episode, perhaps somewhat obscure in the published form, is transparently clear in an earlier manuscript version:

Grip'd Wrestler! do you keep the hardest pull for the last?
Must you bite with your teeth with the worst spasms at parting?
Will you struggle worst when I plunge you from the threshold?
Does it make you ache so to leave me?
Take what you like, I can resist you no longer.
I think I shall sink.
Take drops of my life, if that is what you are after.
Only pass to someone else, for I will contain you no longer.
Pass to someone else; leap to the nearest landing.
Little as your mouth is, it has drained me dry of my strength.
I am faintish.[3]

Although Whitman does not dwell upon adhesiveness in the first two editions of *Leaves of Grass*, he comments in his public letter to Emerson in 1856: "as to manly friendship, everywhere observed in The States, there is not the first breath of it to be observed in print." No one else, so far as I know, was so aware as Whitman of the pervasiveness of "manly friendship" in American life, and of course he ignored the fact that Cooper, Melville, and Thoreau, to cite only three examples, as well as his own early tales, celebrated friendship, without, of course, employing phrenological terminology. Despite Whitman's compulsive discussion of the subject he was duplicitous both in print and in private. At the end of his career, when John Addington Symonds asked about the meaning of "Calamus," Whitman concocted a whopper in reply: he claimed to have fathered six bastards; that he had orphaned them mattered apparently not at all. Yet after replying to Symonds, Whitman observed to Horace Traubel:

I often say to myself about Calamus — perhaps it means more or less than what I thought myself — means different: perhaps I don't know what it all means — perhaps never did know. My first instinct about all that Symonds writes is violently reactionary — is strong and brutal for no, no, no. Then the thought intervenes that I maybe do not know all my own meanings: I say to myself: "You, too, go away, come back, study your own book — an alien or stranger, study your own book, see what it amounts to."[4]

In an unpublished manuscript, now in the collection of Charles E. Feinberg, Whitman comments after reading the Bohn edition of Plato, probably in the 1860s:

Phæ-drus (Plato) purports to be a dialogue between Socrates & Phædrus — the latter a young man, who, coming to Socrates, is full of a discourse by Lysias on *Love* — he reads it to S. — who finally proceeds to give a discourse on the same theme — by love he evidently means the passion inspired in one man by another man, more particularly a beautiful youth. The talk seems to hinge on the question whether such a youth should bestow his "favors" more profitably on a declared "lover," or on one not specially so. . . . His whole treatment assumes the illustration of Love, by the attachment a man has for another man, (a beautiful youth as aforementioned, more especially) — (it is astounding to modern ideas) . . .[5]

This is too disingenuous, even for Whitman. In 1870, in reply to a letter from a young author, Charles Warren Stoddard, which began, "In the name of CALAMUS listen to me!" Whitman approves of Stoddard's thinly veiled homosexual account of his relations with a native in "A South-Sea Idyl": "I have just re-read the sweet story all over, & find it indeed soothing & nourishing after its kind, like the atmosphere. As to you, I do not of course object to your emotional & adhesive nature, & the outlet thereof, but warmly approve them . . ."[6]

Among the manuscripts which Clifton Joseph Furness prints in *Walt Whitman's Workshop* is a projected lecture on the subject of love:

I desire to say to you, and let you ponder well upon it, the fact that under present arrangement, the love and comradeship of a woman, of his wife however welcome, however complete, does not and cannot satisfy the grandest requirements of a manly soul for love and comradeship,— The man he loves, he often loves with more passionate attachment than he ever bestows on any woman, even his wife. — Is it that the growth of love needs the free air — the seasons, perhaps more wildness more rudeness? Why is the love of women so invalid, so transient?[7]

This kind of dubious reasoning, welling out of an absence of experience and of personal frustration, is about as compelling as André Gide's *Corydon,* which is one of the most specious books of our time. The qualities Whitman cites to prove the superiority of male friendship — nature, "wildness," and "rudeness" — are, it cannot be overlooked, the usual attributes of the "fierce" old mother, the sea. Equally dubious is the "dream" he records with ill-concealed intensity in *Democratic Vistas:*

It is to the development, identification, and general prevalence of that fervid comradeship, (the adhesive love, at least rivaling the amative love hitherto possessing imaginative literature, if not going beyond it,) that I look for the counterbalance and offset of our materialistic and vulgar American democracy, and for the spiritualization thereof. Many will say it is a dream, and will not follow my inferences: but I confidently expect a time when there will be seen, running like a half-hid warp through all the myriad audible and visible worldly interests of America, threads of manly friendship, fond and loving, pure and sweet, strong and life-long, carried to degrees hitherto unknown — not only giving tone to individual character, and making it unprecedently emotional, muscular, heroic, and refined, but having the deepest relations to general politics. I say democracy infers such loving comradeship, as its most inevitable twin or counterpart, without which it will be incomplete, in vain, and incapable of perpetuating itself.[8]

Although Whitman's concern with "our materialistic and vulgar American democracy" is comprehensible, his vision is as lonely and futile as Don Quixote's: the singer of the self carries no conviction in the political arena.

In view of Whitman's emotionally starved childhood — the absence of a meaningful male figure and the presence of an overpowering mother — he was almost preconditioned to become the "tenderest lover" of comrades and to create in his art a sublimated environment in which he becomes the lover and the beloved, the older man and the youth. It is surely not without significance, in view of their inability to deal with certain basic human experiences, such as heterosexual love and marriage, that most of the so-called classic American authors lacked normal male identification, either through the premature deaths of their fathers (Irving, Poe, Emerson, Hawthorne, and Melville) or through the dominance of their mothers (Thoreau and Henry James). The consequences were arrestment (the inability to cross "the bridge" to adult commitments and relationships), evasion (the twenty-year sleep of Rip Van Winkle, Natty's flight to the frontier, the escape in Melville into an all-male world at sea), an omnipresent fear just below placid surfaces (the characters, driven in upon themselves, meditate rather than act), and an elegiac tone consonant with the sense of loss originating in youth.

Natty Bumppo is a "father" without paternal obligations — a patriarchal Adam without a troublesome Eve. Gentleman that he is, Natty is unfailingly kind to women, unless they endanger his precious bachelorhood, and passion appears only in the scenes between Natty and his Indian friends, Chingachgook, Uncas, and Hard-Heart. Emerson's essay on "Love" is a pallid affair, but his *Journals* in his twenties breathe emotionally when he discusses friendship. His repressed nature is fully disclosed in a curious entry in 1842: "I have so little vital force that I could not stand the dissipation of a flowing and friendly life; I should die of consumption in three months. But now I husband all my strength in this bachelor life I lead; no doubt I shall be a well-preserved old gentleman."[9] The void in Thoreau's life is poignantly expressed in his poem "I am a parcel of vain strivings tied":

> And here I bloom for a short hour unseen,
> Drinking my juices up,
> With no root in the land
> To keep my branches green,
> But stand
> In a bare cup.[10]

Except for nature, only friendship provides emotional gratification for Thoreau, who in turn reflects most eloquently our sense, and rationalization, of human separateness. The critical glorification of

Melville during the past four decades should not obscure his failure to encompass the full gamut of emotional experience. The magnificent universe unfolded in *Moby-Dick* has the flaws of its principal (castrated) characters: Ahab is a physical and emotional cripple and coward, and his "crazy" pursuit of the white whale, couched as it is in Elizabethan rhetoric, disguises his psychological arrestment and his evasion of adulthood; Ishmael, too, is regressive in his adolescent infatuation with Queequeg (partly concealed by his protective comedy), in his mooning over the sperm oil (which becomes almost a parody of Whitmanesque friendship), and in his final "salvation," the triumphant orphan-bachelor-artist. Even Hawthorne, who at least involves his characters in complex human relationships and who alone in our early literature treats maturely mature emotions, is plagued by his fears of the whipping post and of the senses. His erotic women, Hester Prynne, Beatrice Rappaccini, Georgiana, and Zenobia, are fated to love unwisely clergymen or monomaniacs who jealously guard their intellectual and scientific chastity. Yet the only plausible literary Eden appears in *The House of the Seven Gables,* which critics, cursed with the tragic sense, find unconvincing and sentimental. The American environment, at least as reflected in our serious literature, has not been hospitable to man's emotional development. Rip Van Winkle's arrestment and evasion, unfortunately, characterize our art and perhaps our life.

At least three cultural factors contribute to the situation: the anomaly and isolation of the artist in a materialistic society, the ambivalence of protestantism toward women, and, perhaps most important, the weakening of patriarchal concepts in a land which demanded almost heroic sacrifices from those who wanted to conquer and to fulfill the American dream. The drive to hew a civilization out of a wilderness and later to convert an agrarian culture into an industrial society created an artificial division of sexual functions: men ruled outside the home but in the household women were supreme. Men willingly surrendered to their wives the responsibility of nurturing the young, inculcating moral principles, and cultivating the arts of humane civilization. Since children were coddled into civilization by women, as their fathers sought fame or "the bitch godddess," children understandably had conflicting loyalties and later were confused as to their roles. Reared too exclusively by women, in homes and schools (male

teachers, like Ichabod Crane, were effeminate and culturally suspect), they were later expected to follow "manly" vocations and to
conduct themselves according to a "manly" code, which, like all
codes, camouflaged the insecurity which gave rise to it and crippled
individualism in the name of a phony masculinity. The code could
not conceal the fact that the most awesome power observed by
youths in their formative years was often exercised by living
embodiments of Dame Van Winkle.

Against this background of psychological and social forces
emerged Whitman's "Calamus," with its naive projection of an
agrarian fantasy a century hence at a time when the American
society was steadily and ponderously evolving toward Adams'
multiverse. Although Whitman insisted upon the modernness of
his poetry, declaring to a friend on one occasion that *Leaves of
Grass* presents a "model" of man, "adjusted to the modern, to the
New World, to Democracy, & to science,"[11] it does nothing of the
sort. "Paths untrodden" in "Calamus" lead back (or forward) to a
pastoral society, a new-old Eden, where a loosely knit fraternal
organization replaces political institutions, and where the bonds
between men are affectional, not mechanical. Like *Walden,*
"Calamus" is an act of simplification, an evasive gesture, a retreat
from nineteenth-century, and human, complexity. Its tone is
elegiac, tenderly expressive of the poet's longing for the vanished
love of childhood, both personal and racial. For, like Henry
Adams, Whitman seeks what man will ever seek yet never find, "a
world that sensitive and timid natures could regard without a
shudder."

"Calamus" is a lament for the loss of love. It matters little
whether it records the loss of a specific (unknown) lover (or
lovers), for even if literary detection uncovers names, the poems
will be neither better nor worse. The sequence has no narrative
continuity. Though Whitman shifted the poems about several
times, just as some editors insist upon rearranging Shakespeare's
sonnets in order to establish various unprovable hypotheses, nothing was gained by the alterations. For, however arranged, they
present, in Montaigne-like fashion, the discontinuous continuity
of shifting moods, the instability of an unstable ego, as it grapples
for reality beneath illusion, only to discover that even definitions
themselves are illusory. The poems belie the "impassive" public
appearance of a poet who seethes, sometimes rages, to emerge from

the lonely shell of the self. Their confessional nature is an attempt
to shatter the shell, but at the same time the evasiveness, or "indirections," of the words counteract the confession and protect the
perilous identity of the self against external intrusion. Hands
reach out to touch the beloved — and for a moment lover and
beloved walk "hand in hand" — but almost at once the psychic and
cultural censor intervenes, "Thou shalt not touch." Though love
is, or should be, a dialogue, in these songs hands briefly touch and
eyes meet in a silent exchange, but the poet utters a monologue of
separateness.

In the first poem, "In Paths Untrodden," the "I" seeks the true
self when he escapes "from the pleasures, profits, conformities,"
the dissonant and destructive "clank of the world," to the "pond-
waters," where, like the biblical shepherd and the mythical Narcissus, he looks into the mirror at the eternal human mystery.
Here "in this secluded spot I can respond as I would not dare
elsewhere," and "sing no songs to-day but those of manly attachment." Close to Mother Earth, "Tallying and talked to here by
tongues aromatic," the self finds life-giving food in "this delicious
Ninth Month, in my forty-first year." The imagery links nourish-
ment and birth to the newly discovered freedom from fear that
permits him

To tell the secret of my nights and days,
To celebrate the need of comrades.

Superficially the movement in this poem is from appearance
("clank of the world") to reality ("tongues aromatic"), but actually
the movement is from fear to seeming freedom. The situation and
images are reminiscent of one of the loveliest scenes in American
fiction, when in the forest, beside a strangely murmuring brook,
Hester Prynne sheds the societal stigma and "undrapes" her hair to
justify the "consecration" of a forbidden love, but emancipation in
The Scarlet Letter proves to be abortive, just as subsequent poems
in "Calamus" reveal that the "I's" new reality is illusory.

"Scented Herbage of My Breast" (poem 2 in the series) also
wrestles with the problem of appearance and illusion, but in a far
more complex and daring fashion. On one level it is a beautiful
variation upon poetry's most ancient preoccupation, the permanence of art in a world of flux. Reclining on the earth, once more

clinging to the breast of the ancient mother, the protagonist observes the natural process of growth which he likens to "Scented herbage of my breast," the "leaves" which the poet sends forth into the world from a decaying body. As nature blooms and dies only to renew itself, so artistic "blossoms" confer immortality upon the poet as new generations of readers discover his works: "O I do not know whether many, passing by, will discover you, or inhale your faint odor — but I believe a few will." The "scented herbage" of poetry, then, corresponds to the "tongues aromatic" of nature.

In addition to the immortality theme, Whitman considers the source of art: the poems are "blossoms of my blood! . . . of the heart that is under you." The heart, we discover, is "burning and throbbing":

O I do not know what you mean, there underneath yourselves — you
  are not happiness,
You are often more bitter than I can bear — you burn and sting
  me. . . .

On the one hand he is referring to the pains of artistic creativity, but when we gradually realize that the heart or the breast is a displaced genital analogy, at first somewhat ambiguously presented, we become aware that the poet is simultaneously referring to artistic and personal frustrations. The association of life and art is even clearer when the genital analogy is made explicit:

Grow up taller, sweet leaves, that I may see! Grow up out of my breast!
Spring away from the concealed heart there!
Do not fold yourselves so in your pink-tinged roots, timid leaves!
Do not remain down there so ashamed, herbage of my breast!
Come, I am determined to unbare this broad chest of mine — I have
  long enough stifled and choked. . . .

For, as in other poems, he likens the poetic act to the sexual act, and reminds us that his poetry both exhibits and sublimates his secret, repressed wishes. Thus he asserts that the body must be permitted its natural freedom if he (and man) are to escape "from the sham that was proposed to me" or "from the clank of the world." With this freedom he can discard the evasiveness of "emblematic and capricious blades," or metaphorical indirectness, as well as the artificial injunctions imposed by the whipping post. The "real reality," he is saying, is not the "sham" of the artificial dichotomies created by a fearful world, but the joyous acceptance of the "beautiful" cycle of love and death which is confirmed by the sexual rhythm and the natural rhythm of the universe, and which, organically, is confirmed by his supine position, the posture of love and death. There is a troubling, but characteristic, death-preoccupation in such lines as "faint-tinged roots . . . make me think of Death," and "O I think it is not for life I am chanting here my chant of lovers — I think it must be for Death." Such admissions rarely cloud his prose pronouncements, but when he is most true to himself, in his poetry, he unconsciously acknowledges that he does not expect (and perhaps even avoids) physical fulfillment of his thwarted love, and that the imaginary democracy of comrades is a death wish, personal and cultural. Thus the "real reality" is as problematic as the conclusions of many of Hawthorne's tales.

"Whoever You Are Holding Me Now in Hand" (3) is a strange love poem, seductive and personal but at the same time evasive and impersonal. For the "Me" is simultaneously both *Leaves of Grass* and Walt Whitman, artifact and artist, and the "You" is an unknown reader, out of present time and space. Whitman seeks to transcend the chill of type-face and to transform a book into a seducer or lover, as in "A Song for Occupations":

Come closer to me,
Push close my lovers and take the best I possess,
Yield closer and closer and give me the best you possess.

This is unfinished business with me . . . . how is it with you?
I was chilled with the cold types and cylinder and wet paper between
    us.

At no time is Whitman able to say anything so direct as "Come live with me and be my love." He offers "fair warning" at the outset that "I am not what you supposed, but far different," and toward the conclusion, when he refers to "that which I hinted at," he refuses to be explicit. As Iago "plays" the villain, so Whitman "plays" the elusive lover who searches for "a candidate for my affections." In tempting (or seducing) the "follower" (the reader), the "I" deliberately dwells upon obstacles: "The way is suspicious . . . may-be destructive"; "Your novitiate would even then be long and exhausting," because "you" must abandon "The whole theory of your life, and all conformity to the lives around you."

Therefore release me now, before troubling yourself any further —
    Let go your hand from my shoulders,
Put me down, and depart on your way.

After enticing the "follower" with the prospect of a "novitiate," in preparation for a "suspicious" quest for a grail of some kind, the poet puts the "candidate" off for a moment only to offer another temptation. This temptation is also "suspicious," for it is to take place "by stealth" and "in the open air," far removed from the sight of people — "for trial," he declares, by which he seems to mean something like a trial marriage:

Here to put your lips upon mine I permit you,
With the comrade's long-dwelling kiss, or the new husband's kiss,
For I am the new husband, and I am the comrade.

Characteristically, the "I" suddenly forsakes the role of the aggressor to become the passive recipient of affection, a humble "follower" rather than a leader — a point which emerges in the regressive imagery in the following stanza:

Or, if you will, thrusting me beneath your clothing,
Where I may feel the throbs of your heart, or rest upon your hip,
Carry me when you go forth over land or sea;
For thus, merely touching you, is enough — is best,
And thus, touching you, would I silently sleep and be carried eternally.

Thus the "follower" or the reader (the passage is wonderfully ambiguous) becomes the equivalent of the mother, and the "I" is the protected child. Again the narrator warns the "follower" of his "peril," and declares: "Already you see I have escaped you" — but this, like similar passages in "Song of Myself," is a kind of perverse erotic titillation which stimulates desire rather than dampens it. In the final stanza there is an admission or warning — or perhaps

even a third temptation — "Nor will my poems do good only —
they will do just as much evil, perhaps more." The poem ends as
it begins, for Whitman acknowledges that this imaginary relationship leads nowhere, "Therefore release me, and depart on your
way." There is but the silence of separateness and of resignation,
the chill of the type-face.

The meaning of the "one thing" twice hinted at in "Whoever
You Are Holding Me Now in Hand" emerges in "These I Singing
in Spring" (4). The poet, as in "In Paths Untrodden," again
abandons "the world" to go to the "pond-side," where, "Solitary,
smelling the earthy smell" (note the recurrence of olfactory
images), he is surrounded and embraced by "the spirits of friends,
dead or alive." For this "silent troop" he, like a phallic deity,
plucks "tokens":

Here! lilac, with a branch of pine,
Here, out of my pocket, some moss which I pulled off a live-oak in
    Florida, as it hung trailing down,
Here, some pinks and laurel leaves, and a handful of sage,
And here what I now draw from the water, wading in the pond-side,
(O here I last saw him that tenderly loves me — and returns again,
    never to separate from me,
And this, O this shall henceforth be the token of comrades — this
    calamus-root shall,
Interchange it, youths, with each other! Let none render it back!)

At the "pond-side," then, an ancient ceremony takes place, reminiscent of the birth perhaps of Eros, or of a messiah-like figure
conducting a baptismal rite for initiates, or of a hero like King
Arthur extracting from the waters a magical symbol. But, as in
"The Sleepers," it is a parody of cultural rites, since the "troop" is
silent, which is to say nonexistent.

The scene is also reminiscent of a group of youths at the old
swimming hole, as Eakins, for instance, recaptures it in one of his
paintings — of that period in a boy's life when he cavorts with his
pals in uninhibited "horseplay," and still has the security of the
protective embrace of the mother — the most perfect of all worlds,
at least in the fantasy of the mature man in search of a lost Eden.
That such a fantasy lies behind Whitman's vision is implicit in
"For You O Democracy" (5), a rhetorical poem in which the "I"
becomes again a son rendering homage to a maternal figure (first

the earth, then the intimacy with the lover-mother, and now
democracy):

O mother! have you done much for me?
Behold, there shall from me be much done for you.

Whitman foresees an era in which men will be (again) loving
children under the aegis of "ma femme." The code of this new
society, not unlike Hemingway's, is but childhood's code transferred to man's estate: such love will these comrades have that
"The Kanuck shall be willing to lay down his life for the Kansian";
they will display "manly affection," saluting each other "with a
kiss": "There shall be countless linked hands"; and, finally, there
will be complete "Equality" ("The most dauntless and rude shall
touch face to face lightly"). Thus the tactile bonds of youth are
restored:

These shall tie and band stronger than hoops of iron,
I, extatic, O partners! O lands! henceforth with the love of lovers
   tie you.

In this society the "extatic" poet will no longer have to hide his
craving for touch, be unprotected in a clanking world of inhuman
dynamos ("O Democracy, to serve you, ma femme!"), or even be
an isolate at a secluded "pond-side" with imaginary "spirits of
friends, dead or alive."
    Whatever the future may hold for comrades, a series of negative
statements in "Not Heaving from My Ribb'd Breast Only" (6)
reveals that the "I," like one of Sherwood Anderson's gargoyles, is
frozen in fear and, perhaps more important, in a repressed anger
that is internally racking although it is concealed from public
inspection: "in rage, dissatisfied with myself," "long-drawn, ill-
suppressed sighs," "beating and pounding at my temples," "many
a hungry wish, told to the skies only," "husky pantings through
clenched teeth." (The latent rage here as well as in the "Black
Lucifer" passages in "The Sleepers" and in Sections 28 and 29 of
"Song of Myself" is seldom noted by commentators, although it is
part of the agitation that stirs us subconsciously in Whitman's
poetry.) Suddenly — and again the transformation is electric —

the caged man attains release, not through physical realization of his desire, but through the sublimation afforded by art:

> Not there,
> Not in any or all of them, O adhesiveness! O pulse of my life!
> Need I that you exist and show yourself, any more than in these songs.

This release is but an illusion, however, as the next two poems reveal: art provides only a temporary catharsis. Uncertainties reappear in "Of the Terrible Doubt of Appearances" (7), when the "I" admits that "may-be reliance and hope are but speculations after all," immortality "a beautiful fable only," and the phenomenal world "only apparitions." His doubts become terrifying as he conceives of a universe as black and valueless as Melville's in *The Confidence-Man*:

> May-be they only seem to me what they are, (as doubtless they indeed but seem,) as from my present point of view — And might prove, (as of course they would,) naught of what they appear, or naught any how, from entirely changed points of view. . . .

For a moment even his own identity is in peril until he is saved from Melvillean despair by the magic of touch:

> I cannot answer the question of appearances, or that of identity beyond the grave,
> But I walk or sit indifferent — I am satisfied,
> He ahold of my hand has completely satisfied me.

Similarly, the eighth chant (deleted in 1867), after surveying his previous life and his quest for fame as the singer of "the New World," concludes:

> I am indifferent to my own songs — I will go with him I love,
> It is to be enough for us that we are together — We never separate again.

"We never separate again" is but another illusion; the reality is recorded in the ninth song, in what appears to be one of Whitman's most autobiographical poems, which he rejected after a single appearance. "Hours continuing long, sore and heavy-hearted" is one of the most affective and successful songs in the series: the repetitive use of "Hours" at the beginning of the first five lines, together with the heavy vowel sounds, makes auditory the slowness of time's passage for the "distracted" lover who has observed his beloved "content himself without me"; and the rhetorical questions which the "I" propounds in the concluding six lines dramatize his jealous doubts and agitated despair. In his suffering he exclaims:

Sullen and suffering hours! (I am ashamed — but it is useless — I am
    what I am;)
Hours of my torment — I wonder if other men ever have the like, out
    of the like feelings?
Is there even one other like me — distracted — his friend, his lover,
    lost to him?

"I am what I am" perhaps explains the earlier "I am not what you supposed, but far different," though the reminder of Iago's duplicity may be unintentional. The "distracted" state of the "I" here foreshadows the "perturbation" which Whitman confessed in a notebook in 1870 during his relationship with the former Southern soldier and motorman, Peter Doyle, whose initials he attempted to conceal in the numerals 164 and whose sex he denied through the use of the feminine pronoun:

It is IMPERATIVE, that I obviate & remove myself (& my orbit) *at
all hazards* from this *incessant enormous* & PERTURBATION. . . .
    TO GIVE UP ABSOLUTELY & *for good, from this present* hour,
this FEVERISH, FLUCTUATING, *useless undignified pursuit of 164
— too long,* (*much too long*) persevered in, — so humiliating — *It
must come at last* & had better come now — (*It cannot possibly be a
success*) LET THERE FROM THIS HOUR BE NO FALTERING,
NO GETTING ———————— *at all henceforth,* (NOT ONCE,
under any circumstances) — *avoid seeing her, or meeting her, or any
talk or explanations* — *or* ANY MEETING WHATEVER, FROM
THIS HOUR FORTH, FOR LIFE.
                                   July 15, '70.[12]

In "Recorders Ages Hence" (10) Whitman invites readers to look "underneath this impassive exterior," which countless photographs and portraits were later to freeze into the image of "the good gray poet," whose olympian serenity bears little resemblance to "the tenderest lover" of the "Calamus" poems. He is not, he declares, "proud of his songs, but of the measureless ocean of love within him." This untapped "ocean" finds release in the eleventh chant, "When I Heard at the Close of the Day," one of the few poems in the sequence in which the "I's" joy is unmarred by perplexing doubts about the nature of reality or by "sick, sick dread." One day at sunrise, "inhaling the ripe breath of autumn" (recalling "this delicious Ninth Month" in "In Paths Untrodden"), he bathes alone at the beach and happily contemplates the arrival on the third day of "my dear friend, my lover." The recurrent olfactory and oral images merge with the ever-present erotic waters in this fleeting idyllic interlude:

O then each breath tasted sweeter — and all that day my food nourished me more — And the beautiful day passed well,
And the next came with equal joy — And with the next, at evening, came my friend;
And that night, while all was still, I heard the waters roll slowly continually up the shores,
I heard the hissing rustle of the liquid and sands, as directed to me, whispering, to congratulate me,
For the one I love most lay sleeping by me under the same cover in the cool night
In the stillness, in the autumn moonbeams, his face was inclined toward me,
And his arm lay lightly around my breast — And that night I was happy.

In the next chant, "Are You the New Person Drawn toward Me?" (12), Whitman repeats his earlier admonition: "I am probably far different from what you suppose." Behind this "façade," he declares, is no "trusty and faithful" person. When he asks, "Have you no thought, O dreamer, that it may be all maya, illusion?" is he addressing his imaginary follower or pursuer, who exists only in the poet's mind, or is he unwittingly acknowledging that his amorous encounters are only daydreams? A similar question arises as to the interpretation of the concluding lines of this poem, which he omitted in the next edition of *Leaves of Grass*:

O the next step may precipitate you!
O let some past deceived one hiss in your ears, how many have prest
    on the same as you are pressing now,
How many have fondly supposed what you are supposing now — only
    to be disappointed.

For it is hardly the nonexistent lovers who are "disappointed," but
the poet himself. Thus "the tenderest lover" advances and then
retreats, seduces and then warns, in a consistent pattern of erotic
titillation, or self-titillation.

Abruptly in the thirteenth chant he alters the mood:

Calamus taste,
(For I must change the strain — these are not to be pensive leaves, but
    leaves of joy,) . . .

Despite his assertion that he will depict "Roots and leaves unlike
any but themselves," nature is transformed into an erotic landscape
that reflects his own amorous and sensuous hunger: "Calamus
taste," "Scents . . . from the wild woods," "Breast-sorrel and pinks
of love — fingers that wind around tighter than vines," "Gushes
from the throats of birds," "Breezes set from living shores out to
you on the living sea — to you, O sailors!" The veiled phallicism
implicit in "Calamus" and "Roots and leaves" leads to a description
of spring in terms of impregnation and birth, quite different from
the moral and social ominousness of "April is the cruellest month":

Frost-mellowed berries, and Third Month twigs, offered fresh to young
    persons wandering out in the fields when the winter breaks up,
Love-buds, put before you and within you, whoever you are,
Buds to be unfolded on the old terms,
If you bring the warmth of the sun to them, they will open, and bring
    form, color, perfume, to you,
If you become the aliment and the wet, they will become flowers, fruits,
    tall branches and trees,
They are comprised in you just as much as in themselves — perhaps
    more than in themselves,
They are not comprised in one season or succession, but many succes-
    sions,
They have come slowly up out of the earth and me, and are to come
    slowly up out of you.

The insemination theme is further elaborated in the next two poems. "Not Heat Flames Up and Consumes" (14) is constructed around three simple images — flames (fire), "sea-waves" which "hurry in and out" (water), and "white down-balls of myriads of seeds" (air) — or passion, coitus, and fertilization. The lover-poet is "burning for his love," "seeking something" like the hurrying and unwearying "tide," and emulating "rain-emitting clouds," since

> my Soul is borne through the open air,
> Wafted in all directions, O love, for friendship, for you.

"Trickle Drops" (15) transfers the insemination theme from the general and impersonal to the specific and personal, from "white down-balls of myriads of seeds, wafted, sailing gracefully, to drop where they may," to the red "drops of me," which break forth from their prison (the body), "all ashamed and wet." The poem, as noted in the preceding chapter, presents a daring association of onanism and the creative process as well as an unusually candid admission of the autobiographical nature of his poetry:

> Stain every page — stain every song I sing, every word I say, bloody drops,
> Let them know your scarlet heat — let them glisten,
> Saturate them with yourself, all ashamed and wet,
> Glow upon all I have written or shall write, bleeding drops,
> Let it all be seen in your light, blushing drops.

Yet what Whitman says in these lines is but a variation upon a theme, for the floating or flying imagery he associates with the soul in the previous poem is, as Freud suggests, "the longing for the ability of sexual accomplishment."[13] Or perhaps it is more accurate to say that "Trickle Drops" is Whitman's conscious recognition of the fact that he is sublimating his thwarted sexuality.

In the sixteenth song the protagonist discards metaphorical indirectness for direct autobiographical statement:

> Who is now reading this?

> May-be one is now reading this who knows some wrong-doing of my past life,

Or may-be a stranger is reading this who has secretly loved me,
Or may-be one who meets all my grand assumptions and egotisms with
    derision,
Or may-be one who is puzzled at me.

As if I were not puzzled at myself!
Or as if I never deride myself! (O conscience-struck! O self-convicted!)
Or as if I do not secretly love strangers! (O tenderly, a long time, and
    never avow it;)
Or as if I did not see, perfectly well, interior in myself, the stuff of
    wrong-doing,
Or as if it could cease transpiring from me until it must cease.

This poem, which was removed from *Leaves of Grass* in 1867, is
typical Whitmanesque deception; while proclaiming his personal
confusion, he acknowledges his awareness of his motivations and
his psychic complexity: Whitman was rarely self-deceived. Even
more significant, however, is the admission of feelings of guilt
("O conscience-struck!"), for though guilt often lies just below
the surface, it is not often permitted verbalization. Also noteworthy is the admission of "stern necessity" in the concluding line
— the protagonist's inability to alter his course, to abandon his
"wrong-doing." His deviant course he must compulsively pursue,
and in his art he must compulsively "undrape," so that simultaneously he justifies himself and punishes himself: he is both
criminal and judge, satan and god.
    The next song, "Of Him I Love Day and Night" (17), which
later was transferred to "Whispers of Heavenly Death," relates
how the protagonist in a dream searches for the burial place of his
beloved, only to discover that everywhere the streets are "fuller,
O vastly fuller, of the dead than of the living." Then he declares,
"I stand henceforth bound to what I dreamed," by which he seems
to suggest, as in "Scented Herbage of My Breast" and "Out of the
Cradle Endlessly Rocking," that in the absence of requited love he
welcomes death, where the illusions of the living and the torments
of physical love have no existence. But Whitman again quickly
changes "the strain" in order to describe the "City of Orgies" (18),
which, despite the opening line, "City of my walks and joys!", substitutes the lonely urban landscape for the lonely rural landscape
beside "margins of pond-waters." The "orgies" are hardly reminiscent of a Dionysian rite; they are, almost pathetically, the desperate
delights of an isolate —

> as I pass, O Manhattan! your frequent and swift flash of
> eyes offering me love,
> Offering me the response of my own — these repay me,
> Lovers, continual lovers, only repay me —

who is satisfied, or so he alleges, with the "swift flash of eyes."
Similarly, the protagonist in "Song of the Open Road" observes:

> Do you know what it is, as you pass, to be loved by strangers?
> Do you know the talk of those turning eye-balls?

The "élève" mentioned in "To a Western Boy" (42) is not admitted
to the group, "If he be not silently selected by lovers, and do not
silently select lovers." So too in "Among the Multitude" (41) "I
perceive one picking me out by secret and divine signs," for "I
meant that you should discover me so, by my faint indirections."
To the uninitiated these seem unsatisfactory erotic encounters,
perhaps simply the projections of the "I's" love-consumed mind,
until one finds an explanation in John Addington Symonds' *Studies
in Sexual Inversion:*

> In antiquity the members of the sect had their own means of mutual
> recognition. And at the present time, these men know each other at
> first sight; moreover, they are found everywhere, in every station of
> society; without a single exception. "We recognize each other at
> once," says the writer of a report. . . "A mere glance of the eye
> suffices; and I have never been deceived. . . . [Everywhere] I have
> found people, never seen by me before, and whom I discriminated in a
> second."[14]

Then one understands why the fleeting relationship in "City of
Orgies" is thrice referred to as repayment: the "I" has the gratification, fleeting though it is, of discovering and being discovered by
his kind, of momentarily achieving identity among fellow outlaws.
   "Behold This Swarthy Face" (19), particularly in its original
version, resounds with verbal aggression (these lines disappeared
in 1867):

> Mind you the timid models of the rest, the majority?
> Long I minded them, but hence I will not — for I have adopted
>   models for myself, and now offer them to The Lands.

But the aggression amounts finally to the right of "two natural and nonchalant persons" to salute each other "lightly on the lips with robust love." The bombast seems excessive, but in a generally sympathetic review of *Leaves of Grass* in the *New York Sun* on November 19, 1881, the critic censures "the abstract idea of universal brotherhood, of which the kiss between man and man is his not agreeable poetic type." Whitman was violating a fiercely held cultural concept of male behavior, which is no less rigid one hundred years after "Calamus" was written.

"I Saw in Louisiana a Live-Oak Growing" (20) is a cameo-like statement of Whitman's and American loneliness, so fragile and so perfect that it makes any commentary an impertinence.

I saw in Louisiana a live-oak growing,
All alone stood it, and the moss hung down from the branches,
Without any companion it grew there, uttering joyous leaves of dark
    green,
And its look, rude, unbending, lusty, made me think of myself,
But I wondered how it could utter joyous leaves, standing alone there,
    without its friend, its lover near — for I knew I could not,
And I broke off a twig with a certain number of leaves upon it, and
    twined around it a little moss,
And brought it away — and I have placed it in sight in my room,
It is not needed to remind me as of my own dear friends,
(For I believe lately I think of little else than of them,)
Yet it remains to me a curious token — it makes me think of manly
    love;
For all that, and though the live-oak glistens there in Louisiana, solitary,
    in a wide flat space,
Uttering joyous leaves all its life, without a friend, a lover, near,
I know very well I could not.

But, of course, the opposite is true: Whitman's life resembles that of the live-oak, for he sings his songs of joy "without a friend, a lover, near," and his fortitude is confirmed by the dignity and absence of self-pity in his verse. The phallicism that he discovers in the oak parallels the phallic explanation of his own art, and the castration analogy symbolizes the separation of the artist as well as the man from society and, on a deeper level, the poet's arrestment that keeps him and his poetry from crossing the "bridge" to maturity.

"That Music Always Round Me" (21), later removed from the sequence, provides a brief interlude in which music is likened to an erotic encounter or a wrestling contest, which, as evidenced in passages quoted earlier, for Whitman had sexual associations: "I listen to the different voices winding in and out, striving, contending with fiery vehemence to excel each other in emotion." Then Whitman returns to his hunger in "To a Stranger" (22) and "This Moment Yearning and Thoughtful" (23), first, as in "a dream," conjuring up a relationship with a passing stranger and then with "brethren and lovers" in other lands. In "I Hear It Was Charged against Me" (24) he denies the charge "that I seek to destroy institutions": "I am neither for nor against institutions." He has but one goal, "The institution of the dear love of comrades." His refutation is scarcely convincing, nor is the "spiritual corresponding" he mentions in "The Prairie-Grass Dividing" (25), for "adhesiveness," a dubious biological and social concept, seems sophomoric when defended in specious argumentation. Nor can one ignore the special pleading, or the fear of censure, when Whitman makes his comrades into muscular saints, describing their relationships as "fluid, affectionate, chaste, matured" in "To a Stranger," and depicting in "The Prairie-Grass Dividing" fearless men who "look carelessly in the faces of Presidents and Governors, as to say, *Who are You?*" but who are, "with sweet and lusty flesh, clear of taint, choice and chary of its love-power." Natty Bumppo is their tragicomic ancestor.

"We Two Boys Together Clinging" (26) is an extraordinarily revealing poem that wells out of Whitman's unconscious. The mature man in "I Hear It Was Charged against Me" asserts that he seeks only brotherly love, but when, as here, fantasy is unchecked by social and rational controls, the poet recreates an adolescent's world in which two "armed and fearless" boys run roughshod over all external restraints, social, familial, religious, and political: "No laws less than ourselves owning," "priests alarming," "cities wrenching," "statutes mocking." They play successfully (so they think) at all the male games — "sailing, soldiering, thieving, threatening," but at the next moment they are frolicsome hermaphrodites "on the turf or the sea-beach dancing." And so while they thumb their noses at society — "eating, drinking, sleeping, loving" — their virility is but the wish of two very fearful lads who cling to each other: "We two boys together clinging, / One the other never leaving."

In "O Living Always, Always Dying" (27) Whitman once again makes his familiar assertion of the freedom of the self, which is made suspect by his reiterations.

O me, what I was for years, now dead, (I lament not — I am content;)
O to disengage myself from those corpses of me, which I turn and
    look at, where I cast them!
To pass on, (O living! always living!) and leave the corpses behind!

If the "corpses" are the conventionalisms of Walter Whitman, editor and hack writer, Walt Whitman achieves partial emancipation; but if the "corpses" are the fantasies, anxieties, and insecurities of his youth, such as appear in the preceding poem, then he is eschewing some of his richest subject matter, as he was shortly to do when he assumed a more public (but less successful) voice in his poetry. The title itself and even the gesture, like that of Lot's wife, of turning to look "where I cast them," reestablish the continuum.

One cannot help observing that Whitman talks obsessively about freedom, nonconformity, the bestowal of kisses, and so forth. And the deviancy of the behavior is sheltered from public view by retreats to ponds or by silent exchanges of "turning eye-balls." In other words, the fears of the protagonist are conspicuous. Repeated injunctions to be contemptuous of society's norms may lead to the suspicion that Whitman is lashing not society but, surreptitiously, his own cowardice, his own fear of rebellious conduct that will further alienate him from a society which he desires to lead to his own version of a promised land.

"A Glimpse" (29) repeats a situation in the early tale "The Child and the Profligate" (1841). The poem relates how the "I" and a youth sit hand in hand "in a bar-room" amid "drinking and oath and smutty jest." Uncontaminated but in an all-male environment, "There we two, content, happy in being together, speaking little, perhaps not a word." The gratification of the young (and they never mature) lovers begins and ends with innocent tactile contact. The relationship here and elsewhere is nonverbal. It is almost as though words would dissipate the tenuous affection, as though dialogue would make the union explicit and public when its existence depends upon its secretiveness. In "To a Stranger" (22), "I am not to speak to you — I am to think of you when I sit alone, or wake at night alone." Except for retreats to the "pond-side," where communication is possible, although there is none, the comrades are either strangers in a protective and anonymous crowd or silent companions in a male club like a saloon, where their purity is set off against the ribaldry of men playing at being men (as perhaps they are playing at being lovers), and where their presence will be unnoted and uncensured. And this is the "robust American love" that the poet wants to transmit to all the states, in "A Promise to California" (30), and expects to find openly acclaimed in "the new City of Friends," in "I Dream'd in a Dream" (34): "Nothing was greater there than the quality of robust love."

After indulging himself, in poems 30 to 35, in an evangelical and affected celebration of "a superb friendship, exalté, previously unknown" (the word *exalté* to persuade frontiersmen!), he abandons this unfortunate "strain" to sing of himself in "Earth, My Likeness" (36), where, as in "I Saw in Louisiana a Live-Oak Growing," he not only makes nature over in his own image but also seeks to make his physical desire natural:

Earth! my likeness!
Though you look so impassive, ample and spheric there,
I now suspect that is not all;
I now suspect there is something fierce in you, eligible to burst forth;
For an athlete is enamoured of me — and I of him,
But toward him there is something fierce and terrible in me, eligible to
    burst forth,
I dare not tell it in words — not even in these songs.

Although Whitman's depiction of sexuality often exhibits, perhaps deliberately, a child's misunderstanding of genital functions, here, as Basil de Selincourt pointed out years ago,[15] he appears to suggest sodomy, although oral sexuality is more usual in his poetry. Such is Whitman's honesty in depicting the self that he is driven to poetic and therefore public confession, but such are his shame and fear of censure that he invariably hints only to retreat into silence or "faint indirections."

"Fast-Anchor'd Eternal O Love!" (38) is the Whitmanesque treatment of friendship-versus-marriage. His tribute to woman is unusually ecstatic: "O bride! O wife! more resistless, more enduring than I can tell, the thought of you!" His revision in 1867 of the first line of the poem — "Primeval my love for the woman I

love" — to "Fast-anchor'd eternal O love! O woman I love!" makes
clearer the distinction he wants to draw: love of man for woman is
limited and earthbound ("Fast-anchor'd"), while love of man for
man is emancipating and "disembodied":

Then separate, as disembodied, the purest born,
The ethereal, the last athletic reality, my consolation,
I ascend — I float in the regions of your love, O man,
O sharer of my roving life.

Removed from the "Calamus" context, the poem may point to the
superiority of the soul (imagination) or male principle over the
body or feminine principle, and the floating image may suggest the
flight of the soul freed from physical anchorage. Interpreted in the
context of the sequence, the poem is another variation upon a
theme stated at the outset of the series. The "I" seeks freedom
from a restrictive society (the feminine or maternal principle),
and envisages a male world in which his need and his love can be
gratified. "The last athletic reality" recalls the "athlete . . . enamoured of me," and the floating imagery, as in "Not Heat Flames
Up and Consumes," indicates sexual longing.

That "Fast-Anchor'd Eternal O Love!" is to be interpreted as
personal statement rather than as mysticism is supported by the
following poem, "Sometimes with One I Love" (39), in which the
poet declares, in appropriate economic imagery, that, whether his
love is returned or not, "the pay is certain," since even "unreturned
love" provides subject matter for his art:

Doubtless I could not have perceived the universe, or written one of my
    poems, if I had not freely given myself to comrades, to love.

This version is more meaningful than the revision of 1867 —

(I loved a certain person ardently and my love was not return'd,
Yet out of that I have written these songs.) —

since, though Whitman may have been influenced by his intimacy
with Peter Doyle in 1867, love as depicted in "Calamus" is diffuse,
not focused, a fact which contributes to the restless poignancy and

the "irritable" tensions of the chants. "That Shadow My Likeness" (40), another variation on the illusion-and-reality motif, is likewise earthbound and nonmystical. Whitman describes his "shadow . . . that goes to and fro, seeking a livelihood, chattering, chaffering," and doubts "whether that is really me," but "among my lovers, and carolling my songs, / O I never doubt whether that is really me."

In the next three poems Whitman reiterates previous points. In "Among the Multitude" (41) he assumes once more the stance of a lover beyond ordinary social and familial obligations: "Acknowledging none else — not parent, wife, husband, brother, child, any nearer than I am" — which is a kind of "wicked" parody, as Whitman no doubt realized, of some famous words of Jesus. In "To a Western Boy" (42) the "élève" (another unfortunate affectation) "silently select[s] lovers"; and "O You Whom I Often and Silently Come" (43) dwells on the nonverbal bonds and the "subtle electric fire that for your sake is playing within me."

The penultimate poem confirms explicitly the autobiographical nature of the "Calamus" poems:

Here my last words, and the most baffling,
Here the frailest leaves of me, and yet my strongest-lasting,
Here I shade down and hide my thoughts — I do not expose them,
And yet they expose me more than all my other poems.

What a wonderful piece of comic exhibitionism! In "baffling" his readers, Whitman cannot resist another veiled genital analogy, the aggressiveness of which he knew would escape his disciples but the appropriateness of which in the exhibitionistic "Calamus" context is indisputable.

As in "Song of Myself," the "I" disappears but his art transcends time, to "itch" at the ears of readers "yet unborn."

Full of life, sweet-blooded, compact, visible,
I, forty years old the Eighty-third Year of The States,
To one a century hence, or any number of centuries hence,
To you, yet unborn, these, seeking you.

When you read these, I, that was visible, am become invisible;
Now it is you, compact, visible, realizing my poems, seeking me,

Fancying how happy you were, if I could be with you, and become your
    lover;
Be it as if I were with you. Be not too cetrain but I am now with you.

The last line teases amorously as the final seductive note in the
sequence is sounded.

The joyous rhythm celebrating future unions (or reunions)
momentarily diverts attention from the fact that "Calamus" is a
meditation on the pathos of unfulfilled and perhaps unfulfillable
love. The dialogue of reciprocal love still remains unspoken and
unheard. Such is the "I's" fate and his defiance of logic and consistency — but Whitman cocks his hat to logic and flaunts his
inconsistency — that he is compelled to rejoice in nontactile union
and monologue with "unborn" lovers.

"Calamus," despite the artful mingling of strains, reflects fear
more than joy, loneliness more than union, seeking rather than
finding. The "I" in "Calamus" is, in final analysis, little different
from the lonely Ahab: both create a landscape (or seascape) according to their emotional needs and out of their maladjustments;
both as articulate rebels defy the mores of their societies; and both
hunger for a security or Eden found only in death. Whitman's
protagonist and Melville's problematical hero, with their "crazy"
visions, like Don Quixote's, utter lonely cries but fail to impose
their fantasies upon reality: the same sea still resounds and the
live-oak still grows in Louisiana. But their failures are successes,
since their elegiac meditations on man's finiteness and forlorn-
ness continue to reverberate in our hearts through the transcendence of art.

8

"the low and delicious word DEATH"

In the future of these States must arise poets immenser far, and make great poems of death. The poems of life are great, but there must be the poems of the purports of life, not only in itself, but beyond itself.

— Democratic Vistas

In *A Backward Glance* Edith Wharton records a memorable moment in the history of American literature — Henry James reading the poetry of Walt Whitman.

Another day some one spoke of Whitman, and it was a joy to me to discover that James thought him, as I did, the greatest of American poets. "Leaves of Grass" was put into his hands, and all that evening we sat rapt while he wandered from "The Song of Myself" to "When lilacs last in the door-yard bloomed" (when he read "Lovely and soothing Death" his voice filled the hushed room like an organ adagio), and thence let himself be lured on to the mysterious music of "Out of the Cradle," reading, or rather crooning it in a mood of subdued ecstasy till the fivefold invocation to Death tolled out like the knocks in the opening bars of the Fifth Symphony.[1]

171

One of James's earliest critical pieces was an unfriendly review of *Drum-Taps* in *The Nation* in 1865, written, as Leon Edel suggests, under the influence of Matthew Arnold and biased by the novelist's foolish, and somewhat arrogant, attempt to judge the poet according to his own belief in the impersonality of art. James, however, unlike some of his followers in the Age of James and Eliot, was not a victim of his orthodoxy, and, like Ezra Pound, he eventually made a "pact" with Whitman.

If Mrs. Wharton's recollection of the reading is accurate, James captured the mood of "Out of the Cradle Endlessly Rocking," "crooning it in a mood of subdued ecstasy," at least until he came to the "death" refrain. To make Whitman sound like "the opening bars of the Fifth Symphony," however, is to substitute Jamesian melodrama for the poet's understatement. For surely Whitman, who manages his poetic effects every bit as skillfully as the weaver of the most subtle prose in our literature, did not wrench the mood by such romantic histrionics: the "death" refrain has the soothing intonations of a lullaby uttered by the eternal mother as she rocks the cradle of the boy-poet. "Fate" does not knock in Whitman's poem; the "key" is the verbalization of the awakening consciousness of the protagonist as he learns to view and to accept loss or separation in the continuum of life-death, cradle-coffin, or, to put it another way, to go beyond tragedy to the everlasting comedy of renewal and rebirth.

In "Song of Myself" the protagonist's supine position as he contemplates "a spear of summer grass" suggests love and death, two of his major themes, and the grass, as we have noted, is associated with fertility and the grave. But despite lovely passages on death, the primary thrust of "Song of Myself" is the return to the child's polymorphous landscape in order to resurrect the body, or Eros, buried beneath the weight of long-sanctioned repressions; hence there are "Landscapes projected masculine full-sized and golden." The "I" revels in the physical delights of the body and in tactile relatedness, but Whitman does not dwell in "Song of Myself" on the fact that the body is subject to decay, although his awareness of the missing element is evident in the closing lines of "Great Are the Myths" (1855):

Great is life . . and real and mystical . . wherever and whoever,
Great is death . . . . Sure as life holds all parts together, death holds
    all parts together;

Such as the stars return again after they merge in the light, de[...]
great as life.

These lines introduce a danger inherent in Whitman's position,
which Richard Chase forcefully elaborates upon:

When we look below the surface of "Out of the Cradle" we seem to see
the dark workings-out of a human drama being played on a stage set
by a dramatist with a dubious moral to propose, namely that we should
accept death and that this acceptance may be the origin of such creations as Whitman's poetry. . . . He is titillated by death and he forms
a sentimental attachment to it.[2]

Death, as in Poe's poetry, *almost* becomes a state devoutly to be
wished, since it solves the unsolvable, soothes the anguish caused
by thwarted relationships, and reduces the heterogeneous dissonance of democracy and of life itself to an eternal harmony. The
protagonist in "Song of Myself," it will be recalled, can "resume
the overstaid fraction" only by an act of will, since tragedy and
self-pity exert a paralyzing attraction. Whitman's love chants in
the "Calamus" sequence are frequently in danger of becoming
death chants, as in "Scented Herbage of My Breast":

Yet you are very beautiful to me, you faint-tinged roots — you make
me think of Death,
Death is beautiful from you — (what indeed is beautiful, except
Death and Love?)
O I think it is not for life I am chanting here my chant of lovers —
I think it must be for Death,
For how calm, how solemn it grows, to ascend to the atmosphere of
lovers,
Death or life I am then indifferent — my Soul declines to prefer,
I am not sure but the high Soul of lovers welcomes death most. . . .

Such is the fascination of death for Whitman, as in this trial line
for *Leaves of Grass* — "O Mystery of Death, I pant for the time
when I shall solve you" — that he is in danger of succumbing to
the death wish. But he usually manages to maintain an admittedly
precarious equilibrium.

Whitman's first extended meditation on death is "Out of the
Cradle Endlessly Rocking." Its original title, "A Child's Reminiscence" (1859), indicates that once again the poet returns to the
infantile world — "the rocked cradle" — and consciously reopens

and explores the wound of wounds, the child's loss of maternal love, not to dwell upon man's first tragedy for purpose of self-pity, but to find (or at any rate to assert) an order in which death, like love or life, has its place: "I, chanter of pains and joys, uniter of here and hereafter." Or, in the words of Norman O. Brown, "the primal unity Eros seeks to reinstate is its unity with its own opposite, the death instinct."[3]

Brown's Freudian formulation seems a reasonably exact statement of Whitman's purpose in this particular poem and in his poetry in general: not only is the body resurrected but also death is accepted as part of the "life rhythm." Henry Miller, who rightly sees himself as the heir of Whitman and Emerson, expresses the same conception in his own eccentric and aggressive way in *Tropic of Capricorn*:

The ovarian world is the product of a life rhythm. The moment a child is born it becomes part of a world in which there is not only the life rhythm but the death rhythm. The frantic desire to live, to live at any cost, is not a result of the life rhythm in us, but of the death rhythm. There is not only no need to keep alive at any price, but, if life is undesirable, it is absolutely wrong. This keeping oneself alive, out of a blind urge to defeat death, is in itself a means of sowing death. Every one who has not fully accepted life, who is not incrementing life, is helping to fill the world with death. To make the simplest gesture with the hand can convey the utmost sense of life; a word spoken with the whole being can give life. Activity in itself means nothing: it is often a sign of death. By simple external pressure, by force of surroundings and example, by the very climate which activity engenders, one can become part of a monstrous death machine, such as America, for example.[4]

Brown and Miller, in effect, answer Chase's charge of sentimentality. It is scarcely sentimental to recognize that life is constructed upon death (there is no other foundation), and that whatever order an artist discovers or assumes is an order in which death (that final order) must be accounted for. Whitman's position is not only tenable but also basically sane and life-affirming. He perceives as clearly as Hawthorne and Melville what Chase terms "disorder and dread," but unlike them he resumes "the over-staid fraction" because he "prefers not to" overvalue tragedy and "ambiguities."

Attempts to find the origin of "Out of the Cradle Endlessly
Rocking" in a personal experience about 1858 or 1859 strike me
as misguided and irrelevant, since the significance of an unsuccessful love affair (if one could be proved) would be not so much
the event itself as the reactivation of the experience of loss, ultimately the loss of the beloved mother, Whitman always, as observed earlier, intuitively arriving at a profound psychological
insight. (If one must seek a specific event, I suggest, once again,
that the death of his father in 1855 cannot be overlooked: it is
perhaps more than coincidental that only after his death does the
poet meditate upon the subject, and that reconciliation with death
may be part of his reconciliation with the father.) Thus Bychowski's explanation comes closest to describing the affect of the poem:

When we reduce the poignant beauty of this poem to its unconscious
core, we see the first separation of infancy, the first anguish of infantile
love underlying all the future pain of love. Sweet death emerges then
as the great benefactor, as a supreme salvation, since it promises a
reunion with the beloved mother, earth, sea, and maybe the universe.[5]

Influenced by the fact that the bird's song is called an "aria,"
critics have likened the "trio" — the male bird that has lost its
mate, the sea, and the boy-poet — to the Italian opera which
Whitman attended and admired most of his life. The analogy is
misleading, since, except for the "aria," the poem does not contain
the set pieces and brilliant virtuosity of Donizetti and Bellini. In
an anonymous defense of the poem shortly after its publication,
Whitman himself carefully refrains from stressing the operatic
qualities of the bird's "aria": "the purport of this wild and plaintive
song, well-enveloped, and eluding definition, is positive and un-
questionable, like the effect of music"[6] — an explanation which,
to say the least, explains little.

Although a few of Whitman's friends, as he reported to Horace
Traubel in 1888, said that "Wagner is Leaves of Grass done into
music," the poet's initial response to the comparison was "adverse,
critical." He was apparently troubled that Wagner, according to
rumor, was not a democrat, that his "art was distinctly the art of
caste," and that his "Jack and the Beanstalk stories" were unsuit-
able to "this modern medium." The poet had to "confess that I
have heard bits here and there at concerts, from orchestras, bands,

which have astonished, ravished me, like the discovery of a new world." Mostly on the basis of the enthusiasm of his friends, Whitman came to the conclusion, in 1889, that Wagner's operas "are constructed on my lines — attach themselves to the same theories of art that have been responsible for Leaves of Grass."[7]

Although the poet and his admirers finally agreed on the question, neither condescended to specificity in indicating the artistic and thematic bonds between the two artists. In one of the most perceptive discussions of Whitman's poem, Leo Spitzer points to the coincidence (also noted by Bychowski) of the appearance in 1857 of *Tristan und Isolde* and in 1859 of "A Child's Reminiscence" (the original title). Noting the "Wagnerian orchestration," Spitzer terms the rhyming participial forms a *leitmotif* and observes in both artists "the same feeling for the voluptuousness of death and the death-like quality of love."[8] Spitzer's insights are suggestive rather than developed, perhaps because he is primarily interested in establishing "Out of the Cradle Endlessly Rocking" as a modern elaboration upon the ancient ode.

Unlike Italian opera, "Out of the Cradle Endlessly Rocking" is an introspective "portrait of the artist as a young man," a very personal meditation which is not given a conventional public form for the obvious reason that the subject matter demands a form and a rhythm consonant with its evocation of psychic depths and infantile trauma. From the opening line — in the earlier version, "Out of the rocked cradle" — technique mirrors meaning and sound mirrors sense in a fusion such as few artists have achieved. The musical equivalent of the literal motion of the cradle is the rocking quality of the crescendos and decrescendos, the ecstatic fortissimos and "laving" pianissimos, with their human counterparts in the emotional state of the bird and, more particularly, of the youth. To the final line, "The sea whispered me," which counteracts the despair of "The aria sinking," the poem rocks, not only through the use of -*ing* forms or recurring images like the moon, but also in the rising and falling sounds of the bird's grief and disappointed hopes, the birth imagery ("Out of the boy's mother's womb"), the comfort and loss of the mother's breast, the literal movements of the moon and the waves, the boy's transformation from despondency to an "extatic" state, and the life-journey itself, from the cradle to the coffin.

Unlike, for example, Thomas Mann, who laboriously and self-consciously approximates the Wagnerian texture and density in his prose, Whitman rarely calls attention to his artistic trickery, although his poem is an intricately woven fabric. More important, Whitman does not make suspect the emotionality inherent in the *leitmotif* by recourse to Mann's defensive and evasive irony. Whitman's sound, like Wagner's, completely expresses content or idea, for neither is plagued by an unresolved (or unresolvable) battle between mind and heart, meaning and feeling. Read aloud — and the poem, like music, refuses to remain silent on the printed page — without the intrusion of a rational mind decreeing sense or a critical intelligence attempting explication, "Out of the Cradle Endlessly Rocking" interprets itself. The erotic sounds and movements, as in Wagner's music, evoke birth, love, loss, and death.

Whitman's poem is a reminiscence of an event in the protagonist's boyhood, when on a September night he wanders along the ocean shore and hears the song of a male mockingbird lamenting the disappearance of his mate, against the (seemingly) agitated music of waves advancing and retreating, not unlike the motions of a cradle. As in "The Sleepers," this is a nighttime experience, here played out beneath an autumnal moon. The fall is the dying season of the year, which harmonizes with the bird's loss of his beloved and with the "aria sinking," but also the time of harvest and of ancient fertility rites, which harmonizes with the "death" of a boy and the birth of a boy-poet. The bird, consumed by his grief, is estranged from his environment. The emergent artist, on the other hand, finds the "key," or underlying unity, which links the grief-stricken bird, "the hoarse surging of the sea," and the youthful observer — death, life, and art.

Although Whitman no doubt observed, as he walked the beaches of Long Island in his youth, the nesting habits of birds — perhaps even those of mockingbirds from Alabama — surely his means of depicting universal loss had unconscious and cultural origins. Elsewhere in his poetry, in "The Sleepers," for instance, he disguises and artistically distances the personal note and anguish through projection — a point he makes himself when he says of the bird, "O you demon, singing by yourself — projecting me." The he-bird ("my brother") — not the boy-poet — directly experiences man's fate, abandonment by woman (mother). For the she-bird mysteriously abandons the eggs in her nest, as the mother appears to abandon the child when other offspring arrive, or when the mother appears to permit the father to supplant the child in her affections.

In view of the folklore which "explains" biological realities through tales of the stork, part of the charm of the poem is the simple fact that the child-poet begins to learn about life by observing the habits of birds, but, like all children, arrives at understanding only when he experiences another loss — the abandonment of cultural "lies." The not-so-simple fact about the poem, if we accept Freud's brilliant speculations about the boyhood of Leonardo da Vinci, is that the bird analogy, with its ancient association of the winged phallus, not only accounts for the orgiastic rhythm of the poem, but also harmonizes with the erotic nature of knowledge itself, which is expressed in the boy's longing to be "the outsetting bard of love" and in the mature man's sublimation in his art of "the cries of unsatisfied love." (Like Picasso, Whitman invariably dramatizes art in sexual terms.) With subtlety and insight Whitman remains faithful to the human drama of childhood and maturity, even to the substitution of the artistic lie for the cultural lie: the poem, on all levels, depicts rejection and ultimate reconciliation.

The "trio," as Chase observes, more than hints that the event is a veiled reenactment of the oedipal conflict, the female bird seemingly returning as "the fierce old mother," the sea, that threatens but eventually soothes when the boy begins to comprehend the "life rhythm." The male bird is both "brother" and "dusky demon," child and father. Significantly — and how accurate Whitman's language is! — the boy-poet is "Cautiously peering, absorbing, translating." Timidly, because of the complex nature of the emotional conflict, the youth observes from a safe distance, ingests literally and symbolically — "from the nipples of her breasts" in the third line (omitted in 1867) to the return to the universal mother depicted in the concluding lines — and then orders the experience artistically. Since the he-bird, like the males in "The Sleepers" and "As I Ebb'd with the Ocean of Life," is impotent in his grief, the boy in Whitmanesque fashion must discover the "key" — that is, the eternal erotic principle — without external assistance, paternal or historical.

The child, like the bird, at first knows only love, the mother bending over him in the cradle in an edenic relationship, and complacently thinks that "we two together" will always be together, that all nature conspires to insure the permanence of this idyllic relationship.

Shine! Shine!
Pour down your warmth, great Sun!
While we bask — we two together.

Two together!
Winds blow South, or winds blow North,
Day come white, or night come black,
Home, or rivers and mountains from home,
Singing all time, minding no time,
If we two but keep together.

The ominous words "Till of a sudden" introduce the bird to the pain and riddle of separation or loss. For the she-bird unaccountably abandons her nest and her "four light-green eggs, spotted with brown." The bird, suddenly in a new world devoid of pleasure and love, refuses to accept the finality of the situation. He breaks out into a lament in which he cries, like a child, for consolation — "Soothe! Soothe!" — but the waves, the stars, and the moon return no answer. And eventually, his voice echoing in what appears to him a waste land, he moans:

Loved! Loved! Loved! Loved! Loved!
Loved — but no more with me,
We two together no more.

The moon is "sinking" on the horizon, the sound of his voice is "sinking," and his confidence is gone.

One of the most glowing descriptions of the bird's "aria" is that of John Cowper Powys in *Visions and Revisions:*

The most devastating love-cry ever uttered, except that of King David over his friend, is the cry this American poet dares to put into the heart of "a wild-bird from Alabama" that has lost its mate. I wonder if critics have done justice to the incredible genius of this man who can find words for that aching of the soul we do not confess even to our dearest?[9]

But Powys' praise, inadvertently, does an injustice to Whitman's poem since he removes the song from its context and overemphasizes the (negative) "aching of the soul." Although the bird's loss is also the boy's loss, this is not a poem of self-pity but of a

developing consciousness. And so the rocking participles in the
passage immediately following —

The aria sinking,
All else continuing — the stars shining,
The winds blowing — the notes of the wondrous bird echoing,
With angry moans the fierce old mother yet, as ever, incessantly moan-
ing,
On the sands of Paumanok's shore gray and rustling —

reintroduce the movement of the cradle: life is endless motion.
The poem itself, organically, reflects this motion, as Mrs. Dallo-
way's needles duplicate the movement of the waves, and the boy's
consciousness moves beyond empathy (or stasis) to awareness. As
the song dies away, an artist is born.

The imagery of the poem is unobtrusively but intricately related
to the exposition of the bird's despair and the boy's awakening.
The moon, introduced in the eleventh line, moves across the
heaven, rising and falling according to its erotic rhythm, and, like
Wagner's restless and orgiastic musical patterns, reflects the emotional tensions of the participants: "From under that yellow half-
moon, late-risen, and swollen as if with tears." (Subsequently we
read, "by these tears a little boy again"; "Sat the lone singer [the
bird], wonderful, causing tears"; and of "the boy extatic," "The
strange tears down the cheeks coursing.") In a long aria the male
bird four times associates himself and his loss with the moon:

Low hangs the moon — it rose late,
O it is lagging — O I think it is heavy with love.

· ·

Low-hanging moon!
What is that dusky spot in your brown yellow?
O it is the shape of my mate!
O moon, do not keep her from me any longer.

· ·

Carols of lonesome love! Death's carols!
Carols under that lagging, yellow, waning moon!
O, under that moon, where she droops almost down into the sea!

· ·

O brown halo in the sky, near the moon, drooping upon the sea!
O troubled reflection in the sea!

Not only do the bird and the moon appear to droop simultaneously, but also darkness appears to settle over the world. But
this is the bird's reality, not that of the almost forgotten youth who
has been observing and listening on the "sands of Paumanok's
shore," under the same moon and in the same shadows. Unlike
the bird fixated in his grief and physically and emotionally arrested
on a lonely perch —

All night long, on the prong of a moss-scallop'd stake,
Down, almost amid the slapping waves,
Sat the lone singer, wonderful, causing tears —

the lad is about to experience a miraculous transformation which
will lead him to a reality beyond the bird's comprehension.

The yellow half-moon, enlarged, sagging down, drooping, the face of
    the sea almost touching,
The boy extatic — with his bare feet the waves, with his hair the
    atmosphere dallying,
The love in the heart pent, now loose, now at last tumultuously
    bursting. . . .

The erotic and birth images, as in "There Was a Child Went
Forth," appropriately characterize the metamorphosis. "Extatic"
is a most expressive (Whitman would say "delicious") word to
describe the adventure which is both intellectual and orgiastic.
For the boy knows, as the bird does not, that the setting (or dying)
moon will rise again on the morrow, but on a deeper level he
senses that the moon's erotic union with the ocean — "the face of
the sea almost touching" — is part of "the procreant urge." The
falling and rising of the tides, the erotic rhythm of the universe,
he *senses,* contain an insight beyond that of the bird's tragic perspective, which projects its loss or betrayal upon the cosmos.
    At this point the "extatic" youth's insight is limited and amor-
phous. In sharing the bird's grief, the boy, symbolically, enters
into a brotherhood and acknowledges the universal loss upon which

life rests: he has, in short, accepted "things as they are," which
will be the subject matter of his art.

Bird! (then said the boy's Soul,)
Is it indeed toward your mate you sing? or is it mostly to me?
For I that was a child, my tongue's use sleeping,
Now that I have heard you,
Now in a moment I know what I am for — I awake,
And already a thousand singers —a thousand songs, clearer, louder,
    more sorrowful than yours,
A thousand warbling echoes have started to life within me,
Never to die.

But the vision or illumination which will enable the artist to
reconcile disparities and to rediscover the eternal order does not
come at once, because the third member of the trio — the sea —
has not spoken, although it has been sounding ceaselessly in the
background as the bird voices its grief and as the boy is transformed
into a poet.

The youth seems about to duplicate the bird's experience, the
delights of "Two together" and then insurmountable grief: since
he, unlike the bird, has the ability to generalize, he imagines that
the "destination" of man may be universal "chaos":

O give me some clew!
O if I am to have so much, let me have more!
O a word! O what is my destination?
O I fear it is henceforth chaos!
O how joys, dreads, convolutions, human shapes, and all shapes, spring
    as from graves around me!
O phantoms! you cover all the land, and all the sea!
O I cannot see in the dimness whether you smile or frown upon me;
O vapor, a look, a word! O well-beloved!
O you dear women's and men's phantoms!

(All but the first two lines disappeared in the revised version of
1881, when, as was his practice later in life, Whitman smoothed
out the tensions in his earlier poems.) Now, for the first time, the
boy listens to the "whispering" of the sea: "Is that it from your
liquid rims and wet sands?"

Thus at last the sea emerges, literally and artistically, as the most
powerful member of the "trio" around whom the action revolves.

It voices no words, but its unuttered sounds speak as the bird's song cannot. It never alters its endless motions, which are variously viewed as invasions or embraces of the shore, depending upon the observer's predisposition, but gradually it envelops the boy-poet and the bird as the mother envelops her offspring. For the sea is eternal woman, the bird's mate as well as the mother introduced in the opening lines of the poem —

Out of the rocked cradle,
Out of the mocking-bird's throat, the musical shuttle,
Out of the boy's mother's womb, and from the nipples of her breasts —

at the beginning of what Spitzer felicitously calls an " 'oceanic' sentence." The time-burdened cradle has its timeless counterpart in the motions of the waves. The event recorded in "Out of the Cradle Endlessly Rocking" occurs along Paumanok's shore, but the event that is life begins in the amniotic waters and culminates in the grave, only to repeat itself time without end.

After the she-bird's disappearance, when grief pervades and colors the atmosphere, the protagonist refers casually to "the hoarse surging of the sea" and to "slapping waves" — obliquely attributing disaster to the terrifying sea, particularly in one graphic picture of loss, "The white arms out in the breakers tirelessly tossing." But, as it turns out, the "white arms" will eventually soothe and heal the pain. In the "aria" the bird looks across the dark waters in search of his beloved and even imagines that he hears her voice above the "husky-noised sea," which, of course, is only the echo of his own lonely voice. (However, "A thousand warbling echoes have started to life within me.") The sea as a character in the dramatic action is not directly present until the bird's song is over —

The colloquy there — the trio — each uttering,
The undertone — the savage old mother, incessantly crying,
To the boy's Soul's questions sullenly timing — some drowned secret hissing,
To the outsetting bard of love.

Caught up in the bird's tragedy, the emergent artist equates the bird's song and the sound of the sea: "With angry moans the fierce

old mother yet, as ever, incessantly moaning." The "moaning,"
however, is the bird's as well as the boy's empathetic response.
"Fierce old mother" is projection of uncomprehended despair upon
the ocean, or eternal mother — an unsatisfactory handling of the
universal loss upon which the poem is predicated.

As the lad seeks "some clew," the sea loses its fierceness and
reintroduces the enveloping mother in a remarkable stanza.

Answering, the sea,
Delaying not, hurrying not,
Whispered me through the night, and very plainly before daybreak,
Lisped to me constantly the low and delicious word DEATH,
And again Death — ever Death, Death, Death,
Hissing melodious, neither like the bird, nor like my aroused child's
    heart,
But edging near, as privately for me, rustling at my feet,
And creeping thence steadily up to my ears,
Death, Death, Death, Death, Death.

The wonderful dactyls in the first two lines, reminiscent of those
at the opening of the poem, quietly prepare us for the inevitable
resolution. "Lisped" is extraordinarily right in the context: it is
both sound as dimly understood by a child in a mother's embrace
and imitative vocalization of a child learning to make sounds, "my
tongue's use sleeping." The sound or word is delicious as is any
sound in an affectional context where the intonation of love speaks
with a clarity rarely given to uttered syllables. The sound of the
word, like the waves, engulfs the boy-poet — "edging near," "rustling at my feet," "creeping." The bird's song was intellectually
comprehended: "The aria's meaning, the ears, the Soul, swiftly
depositing" — but the water physically and emotionally is like the
all-inclusive embrace of the mother: "And creeping thence steadily
up to my ears." And the five-times repeated word rocks like the
cradle itself.

As the boy-poet, who has absorbed the plight of "my brother,"
and the ocean become one, life (bird), art (boy), and immortality
(sea) are a trio or a trinity that is one. The fertility rite beneath
the autumnal moon is completed — "the key, the word up from
the waves." Mythically, the artist, like Aphrodite and Everyman,
springs from the water. And the rhythm of the poem (and of life)
rises and falls, until the joyous but subdued decrescendo in the

final line — uttered with the quiet triumph and contented satisfaction of the child-man in the arms of the eternal mother.

Which I do not forget,
But fuse the song of two together,
That was sung to me in the moonlight on Paumanok's gray beach,
With the thousand responsive songs, at random,
My own songs, awaked from that hour,
And with them the key, the word up from the waves,
The word of the sweetest song, and all songs,
That strong and delicious word which, creeping to my feet,
The sea whispered me.

Whicher observes that the sea offers "no consoling revelations but simply reality. . . . The outsetting bard of love will be the bard of unsatisfied love because there is no other kind."¹⁰ But Whitman's music refutes Whicher's reading: the "delicious word" *sounds* its consolation. As the poem makes clear in the story of the birds and as the "Calamus" poems prove, "cries of unsatisfied love" characterize the poet's and man's lot, but "Out of the Cradle Endlessly Rocking" is, to quote D. H. Lawrence, "the perfect utterance of a concentrated, spontaneous soul," in which the poet endeavors to place thwarted love and death in perspective and to create a meaningful artifact and a meaningful life out of universal psychic loss. The body, life itself, and art, Whitman asserts, can be free only when death is acknowledged. Without recourse to God or mysticism, Whitman fuses, as psychologists were to do, Eros and Thanatos, repudiates the stasis of romantic despair or pessimism, and celebrates the eternal human comedy.

Structurally, the restless "oceanic" opening sentence finds rest in the quiet final line. Psychologically, the mature man has reaffirmed his faith in his artistic powers by this return to childhood experience, the source of his art (and all art) and the source of the pain which he will transcend in his intellectual-emotional insight and in creative sublimation. Finally, "Out of the Cradle Endlessly Rocking" provides an artistic and human catharsis: the poem evokes pain as we read but at the same time makes the pain endurable because it offers a metaphorical and psychological order. It moves us viscerally and emotionally when it traverses psychic depths, but consoles because we assert our humanity, not in vicarious admiration of great deeds performed by tragic heroes, which few of us will have occasion to emulate, but in the realization that the great and the mediocre can live creatively if they accept the "life rhythm."

Of Whitman's major poems the most admired has always been "When Lilacs Last in the Dooryard Bloom'd." Although there have been a few dissenting voices, Swinburne's praise has been reechoed through the years, even by T. S. Eliot, who, unlike Ezra Pound, never made a "pact" with his greatest American predecessor. The popularity is not difficult to explain. "When Lilacs Last in the Dooryard Bloom'd" is seldom considered out of the emotional context, national and personal, of the "captain" whose loss it memorializes in a semi-traditional form. In times of national sorrow, as after the untimely deaths of Franklin D. Roosevelt and John F. Kennedy, commentators invariably quote from the greatest American elegy. It is also one of the facts of modern literary history that no other national political leader has been commemorated in a poem at once worthy of the man and consoling to the bereaved nation. But rare have been the heroes so warmly engaging as the homely Lincoln, who has borne without loss of dignity a nickname that humanizes the patriarch after whom he was named. Even rarer in a century of "estrangement" have been poets like Whitman, a poet laureate who wrote verse worthy of his (imaginary) position.

It probably is not true that Lincoln saw Whitman passing the White House one day and, after inquiring who he was, said: "Well, *he* looks like a *man*."[11] But it is a legend that reflects credit upon its creator, and surely some poet should have created an "imaginary conversation" between two of the greatest men of their generation.

Another reason for the acclaim of "When Lilacs Last in the Dooryard Bloom'd" is its anticipation of twentieth-century poetic tendencies. The least personal, at least superficially, of Whitman's great poems, it does not offend those people (the latter-day puritans) who cringe when he unabashedly "dotes" on his anatomical assets, and who prefer an art distanced by the transparent fiction of impersonality or objectivity. The structure, often erroneously likened to that of formal music, and the symbolic schematization of the poem appeal to a generation that has reveled too much in

cerebral artistic devices in order to depict the (exaggerated) dead-
ness of the modern world and that has contributed to the dehuman-
ization of art, to borrow from Ortega y Gasset, much as the modern
economic system has created institutional man in its own image.

The symbols in the poem — the lilacs, the western star, and
the "gray-brown" thrush — have been endlessly scrutinized despite their apparent simplicity, and understandably so, since, as is
usually the case, Whitman is more subtle than his interpreters.
The Long Island lilacs have been said to represent Whitman's
youth, Lincoln the man as opposed to Lincoln the ideal (the star),
spring as the season of rebirth, the sense of smell (the "mastering
odor"), day and physical life, love as the remembrance of death
(the lilac as a floral tribute on the coffin). The star has elicited
greater agreement because of its obvious association with the President's death, although the symbol has been extended to include
death itself or the Western conception of death, Lincoln as an
ideal, and the "Calamus" theme. The bird has been associated
with love, insight as knowledge of death, the "thought of mor-
tality," and the poetic process itself (the bird as the "brother" of
the protagonist). A few commentators, not without justification,
have added to Whitman's "trinity" the cloud, which is introduced
in Section 2, and night itself, relating them to the death theme.
The cloud, not unlike Hawthorne's veil imagery in *The Blithedale
Romance*, is skillfully manipulated from its first appearance as
a "harsh surrounding cloud" (2) to its disguised reappearance as
the "shroud" (5) from which new plants emerge in the spring and
as the "crape-veil'd women" in "cities draped in black" (6) who
watch Lincoln's casket pass by, to its literal reappearance in Section
14, where it is transformed by the awakening awareness of the
protagonist:

Appear'd the cloud, appear'd the long black trail;
And I knew Death, its thought, and the sacred knowledge of death;

and finally it fuses, even coloristically, with the "Dark Mother" in
the bird's "carol": "O vast and well-veil'd Death."

Whitman's treatment of the cloud not only invalidates the rigid
categories of some critics, but also points to the conclusion which
Feidelson draws in *Symbolism and American Literature:* "the lilac
and the star enter the poem not as objects to which the poet assigns

a meaning but as elements in the undifferentiated stream of thoughts and things."[12] For the symbols do not have specific meanings and separate functions: they merge with each other in endless patterns as the protagonist attempts to transcend the specific event (Lincoln's death) in order to include all deaths and to understand death itself, and to transcend chronological time (1865) in order to place the tragedy in the perspective of eternity, which is beyond tragedy. In their attempts to impose rigid schemes upon the poem, critics have confirmed the fluidity of the symbols when they have assigned "love" to the lilacs, the star, and the bird —and rightly so, for the shrub has "heart-shaped leaves," the star is Venus, and the bird sings of the "Dark Mother," who, like the sea in "Out of the Cradle Endlessly Rocking," croons to her offspring.

Gay Wilson Allen, noting that Lincoln's death occurred during Easter week, observes that the "trinity" provides suggestive associations not only with the Christian resurrection but also with the rebirth or awakening of nature: the landscape which the coffin crosses is in the process of self-renewal, Venus is in the western sky at this time of the year, and the thrush ordinarily sings only in the spring. Kenneth Burke also indicates many examples of Whitman's "undifferentiated stream of thoughts and things": the protagonist's "pouring" lilacs upon the coffin and the bird which is to "pour your chant from the bushes" (he might have noted the dirges of the grief-stricken people that "pour'd around the coffin," which also links the shrub and the bird's "carol"); the "drooping" star, the broken "sprig" of lilac, and the protagonist's soul before the assassination which "sank" as the star "dropt in the night"; the "perfume strong" of the lilacs "in the dooryard fronting an old farm-house," the odor of the "bouquets" placed upon the casket, the poet's question, "what shall my perfume be, for the grave of him I love?", the song of the bird among "the fragrant cedars," and the final line, "There in the fragrant pines, and the cedars dusk and dim." Arguing by analogy, Burke points out that scent in Whitman's poetry usually has a maternal association (the mother, in "There Was a Child Went Forth," it will be recalled, has "a wholesome odor falling off her person"), but also sometimes a "Calamus" association, as in "Scented Herbage of My Breast," which actually combines both.[13] In "When Lilacs Last in the Dooryard Bloom'd," the "comrades three" seek out the bird that sings from its perfumed retreat of the "Dark Mother," the fragrance of whose love enfolds the trio and all of life in its embrace.

In richly suggestive fashion the lilac is more than a perfume, a heart image, and a sign of emergent spring. Maud Bodkin's association of the "spring" with the "golden bough" of Frazer and Vergil adds a mythic dimension and relevancy:

The single branch chosen in the spring festival to be set up before one's door brings the spirit and power that is stirring in every branch within the woods, to bless and strengthen the householder shut away within his dwelling. So, the blossoming branch offered to the dead as part of the ritual of interment, brings in symbol the power that reawakens forest and garden, to keep watch beside the corpse or accompany the freed spirit.[14]

The protagonist breaks off the phallic flower ("a pointed blossom, rising, delicate") because he wants to bestow upon the coffin of the beloved an aromatic token, a fertility symbol as well as a love token like those the "I" gives to his comrades in the "Calamus" poem "These I Singing in Spring":

Plucking something for tokens — something for these, till I hit upon
    a name — tossing toward whoever is near me,
Here! lilac, with a branch of pine. . . .

At the same time the broken branch is not unrelated to Lincoln's death in the fullness of his life. On an unconscious level the act is a castration rite — the wound, the acceptance of tradition in the public act of placing an offering on the casket, and the gradual growth of the protagonist to man's estate, which is to say to awareness.

The thrush also has a complex symbolic purpose: it is death, love, poetic process, but more. Traditionally the bird is associated with the flight of the soul after the death of the body; the bird iconography of New England gravestones reflects this belief. The birdlike flight of the artist's imagination, in the Daedalus-Icarus legend and in James Joyce's epiphany scene in *Portrait of the Artist as a Young Man,* is a commonplace. And it is hardly farfetched to suggest once again the winged phallus and its potency, which, interestingly enough, is treated in detail in Thomas Wright's *The*

Worship of the Generative Powers, privately printed about 1866. Furthermore, if, because of the explicit association of bird and poet — "O how shall I warble myself for the dead one there I loved?" — we create a composite bird-poet, then we can scarcely avoid recalling the birdmen of Egyptian lore and the gods with bird heads that often adorned the tombs of pharaohs and presumably promised another life after death. This association is not implausible in view of Whitman's well-established interest in Egyptology. (Section 11 is generally considered to have been inspired by an Egyptian tomb.) Without an adequate Amercian equivalent, or so he supposed, Whitman gave to his hero, as Allen suggests, the esthetic grandeur the Egyptians accorded to their leaders.

Because of his ignorance of American iconography, a weakness shared by most of our writers and literary critics, Whitman missed the opportunity to incorporate the symbols of early tombstones into this section of his poem. As the seminal study of Allen I. Ludwig in *Graven Images: New England Stonecarving and Its Symbols, 1650–1815* indicates, Whitman could have drawn upon puritan erotic symbolism, particularly the conventionalization of the maternal breast, and not only foreshadowed the appearance of the "Dark Mother" but also linked once again Eros and Thanatos, this time in a traditionally American fashion. Whitman, however, solved his artistic problem in two ways. First, he naturalized the Egyptian tradition by having his tomb-pictures present American "scenes," rural and urban, which assert the continuity of life in the face of seemingly irreparable loss, particularly in the final line, "And all the scenes of life, and the workshops, and the workmen homeward returning," which fuses Egyptian and American "workshops" and simultaneously weaves the scene into the ever-present journey motif. Second, on the psychological level, the tomb (womb) is part of the symbolic substructure which unobtrusively keeps before us at all times the dominancy and all-inclusiveness of the maternal principle, which will culminate in the advent of the mother. There is at the beginning of the poem "the old farm-house" near which the lilac grows and which no doubt derives from Whitman's youth on Long Island; then there is the description of mother earth covered with the emerging vegetation of spring; shortly thereafter follows the account of the coffin (cradle) and of its adornment with flowers; and throughout the poem the bird warbles in the swamp, to which the protagonist finally goes in order to hear the "oceanic" lullaby of the mother who eternally bestows her affections without differentiation or distinctions of any sort.

One of the few flaws Matthiessen finds in the poem is the use of the word "orb" in reference to the star, which he terms an "orator's word." Although Whitman's diction is sometimes affected, a point which hostile critics delight to make, is it not reasonable to suppose that the poet more often than not knew exactly what he was doing, and that the alleged failure in taste is actually the critic's failure of insight? "Orb" as related to "orbit" harmonizes with the journey theme, particularly with the protagonist's developing awareness. "Orb" with its evocation of the heart or, more specifically, the breast, is related to the "heart-shaped" leaves of the lilac, Venus, and the "Dark Mother." "Orb" as an "orator's word" is consonant with the shape of the mouth, "Song of the bleeding throat! / Death's outlet song of life," and the "carol," especially with the line, "Undulate round the world." Thus it harmonizes with the protagonist's quest for appropriate language to voice his and the nation's grief and abiding faith.

In a perceptive attempt to explain the physiological aspects of the poem, Matthiessen points out that flower, star, and bird correspond to the three senses, smell, sight, and hearing, but, as previously noted, this categorization ignores the fluidity of the symbols. In addition, it does not take into account the sense of touch, which, although it cannot be attributed to any one of the main symbols, characterizes all of them. For tactility, as one would expect, is an integral part of the dramatization of the awakening consciousness. In Section 2 the protagonist says of his grief: "O cruel hands that hold me powerless!" In describing his vague presentiments before Lincoln's murder, in Section 8, he speaks of the star "as you bent to me night after night, / . . . as if to my side." Twice, in Sections 9 and 13, he alludes to the fact that star and lilac detain him and keep him from visiting the bird in the swamp, which, of course, suggests that overwhelming personal grief paralyzes him. But when he "resumes the overstaid fraction" in Section 15, he goes forth

> with the knowledge of death as walking one side of me,
> And the thought of death close-walking the other side of me,
> And I in the middle, as with companions, and as holding the hands of companions. . . .

Then the thrush sings caressingly of "the sure-enwinding arms of cool-enfolding death" and of "the body gratefully nestling close to thee." (How right, artistically and psychologically, "nestling" is!) With "eyes unclosed" the protagonist is now "unloosing the hold of my comrades' hands" (19), for "the tally" of his soul enables him to bear his grief. In the concluding section he is content with the "memory ever I keep": "With the holders holding my hand."

The tactile imagery not only heightens the sensuous appeal of the poem but also illustrates Whitman's characteristic preoccupation with human relatedness. The star is "my comrade," the bird is "my brother." "Comrades three" (presumably star, lilac, and protagonist) go together to the swamp, and the poem is a tribute to "the sweetest, wisest soul of all my days and lands." As Burke suggests, the relationship between the star and the "I" is that of father and son. The protagonist imagines the star bending "as if to my side," which may or may not be an instance of the pathetic fallacy, although the use of the qualifying *as if* indicates Whitman's awareness of the illusoriness of the relationship. Moreover, the situation duplicates that in "As I Ebb'd with the Ocean of Life," where the "I" attempts to establish an unusually ardent relationship with "father" shore:

Kiss me, my father,
Touch me with your lips, as I touch those I love,
Breathe to me, while I hold you close, the secret of the wondrous
     murmuring I envy,
For I fear I shall become crazed, if I cannot emulate it, and utter
     myself as well as it.

The ineffectual father — even Washington ("The Sleepers") and now Lincoln — cannot offer the "son" security and contentment. Man is fragmentation, unity is woman. Invariably in these scenes Whitman's imagery suggests the longing for a maternal relationship with the father which the father cannot sustain; hence the father fails the son, who recovers the infantile Eden where he is the exclusive possessor of the mother.

In a very real, even visceral, sense, "When Lilacs Last in the Dooryard Bloom'd" is a drama of envelopment or absorption in the mother, a theme present in autobiographical poems like "The Sleepers," but here rendered with no less urgency, although the manifest subject is Lincoln's death. In the first section the protagonist speaks of the "trinity sure to me you bring," although at this point he understands only superficially the nature of the trinity and its oneness. In Section 2 he is physically enveloped and frustrated by his grief — as indicated by the "harsh surrounding cloud that will not free my soul." In the next section he is engulfed by the perfume of the lilac bush in a setting, as noted earlier, vaguely reminiscent of his (lost) childhood, which will be recovered in the "carol." He hears the bird in Section 4, but such is his grief that he is not receptive to "Death's outlet song of life": decorum and present grief do not allow perspective. In Section 5 the earth in spring is covered with the new growth of violets, grass, "yellow-spear'd wheat," and apple blossoms: this is, we are told, "the breast of the spring." The nation, however, mourns the fallen leader — "the great cloud darkening the land" (6). In Section 7 the protagonist brings his offering to the coffins of the dead: "I cover you over with roses and early lilies" — and, filled with grief, he recalls his anticipation of tragedy as he walked alone on a spring night (8). Again the bird calls (9), and again the protagonist is held by his "comrade," the star. In Section 10 he wonders how as a poet he can "perfume the grave of him I love." Eventually "the breath of my chant" — a lovely enveloping image — will encompass grief and life, but not yet.

The tomb in Section 11 is covered with pictures of "growing spring" beneath "floods of the yellow gold of the gorgeous, indolent, sinking sun" and "In the distance the flowing glaze, the breast of the river." Next the protagonist has a vision of the United States "cover'd with grass and corn," as Whitman once again employs the verb "cover." The description of the sun shining over "this land!" anticipates the advent of the "Dark Mother" — "gentle, soft-born, measureless light," "bathing all," "delicious," and "enveloping man and land." For the third time (perhaps another variation upon the "trinity" theme) the protagonist alludes to the bird (13) — "pour your chant from the bushes" — but "the star holds me," and "the lilac, with mastering odor, holds me." Alone, at sundown (14), he observes the harmony of "the heavenly aerial beauty" and the regularity of "many-moving sea-tides" and of the seasons, and the continuity of "daily usages" ("And the infinite separate houses, how they all went on, each with its meals and minutia of daily usages"). Then, in a veiled erotic image,

Falling among them all, and upon them all, enveloping me with the
    rest,
Appear'd the cloud, appear'd the long black trail;
And I knew Death, its thought, and the sacred knowledge of death.

The seemingly "harsh surrounding cloud" (2) is now transformed,
and the moment of awareness (or absorption) has arrived.

    With his companions he goes to the "gray-brown bird": "And
the charm of the singing rapt me." If we construe "rapt" as
"wrapped," we are close to the emotional and visual truth of the
scene. Aurally and rhythmically, the "carol" encompasses us as the
mother the child at her breast.

Come, lovely and soothing Death,
Undulate round the world, serenely arriving, arriving,
In the day, in the night, to all, to each,
Sooner or later, delicate Death.

Prais'd be the fathomless universe,
For life and joy, and for objects and knowledge curious;
And for love, sweet love — But praise! O praise and praise,
For the sure-enwinding arms of cool-enfolding Death.

Dark Mother, always gliding near, with soft feet,
Have none chanted for thee a chant of fullest welcome?
Then I chant it for thee — I glorify thee above all;
I bring thee a song that when thou must indeed come, come un-
    falteringly.

Approach, encompassing Death — strong Deliveress!
When it is so — when thou hast taken them, I joyously sing the dead,
Lost in the loving, floating ocean of thee,
Laved in the flood of thy bliss, O Death.

From me to thee glad serenades,
Dances for thee I propose, saluting thee — adornments and feastings
    for thee;
And the sights of the open landscape, and the high-spread sky, are
    fitting,
And life and the fields, and the huge and thoughtful night.

The night, in silence, under many a star;
The ocean shore, and the husky whispering wave, whose voice I know;

And the soul turning to thee, O vast and well-veil'd Death,
And the body gratefully nestling close to thee.

Over the tree-tops I float thee a song!
Over the rising and sinking waves — over the myriad fields, and the
    prairies wide;
Over the dense-pack'd cities all, and the teeming wharves and ways,
I float this carol with joy, with joy to thee, O Death!

The notes of the thrush, we are told in Section 17, are "filling
the night," as is "the swamp-perfume." Even more important, like
a new-born child, the protagonist begins to see:

While my sight that was bound in my eyes unclosed,
As to long panoramas of vision.

He recalls, in Section 18, "battle-corpses, myriads of them, / And
the white skeletons of young men," covering the earth as "debris,"
which refers back to winter's "gray debris" (5) before the coming
of spring. The dead, he says, are beyond suffering, only the sur-
vivors suffer — a statement which is at once an acknowledgment
of suffering and a perspective from which suffering can be viewed
without despair. And so the "tallying song" is "Covering the earth,
and filling the spread of the heaven" (19). In the final two sections the protagonist is alone, content with his memories — "Lilac
and star and bird, twined with the chant of my soul."

Envelopment, whether in nature's luxuriant growth, the grave
or tomb, the "carol" of the bird-poet, or the coddling arms of the
mother, is expressed in Whitman's usual erotic rhythm. As in
"Out of the Cradle Endlessly Rocking," the "life rhythm" is organically related to the subject matter; participial forms and the
actions, animate as well as inanimate, have the rising and falling
qualities of the sea and of sexuality. The result is that almost every
section of "When Lilacs Last in the Dooryard Bloom'd" rises and
falls and leads to the next section, where the action is repeated.
The first three lines of the opening section consist of images of
mourning, but the first line of the second stanza reads, "O ever-
returning spring!" The "fallen star" (2) is succeeded by the lilac
(3), "rising, delicate with the perfume I love," until the last line,
"A sprig, with its flower, I break." Section 4 introduces the
thrush, "The hermit, withdrawn to himself, avoiding the settle-

ments," but the "hermit" is to warble "Death's outlet song of life." Nature (or mother earth) is in Section 5 "from its shroud in the dark-brown fields uprising," the eye ascending to "the apple-tree blows of white and pink" but then looking down upon another scene:

Carrying a corpse to where it shall rest in the grave,
Night and day journeys a coffin.

There are only falling images in the account of the coffin (6) until the dirges of "the thousand voices" are "rising strong and solemn," at which time the fluctuations are especially marked:

With all the mournful voices of the dirges, pour'd around the coffin,
The dim-lit churches and the shuddering organs — Where amid these
    you journey,
With the tolling, tolling bells' perpetual clang;
Here! coffin that slowly passes,
I give you my sprig of lilac.

Section 7 is a long parenthetical statement which serves two purposes. The protagonist here emerges clearly for the first time as the central character or consciousness in the poem; up to this point he has confined himself to external descriptions of the star, the lilac, the bird, and so forth. Second, within the half-circles of the parentheses, the "I's" reverie introduces a counter circular motion: Lincoln's death is to be viewed as an event in an endless cycle of similar events. The rising-falling fluctuations will continue, but dirges will become "a song for you, O sane and sacred death."

The star (8) narrows the focus of the poem again to Lincoln's death, and the falling images of grief reintroduce personal anguish. Motion is seemingly suspended in the references to the bird (9), although the staccato rhythm — "I hear — I come presently — I understand you" — presages a change in mood and rhythm. In Section 10 the protagonist meditates on the artistic problem of warbling "for the dead one there I loved." His reverie culminates in a lovely erotic passage, played out in anticipatory water imagery:

Sea-winds, blown from east and west,
Blown from the eastern sea, and blown from the western sea, till there
    on the prairies meeting:

These, and with these, and the breath of my chant,
I perfume the grave of him I love.

The descent into the tomb (11) is countered by wall scenes depicting growth. Section 12 is another of the protagonist's meditations, which are now regularly alternating with descriptions of his symbols — thus contributing to the erotic motion as well as to the circular expansion from the particular to the general; he notes "the sparkling and hurrying tides," and "the most excellent sun" is "bathing all." When the bird reappears (13), his song is "liquid, and free, and tender! / O wild and loose to my soul!" The protagonist's third reverie (14) gradually builds to the crescendo of "the sacred knowledge of death." Next the comrades "go under," "Down to the shores of water," surrounded by "the solemn shadowy cedars, and ghostly pines so still." In this primordial setting — essentially the same as in "Song of Myself," "The Sleepers," "Calamus," and "Out of the Cradle Endlessly Rocking" — a new self emerges in a new-old return to the source of life, the mother: and a poet is born,

Lost in the loving, floating ocean of thee,
Laved in the flood of thy bliss, O Death.

Earlier erotic images — "bleeding throat" and "pour your chant from the bushes" — now fall into place in Whitman's intricate artistic plan. Perhaps "the long black trail" of the cloud becomes a "trail" of sound, a kind of umbilical cord. Once again, as in Section 5 of "Song of Myself" — "loose the stop from your throat" — birth is presented in primarily oral terms, foreshadowed in the phrase "the breath of my chant."

The song floats "Over the rising and sinking waves," after which the images rise, except for the protagonist's recollection of battlefields strewn with "the white skeletons of young men," but they have found the calm of which the "Dark Mother" sings. Those "that remain'd suffer'd," since death of one's beloved will always be traumatic, but like the waves

Victorious song, death's outlet song, (yet varying, ever-altering song,
As low and wailing, yet clear the notes, rising and falling, flooding the
    night,

Sadly sinking and fainting, as warning and warning, and yet again
  bursting with joy,). . . .

Momentarily the protagonist despairs,

Must I leave thee, lilac with heart-shaped leaves?
Must I leave thee there in the door-yard, blooming, returning with
  spring?

Must I pass from my song for thee;
From my gaze on thee in the west, fronting the west, communing with
  thee,
O comrade lustrous, with silver face in the night?

But "their memory ever I keep" — of Lincoln, comrades, lost love
— and the final picture is one of erotic harmony, "twined with
the chant of my soul."

For a moment perhaps the erotic harmony conceals a significant
omission: there is no communal joy at the successful completion
of a rite of passage, for there are no human participants in the
ceremonies. There is, in fact, no one even to love, only memories.
And so the "bard of love" undergoes rites that lead to acceptance
of loneliness and lovelessness and to transcendence through art.
Song is sublimation; the rest is resignation.

"Passage to more than India!"

"Crossing Brooklyn Ferry" (1856) is a sustained hymn to joy — the joy of the sensuous body. The poem is as placid as the East River which the ferry crosses eternally (or so it seemed in the nineteenth century) from New York to Brooklyn. The protagonist's associations rise and fall like the gentle "flood-tide" and "ebb-tide" of the river, and imitate the "slow-wheeling circles" of the gulls "floating with motionless wings." There is no "fierce old mother," no ineffectual father, since the poet does not venture into the psychic depths of "The Sleepers" or "Out of the Cradle Endlessly Rocking." Thus the poem cannot record a dramatic "leap" to affirmation, for almost at the outset, in line 7, we are told of "the simple, compact, well-joined scheme." There is little progression, mostly a circular repetition: "Others will enter the gates of the ferry, and cross from shore to shore," which is but another way of stating, "I too had been struck from the float forever held in solution." Beneath the placidity, however, will emerge a muted eroticism, introduced in the first line of the poem, "I watch you, face to face," and Whitman's characteristic preoccupation with birth, human and artistic.

Rather than a mystical experience, the poem is a hedonistic statement of faith, the forerunner of Wallace Stevens' "Sunday Morning," without the latter's explicitly stated conflict between pagan liberation of the senses and "the dark / Encroachment of that old catastrophe," Christianity. Like Stevens' lovely old lady, Whitman is saying, "Divinity must live within herself." The lady seeks no Eden, terrestrial or heavenly, and welcomes flux, for "Death is the mother of beauty." The stasis of paradise is boredom, a sensuous vacuum: she prefers an earthbound expression of joy not unlike that of Hawthorne's Merry Mounters:

> Supple and turbulent, a ring of men
> Shall chant in orgy on a summer morn
> Their boisterous devotion to the sun,
> Not as a god, but as a god might be,
> Naked among them, like a savage source.

Peacefully — her voice never becoming shrill — she concludes her Sunday-morning reverie with a benediction, never heard in formal houses of worship, in which she accepts the delights of a dying body in a dying world.

> Deer walk upon our mountains, and the quail
> Whistle about us their spontaneous cries;
> Sweet berries ripen in the wilderness;
> And, in the isolation of the sky,
> At evening, casual flocks of pigeons make
> Ambiguous undulations as they sink,
> Downward to darkness, on extended wings.

Like "Sunday Morning," "Crossing Brooklyn Ferry" is a serene meditation on mutability in a world no longer concerned with the principle of plenitude or the Great Chain of Being, as Edmund Spenser is in his "Mutability Cantos," but deeply concerned with the devitalization of the body and the senses in the era of the machine. Perhaps deliberately Whitman places his protagonist aboard the nineteenth-century symbol of the dynamo, the ship propelled by steam, and he journeys from one urban sprawl to another, always in sight of the smokestacks of modern "progress."

> On the neighboring shore, the fires from the foundry chimneys burning
> high and glaringly into the night,
> Casting their flicker of black, contrasted with wild red and yellow light,
> over the tops of houses, and down into the clefts of streets.

But "progress" is reduced to colorful pictures and artistic patterns, without the attendant human problems, so that Whitman's protagonist is in final analysis as isolated from the tempo of modern industrial life as Stevens' heroine, who delights in her Matisse-like retreat (an "art nouveau" paradise) far from the grime and tensions of the twentieth century. Whitman's ferry, it need hardly be added, bears little resemblance to the *Fidèle* in Melville's *The Confidence-Man.*

Whitman's "I" contemplates "mackerel-crowded seas": the transiency but the eternal recurrence; the multiplicity without apparent plan but the "simple, compact, well-joined scheme"; the dying or "disintegrated" body but the "float." Everything is in motion: the ferryboat crossing the river, the "flood-tide," the gulls, the shifting reflections on the water, chronological time (the "sun half an hour high" and "the sunset"), historical time (the passengers past, present, and future), the float, and the erotic relationship between the "I" and "you." Grammatically, pronouns shift and tenses change, and the poem turns in upon itself to repeat various passages. "Crossing Brooklyn Ferry" is, organically, part of the flux it depicts. In this respect it is far more subtly organized than "Sunday Morning."

The core of Whitman's lyric and his "philosophy" — and he employs the inevitable oral term "sustenance" — appears in the second section:

> The impalpable sustenance of me from all things, at all hours of the
> day,
> The simple, compact, well-joined scheme — myself disintegrated, every
> one disintegrated, yet part of the scheme,
> The similitudes of the past, and those of the future,
> The glories strung like beads on my smallest sights and hearings — on
> the walk in the street, and the passage over the river,

The current rushing so swiftly, and swimming with me far away,
The others that are to follow me, the ties between me and them,
The certainty of others — the life, love, sight, hearing of others.

And the key line is: "The glories strung like beads on my smallest
sights and hearings." For the "beads" are a hedonist's rosary which
he counts no less reverently than the religious adherent, even
though there is no prescribed (dead) ritual, only the spontaneous
response of "my smallest sights and hearings." The "beads" are
also a kind of democratic Chain of Being that rests upon no
arbitrary differentiations according to rational and aristocratic
schematizations of class-conscious civilizations, and is not premised
either upon long-sanctioned absolutes or upon the existence of a
deity. There is but one absolute: the opening of the bodily senses
to "you dumb, beautiful ministers," which are the commonplaces of
nature, so familiar and immediate that they are generally ignored.
And the gods are "these that clasp me by the hand."

Whitman's protagonist is one of a motley, democratic crowd
aboard a ferry: "Crowds of men and women attired in the usual
costumes!" Stevens' hedonist, on the other hand, is a genteel lady
who in her fashionably expensive attire (her fastidiously nonchalant "peignoir") and in her elegant leisure ("late / Coffee and
oranges in a sunny chair") sits alone as she muses urbanely on
that "old catastrophe," and, not without a bow to William Butler
Yeats, surveys human history with bookish wit ("Jove in the clouds
had his inhuman birth"). Whitman's language in "Crossing
Brooklyn Ferry" fuses a wonderful delicacy with vigorous slang:
"hot wishes I dared not speak," "Bully for you!" and "Blab, blush,
lie, steal." (The last two passages disappeared in 1871.)

Whitman's "beads" of familiar sights and sounds dazzle with
some of the iridescence of Turner's paintings in exquisite passages
which are as simple as the scenes they describe. Here the protagonist does not project his emotional state upon nature.

I watched the Twelfth Month sea-gulls — I saw them high in the air,
    floating with motionless wings, oscillating their bodies,
I saw how the glistening yellow lit up parts of their bodies, and left
    the rest in strong shadow,
I saw the slow-wheeling circles, and the gradual edging toward the
    south.

I too saw the reflection of the summer sky in the water,
Had my eyes dazzled by the shimmering track of beams,
Looked at the fine centrifugal spokes of light round the shape of my
    head in the sun-lit water,
Looked on the haze on the hills southward and south-westward,
Looked on the vapor as it flew in fleeces tinged with violet. . . .

The white wake left by the passage, the quick tremulous whirl of the
    wheels,
The flags of all nations, the falling of them at sun-set,
The scallop-edged waves in the twilight, the ladled cups, the frolicsome
    crests and glistening. . . .

Diverge, fine spokes of light, from the shape of my head, or any one's
    head, in the sun-lit water;
. . . .
Burn high your fires, foundry chimneys! cast black shadows at nightfall!
    cast red and yellow light over the tops of the houses. . . .

Stevens' gracious lady sums up a lifetime as she meditates in her
chair on the patio: hers is the tranquillity of recollected memories.
Whitman's perspective is a re-creation, as in "There Was a Child
Went Forth" and "Out of the Cradle Endlessly Rocking," of the
child's excited curiosity about the miracle that is the world. Of the
people "attired in the usual costumes," he observes, "how curious
you are to me!" and, in the following line, "[you] are more curious
to me than you suppose." Later, as the "I" slowly establishes a
relationship with the "you," the reader — "What is it, then, between us?" — he acknowledges doubts and frustrations: "I too
felt the curious abrupt questionings stir within me" — an emotional (erotic) bond of common experience, which leads directly
to the passage about "the float forever held in solution." Still later,
as the eroticism becomes more explicit ("Closer yet I approach
you"), he observes, still with childlike wonder:

Now I am curious what sight can ever be more stately and admirable
    to me that my mast-hemm'd Manhatta,
. . . .
Curious what Gods can exceed these that clasp me by the hand, and
    with voices I love call me promptly and loudly by my nighest name
    as I approach,

Curious what is more subtle than this which ties me to the woman or
man that looks in my face. . . .

The innocent wonder does not conceal the fact that curiosity, as
one should expect, is a child's desire for sexual knowledge. The
powerfully erotic line immediately following the above passage
makes the clarification: "Which fuses me into you now, and pours
my meaning into you." "Crossing Brooklyn Ferry" presents erotic
fusion simultaneously on many levels: man and nature, body and
soul, and protagonist-poet and reader — the symbolic equivalents
of these interlocking themes are the "beads," "the float," and the
poem itself. A trinity which is one.

"The glories strung like beads" are, as it were, the umbilical cord
between man and nature which is severed when man refuses to
use his sense organs as receivers of miraculous impressions. This
aspect of the threefold erotic motif culminates in "you dumb,
beautiful ministers," led up to through these lines (which were
excised, incidentally, in 1881):

We descend upon you and all things — we arrest you all,
We realize the Soul only by you, you faithful solids and fluids,
Through you color, form, location, sublimity, ideality,
Through you every proof, comparison, and all the suggestions and de-
    terminations of ourselves.

What appears ambiguous when approached intellectually —
whether Whitman is monistic or dualistic in his treatment of body
and soul — is reasonably clear if we observe his imagery closely.
In the celebrated passage concerning "the float" —

I too had been struck from the float forever held in solution,
I too had received identity by my body,
That I was, I knew was of my body — and what I should be, I knew
    I should be of my body —

Whitman describes, not without a suggestion of sexual violence in
the use of the word "struck," the emergence of the fetus from the
"film" of the mother and the beginning of the continuous process
of achieving identity by means of the body. "Sustenance" comes
from "my smallest sights and hearings," which provide the "necessary film":

Appearances, now or henceforth, indicate what you are;
You necessary film, continue to envelop the Soul;
About my body for me, and your body for you, be hung our divinest
    aromas. . . .

In other words, the relationship of body and soul is like that of
mother and fetus: the child emerges from the fertilized womb,
and the soul is the summation of the eroticized body — two but
one.

The sensuous body in relationship to nature and to the soul is,
however, incomplete until human involvements are introduced.
This element Whitman supplies in his depiction of the gradual
growth of intimacy between the poet-protagonist and the reader.
Although this relationship is in many respects illusionary, and even
abstract since it is love out of time and place, it serves two valid
artistic purposes: it concretely dramatizes man's craving for love,
the satisfaction of his "curiosity," and it makes the poem like the
body an erotic instrument.

The earlier versions of "Crossing Brooklyn Ferry" are more
amorous and personal than those revised by "the good gray poet."
For example, in 1881 Whitman excised, ill-advisedly in my
opinion, two lines which served to indicate similarities in experience and to narrow the distance between the protagonist and
his audience: "I project myself — also I return — I am with
you, and know how it is," and "I project myself a moment to tell
you — also I return." But these deletions do not do great damage
to the erotic drama of the merger of the "I" and the "you" into
"we."

What is it, then, between us?
What is the count of the scores or hundreds of years between us?

Whatever it is, it avails not — distance avails not, and place avails not.

After recalling that all men enter the world in the same way, the
protagonist admits that "The dark threw patches down upon me
also," a curious, but lovely, description of "evil," until one realizes
that it wells out of Whitman's unconscious evocation of a child's
terror in the dark and his abrupt introduction to the mysteries and
perhaps (seeming) violence of sexuality. (It is a well-nigh perfect
illustration of how the artist orders unconscious material.) "It is

not you alone who know what it is to be evil," he continues; "I too
knitted the old knot of contrariety" (another veiled erotic reference). With the thoroughness of a John Bunyan, the protagonist
enumerates his vices, which, perhaps intentionally and humor-
ously, pretty much cover the seven deadly sins. (In the 1856
version only, he even terms himself "a solitary committer," which
surely is not unrelated to "knitted the old knot of contrariety.")
The vices of the protagonist establish his ordinariness and his
accessibility. Even this confession to the reader is not without its
amorousness, the sharing of secrets by lovers. (Despite the objec-
tions of some critics to the presence of these personal details in
the poem, Whitman, as usual, introduced them for "reasons" which
are valid artistically and psychologically.)

The confession leads to the recital for the first time of the protagonist's human involvements after being "struck from the float."

But I was a Manhattanese, free, friendly, and proud!
I was called by my nighest name by clear loud voices of young men as
    they saw me approaching or passing,
Felt their arms on my neck as I stood, or the negligent leaning of their
    flesh against me as I sat,
Saw many I loved in the street, or ferry-boat, or public assembly, yet
    never told them a word,
Lived the same life with the rest, the same old laughing, gnawing,
    sleeping,
Played the part that still looks back on the actor or actress,
The same old rôle, the rôle that is what we make it, as great as we like,
Or as small as we like, or both great and small.

(One notes the predominance of "Calamus" attachments, and it is
hardly surprising that in the 1860 edition Whitman placed the
poem after the "Calamus" chants.) Immediately following these
lines he writes, "Closer yet I approach you." And now the erotic
atmosphere, sexually undifferentiated as one would expect, is
heightened, and the curiosity, as indicated before, is clearly sexual.
The protagonist has difficulty imagining "Gods" who can "exceed"
those "young men" "that clasp me by the hand" — a passage recalling "God comes a loving bedfellow" in "Song of Myself." But at
the same time the protagonist-poet sublimates his erotic hunger in
art, in imaginary coitus with an imaginary reader.

Which fuses me into you now, and pours my meaning into you.
We understand, then, do we not?
What I promised without mentioning it, have you not accepted?
What the study could not teach — what the preaching could not ac-
complish is accomplished, is it not?
What the push of reading could not start is started by me personally,
is it not?

(The last line, crude perhaps in its blunt potency but justifiable in
order to establish art as an act of impregnation, disappeared in
1881.)

The rest of the poem is a lovely orchestration of themes introduced earlier, as the hedonist experiences the quiet satisfaction
and glow of personal and sexual fulfillment. Everything, animate
and inanimate, exudes "divinest aromas" as the poem circles to its
conclusion:

You have waited, you always wait, you dumb, beautiful ministers! you
novices!
We receive you with free sense at last, and are insatiate henceforward,
Not you any more shall be able to foil us, or withhold yourselves from
us,
We use you, and do not cast you aside — we plant you permanently
within us,
We fathom you not — we love you — there is perfection in you also,
You furnish your parts toward eternity,
Great or small, you furnish your parts toward the Soul.

What a subtle, unobtrusive art Whitman brings to this lyric!
The artistic surface, never flawed by false notes or by intellectual
pretensions, is richly evocative. The ferry, an ordinary boat used
for transportation, is reminiscent of the journey to the classical
underworld as well as of the journey to the recesses of the human
personality. The ferry is the fetus which moves through the amniotic fluids (the float) and emerges as an individual that creates
soul and gods in its own image. The ferry is, finally, the artifact
"struck" from the poet's imaginative ordering of conscious and unconscious materials. The poem, in turn, is "forever held in solution," renewing itself whenever an empathetic reader relives the
universal experience it records.

"Crossing Brooklyn Ferry" may have at its center the symbol of
the age of the dynamo, but its intent is revealed in the narcissistic
act described in the first line: "Flood-tide below me! I watch you,
face to face." It is an introspective lyric that wells out of Whitman's depths. "When Lilacs Last in the Dooryard Bloom'd" succeeds because the occasion, the death of Lincoln, is converted into
a very personal consideration of the nature of life and death; "O
Captain! My Captain!" fails because it is a trite public expression
of grief in a banal public rhythm. When after the Civil War
Whitman composes primarily occasional poems, the patriotic fervor
is sincere, the faith in evolution or progress is genuine, and the
identification with his era is admirable, if not quite real — but the
poems fail, except for scattered passages. They are not struck from
Whitman's "float," but from the surface of his mind. When he
consciously assumes a public, prophetic role, he is a declaimer of
truisms rather than a prophet: he speaks to the future meaning-
fully only in his songs of the self. Similarly, *Specimen Days,*
admirable as his first-hand accounts of hospitals are, is an unsatisfactory work — a pleasantly superficial autobiography of "man
thinking" not very profound thoughts.

Whitman deals astutely with the origins of his art in "Scented
Herbage of My Breast," "Trickle Drops," "Out of the Cradle Endlessly Rocking," and "When Lilacs Last in the Dooryard Bloom'd,"
but when he indulges in grandiose claims for "the true son of God"
(the poet), one hears in the background, in the rhythm and the
rhetoric, the worst of Henry Wadsworth Longfellow and (more is
the pity) the patriotic merchants of the Fourth of July and "manifest destiny." The strained eloquence of the Preface to the first
edition of *Leaves of Grass* and of "By Blue Ontario's Shore" is bad
enough, but worse is the bathos of the Muse in "Song of the Exposition" (1871):

I say I see, my friends, if you do not, the illustrious emigré, (having it
    is true in her day, although the same, changed, journey'd consid-
    erable,)
Making directly for this rendezvous, vigorously clearing a path for
    herself, striding through the confusion,
By thud of machinery and shrill steam-whistle undismay'd,
Bluff'd not a bit by drain-pipe, gasometers, artificial fertilizers,
Smiling and pleas'd with palpable intent to stay,
She's here, install'd amid the kitchen ware!

Every poet is entitled to his failures and his lapses, but Whitman's "modern" rant taxes our patience and sometimes insults our hearts, unless we recall that Walter Whitman, journalist and patriot, did not die in 1855: he always emerges when the "Song of Myself" is not being sung.

Whitman delights in establishing his modernity by assailing the clichés and irrelevancies of an outdated literature, as in another passage in "Song of the Exposition":

Away with old romance!
Away with novels, plots and plays of foreign courts,
Away with love-verses sugar'd in rhyme, the intrigues, amours of idlers,
Fitted for only banquets of the night where dancers to late music slide,
The unhealthy pleasures, extravagant dissipations of the few,
With perfumes, heat and wine, beneath the dazzling chandeliers.

But then observe (charitably) what he substitutes for this bric-a-brac:

To you ye reverent sane sisters,
I raise a voice for far superber themes for poets and for art,
To exalt the present and the real,
To teach the average man the glory of his daily walk and trade,
To sing in songs how exercise and chemical life are never to be baffled,
To manual work for each and all, to plough, hoe, dig,
To plant and tend the tree, the berry, vegetables, flowers,
For every man to see to it that he really do something, for every woman too;
To use the hammer and the saw, (rip, or cross-cut,)
To cultivate a turn for carpentering, plastering, painting,
To work as tailor, tailoress, nurse, hostler, porter,
To invent a little, something ingenious, to aid the washing, cooking, cleaning,
And hold it no disgrace to take a hand at them themselves.

Apparently Whitman was unaware that in "Song of the Exposition" he was not talking about "the present and the real" in 1871, but of rural life in the early nineteenth century (at the latest) before the emergence of the industrial system that made the Exposition possible. As Leo Marx points out in *The Machine in the Garden,* Whitman's is the "industrialized version of the pastoral ideal": "the new power often is interpreted as a means of realizing the classical, eighteenth-century aims of the Republic."[1]

Worst of all, Whitman knew better, as almost any page of *Democratic Vistas* demonstrates. But he was a prisoner of his own public image, or at least of one aspect of his public image: he wanted to be the poet of affirmation and progress — the serene spokesman of a present and future worthy of Columbus' dream: "The shore thou foundest verifies thy dream." Whitman makes a meaningful affirmation when he deals with the potentialities of the miraculous self and man's (resurrected) bond with nature. (What in part redeems "Passage to India" is that he soon abandons the technological feats which are the occasion for the poem and speaks of the "Soul.") For the simple truth is that Whitman, like his follower Hart Crane, never marries poetry and technology. Perhaps they are not marriageable, but there surely is no poetic passage to the machine or the electronic age if the poet nostalgically hungers for the pastoral ages of Vergil, Spenser, and the eighteenth century, which were but poetic fictions. Whitman never recaptures the "thud of machinery" as he does the throb of the erotic body.

The opening lines of "Passage to India" are impressive but melodically anachronistic, even for a "true son of God":

Singing my days,
Singing the great achievements of the present,
Singing the strong light works of engineers. . . .

His subject is the completion of the Suez Canal, the Northern Pacific Railroad, and the cable across the Pacific Ocean. To say in justification of Whitman that he spiritualizes machinery in order to embrace it in his "plan" is in final analysis a rationalization of his reluctance to accept the facts of the machine and modern civilization; inadvertently, he freezes the poet and man into eternal alienation from his age, an error that Henry Adams does not perpetuate in his autobiography. Despite Whitman's assertion in the fourth line that the three engineering triumphs "the antique ponderous Seven outvied," his real fascination is not with such externals as improved means of transportation or communication, but with one of man's oldest preoccupations, the journey of the self. In Section 3 he allots five lines to the Suez Canal, only one of which refers concretely to the technological feat, "The gigantic dredging machines." Next he presents a seventeen-line catalogue of sights from the new railroad, which is acceptable, but humdrum, geography and which sounds a false pastoral note, particularly in a phrase like "in duplicate slender lines." (To compare this passage with the catalogues in Sections 15 and 33 of "Song of Myself" is to realize how little the event fired Whitman's poetic skills.) Structure and proportion require, one would imagine, that the laying of the cable receive approximately equal treatment, but the only specific reference to it appears in the first stanza of the poem: "The seas inlaid with eloquent gentle wires" — which, like Crane's depiction of Brooklyn Bridge, is false texturally and poetically. Unconsciously, Whitman reduces gigantic machinery to toys of manageable size, a response which is understandable, as is the spiritual veneer with which he coats things of steel, but which evades the problems of man's relationship with his emotionless creations.

"To a Locomotive in Winter" (1876) is more successful than most of his occasional pieces, but it reveals similar flaws. The first line, "Thee for my recitative," while right in "Out of the Cradle Endlessly Rocking," is disturbing in this context: the biblical or Quaker pronoun jars, even if we grant Whitman's intent to spiritualize machinery, and "recitative" conjures up an old-fashioned harmony hardly compatible with the dissonance of the engine's "gyrating" or its "lawless music." The sound of the poem simply does not square with Whitman's assertion: "No sweetness debonair of tearful harp or glib piano thine." Once again he makes an iron monster a toy: "thy knitted frame," "the tremulous twinkle of thy wheels," "The train of cars behind, obedient, merrily following." Whitman calls the locomotive an "emblem of motion and power," when everything in the poem diminishes the power and trivializes the thrust of the motion. (Leo Marx[2] has a perceptive discussion of George Innes' painting entitled "The Lackawanna Valley," 1855, which incorporates a dirtless, "gentle" train into a typical Hudson River School landscape.)

"To a Locomotive in Winter" moves in its declamatory swell to a crescendo which "sounds" not without effectiveness, as long as one forgets the fallacies upon which it is based and shares the poet's unstated fear of the machine:

Fierce-throated beauty!
Roll through my chant with all thy lawless music, thy swinging lamps at night,

Thy madly-whistled laughter, echoing, rumbling like an earthquake,
    rousing all,
Law of thyself complete, thine own track firmly holding,
(No sweetness debonair of tearful harp or glib piano thine,)
Thy trills of shrieks by rocks and hills return'd,
Launch'd o'er the prairies wide, across the lakes,
To the free skies unpent and glad and strong.

The effectiveness of this passage has little to do with the locomotive
as machinery, but the locomotive as an unconscious sexual symbol
leads to another "Song of the bleeding throat" ("When Lilacs Last
in the Dooryard Bloom'd"), to another "hum of your valved voice"
("Song of Myself," Section 5). (A similar unconscious association
is present in Nathaniel Hawthorne's "The Artist of the Beautiful,"
as W. B. Stein points out,[3] when Owen Warland's sexual inadequacy and fear appear in his frightened response to a steam
engine in his youth and later to the pistonlike, brawny arms of
Richard Danforth, the blacksmith-rival for Annie's affections.)
In other words, Whitman's poem is picturesque and superficial
(like the prints of Currier and Ives), perhaps of historical interest
because of his attempt to poeticize the locomotive, but without
affect, until he descends into his private fantasy world and
emerges with psychic equivalents which reverberate in Everyman's
private universe.
    Of his later poems, those written after 1865, "Passage to India"
has received most attention, partly because its length indicates the
significance Whitman himself attached to it but also because many
critics find it the culminating expression of the poet's religious or
mystical sentiments. In a conversation with Horace Traubel in
1888, Whitman observed: "There's more of me, the essential
ultimate me, in that than in any of the poems. There is no philosophy, consistent or inconsistent, in that poem . . . but the burden
of it is evolution — the one thing escaping the other — the un-
folding of cosmic purposes."[4] Like many of his comments upon
his poetry, this one is better as sound than as sense. To unfold
"cosmic purposes" without a philosophy "consistent or inconsistent"
is disingenuous anti-intellectualism. And certainly it is a half
truth (or less) that "the burden of it is evolution," for the poem
has little to do with scientific or even industrial evolution; its emotional core pertains to personal growth (or evolution in a loose

sense), to acceptance or resolution of a personal, but universal, conflict. The admission that the poem delineates "the essential ultimate me," despite its (perhaps deliberate) vagueness, is significant, but probably in ways that Whitman never intended.

"Passage to India" is in effect the swan song of a poet in retreat both in his art and his subject matter. The poem consists of shreds and patches from earlier motifs and lines which his art cannot successfully fuse into a new variation upon old subject matter. The organizing principle is familiar and repetitious: the trio of engineering achievements, later the "Trinitas divine," and finally "Time and Space and Death." But the fusion of symbols is cerebral, imposed from without. Body and soul wrestle once again, but even the syntax is strained and weary: "thou pressing me to thee, I thee to me, O soul." The "Calamus" theme receives almost its final statement — or, more exactly, sublimation. God is now "the Comrade perfect," not a "loving bedfellow." Since the three projects which the poem celebrates involved many laborers, one might have expected Whitman to sing of their achievements in a catalogue-aria as further evidence of the common man's limitless potentials. But he knew that these laborers were the puppets of technicians; they were not the workingmen of his youth, of the vanishing pastoral age to which he always recurs. And so the laborers are not accorded Homeric treatment. Instead, Whitman glorifies a "representative man," Christopher Columbus, who achieves Michelangelesque proportions:

With majestic limbs and pious beaming eyes,
Spreading around with every look of thine a golden world,
Enhuing it with gorgeous hues.

And observe the change from the "I's" identification in "Song of Myself" with an overman who bestrides the cosmos in the flush of his virility to the protagonist's identification with a "sad shade," Columbus, whose "majestic limbs" are "chain'd":

As the chief histrion,
Down to the footlights walks in some great scena,
Dominating the rest I see the Admiral himself,
(History's type of courage, action, faith,)
Behold him sail from Palos leading his little fleet,

His voyage behold, his return, his great fame,
His misfortunes, calumniators, behold him a prisoner, chain'd,
Behold his dejection, poverty, death.

(Curious in time I stand, noting the efforts of heroes,
Is the deferment long? bitter the slander, poverty, death?
Lies the seed unreck'd for centuries in the ground? lo, to God's due
　　occasion,
Uprising in the night, it sprouts, blooms,
And fills the earth with use and beauty.)

In "Prayer of Columbus," written in 1874, the hero is also "A
batter'd, wreck'd old man," of whom Whitman observes in one of
his letters: "As I see it now I shouldn't wonder if I have unconsciously put a sort of autobiographical dash in it."[5]

The muted eroticism of "Passage to India" reveals as graphically
as anything else Whitman's loss of confidence in the sensuous life
and the withering of his artistic powers. Gone are "bodies electric,"
tactile responsiveness to nature, and the exciting and erotic par-
ticularity of his earlier poetry. The festivities, for example, at
"the marriage of continents, climates and oceans" (a somewhat
old-fashioned subject for a "modern" poet) are now decorously
Apollonian rather than Dionysian. Many passages in "Passage to
India" recall earlier lines, only to remind us of the superiority of
his original statements:

Down from the gardens of Asia descending radiating,
Adam and Eve appear, then their myriad progeny after them. . . .

Cooling airs from Caucasus far, soothing cradle of man,
The river Euphrates flowing, the past lit up again.

Amid the wafting winds, (thou pressing me to thee, I thee to me, O
　　soul,)
Caroling free, singing our song of God,
Chanting our chant of pleasant exploration.

With laugh and many a kiss,
(Let others deprecate, let others weep for sin, remorse, humiliation,)
O soul thou pleasest me, I thee.

Whose air I breathe, whose ripples hear, lave me all over,
Bathe me O God in thee, mounting to thee,
I and my soul to range in range of thee.

"Passage to India," it seems to me, is an excellent illustration of Anton Ehrenzweig's astute point in *The Psycho-analysis of Artistic Vision and Hearing*:

The slow evolution of an artist's personal "style" will be based on this constant articulation of his own inarticulate form creations. As he matures his technique will become more and more encrusted with the dead weight of all too beautiful mannerisms which once had been inarticulate Dionysian forms. Only the strongest among the artists will carry this burden with ease and give freedom to his unconscious creative mind to bring forth new inarticulate forms which will die again as they meet the conscious eye.[6]

Although Whitman claims that he sings a "worship new" in "Passage to India," the poem offers nothing new: it is a more indirect and weaker statement of earlier positions that relies excessively on exclamation points in its expression of faith in man's destiny. In fact, it is scarcely unfair to say that "Passage to India" is the Whitmanesque equivalent of Emerson's "Experience," in both of which are evidences of unacknowledged loss of faith in democratic man and of (middle-aged) retreat from the complexities of an industrial civilization.

Whitman still trusts in "the seed unreck'd for centuries in the ground," but "Passage to India" resembles Melville's *The Confidence-Man* or T. S. Eliot's *The Waste Land* in its gloomy survey of human history and its depiction of agitated men in pursuit of elusive (and perhaps illusive) goals. Columbus' life ends in ignominy, and Adam and Eve give birth not to Adamic impregnators of "bodies electric" but to an anxious (we would say neurotic) progeny:

Wandering, yearning, curious, with restless explorations,
With questionings, baffled, formless, feverish, with never-happy hearts,
With that sad incessant refrain, *Wherefore unsatisfied soul?* and
   Whither O mocking life?

What emerges from this and his references in the following stanza to "these feverish children" and to their "restless explorations" is a picture of the human race alienated from nature and love. To be sure, Whitman claims that "the true son of God," the poet, will soothe the hearts "of fretted children," and that "Nature and Man shall be disjoin'd and diffused no more." But this is a poetic cliché, and punctuating assertions with exclamation points may overwhelm the eye but scarcely convinces the mind.

The poem comes to life, and becomes something more than an occasional piece, when Whitman resumes his characteristic preoccupation with the reconciliation of body and soul, or the Me and the Not-Me, which, as I have argued before, is the resolution of personal conflicts originating in childhood. And once more the protagonist establishes a filial relationship. Columbus and Adam are only important in so far as they are father surrogates; as historical characters they are as irrelevant as history itself to the individual's psychic growth and emerging consciousness. The emotional center of the poem is the "I's" relationship to the "Comrade perfect" — this time a paternal rather than a maternal figure. However, just as earlier protagonists only gradually come to accept the eternal mother, so here the "I" evinces at first fear and hesitation: "Swiftly I shrivel at the thought of God," and "I, turning, call to thee O soul, thou actual Me." Thereupon the "soul" prepares the protagonist for union (or reunion) with "God," or, more specifically, with the father. At once the protagonist is filled with an all-inclusive ("oceanic") but vague love of mankind and of good deeds, but the expression of these commonplace moral sentiments is not so important as the final lovely and concrete pictorial image which wells up from the depths of his being:

Greater than stars or suns,
Bounding O soul thou journeyest forth;
What love than thine and ours could wider amplify?
What aspirations, wishes, outvie thine and ours O soul?
What dreams of the ideal? what plans of purity, perfection, strength?
What cheerful willingness for others' sake to give up all?
For others' sake to suffer all?

Reckoning ahead O soul, when thou, the time achiev'd,
The seas all cross'd, weather'd the capes, the voyage done,
Surrounded, copest, frontest God, yieldest, the aim attain'd,
As fill'd with friendship, love complete, the Elder Brother found,
The Younger melts in fondness in his arms.

This is the climax of the poem — but also the culmination of Whitman's poetic career and his psychological journey. Obviously, as the variation upon the Prodigal Son parable indicates, we are observing a rite of reconciliation with the earthly father: the wandering son has come home. And when he "melts" in the father's arms, it follows, both artistically and psychologically, that, as the next line reveals, the "I" can now achieve "Passage to more than India!"

Since Whitman's poetry is of a piece — always the "I" seeks resolution in retreat — the climax of "Passage to India" takes on added significance. As I have noted repeatedly, Whitman's poetry is filled with ineffectual father-figures. And so when in this poem the protagonist is united with the father rather than with the mother, everything is truly in order, for not only has the father been restored to his proper role but also the son can assume his proper filial role. The "Comrade perfect," unlike the father in "There Was a Child Went Forth," is not "strong, selfsufficient, manly, mean, angered, unjust"; he is the antithesis — an ideal father like the grandfather in "I Sing the Body Electric." The father no longer arouses a murderous oedipal response as in "The Sleepers." Now there can be no rivalry: the "I" shrivels in physical and no doubt sexual impotency before the father and then "melts" or dissolves in his embrace. In other words, the "bridge" which puzzles and frightens the protagonist in "The Sleepers" is no longer a threat: what is implied in that poem is now made explicit. In "As I Ebb'd with the Ocean of Life" the "I" screams and begs for the affection which the father-figure is unable to give:

Kiss me, my father,
Touch me with your lips, as I touch those I love,
Breathe to me, while I hold you close, the secret of the wondrous murmuring I envy,
For I fear I shall become crazed, if I cannot emulate it, and utter myself as well as it.

Here the protagonist is on the verge of madness, but in "Passage to India," with a loving father, madness is no longer a possibility.

It is no mistake that this father is the "Comrade perfect" who offers "friendship" to the son. For he is the love object that the protagonist seeks but never finds in "Calamus." "Adhesiveness," as I have suggested earlier, conceals an unconscious desire for a satisfactory relationship between a youth and an older man — between, that is, son and father. It is clear in the "Calamus" sequence that the singer is ready to relinquish physical or sexual gratification, which he at once seeks and fears, for the sake of an abstraction, which is an idealized father who can fulfill his emotional needs. Surely this point emerges clearly in "Fast-Anchor'd Eternal O Love!":

Then separate, as disembodied, the purest born,
The ethereal, the last athletic reality, my consolation,
I ascend — I float in the regions of your love, O man,
O sharer of my roving life.

In "Passage to India" the "roving life" is over, but the "Comrade perfect" is "the last athletic reality."

As one should expect in view of the abortive attempts evident throughout the early poetry to fuse male and female, the reunion in "Passage to India" achieves the ultimate and long-craved fusion or merger. The "Comrade perfect" is both father and mother:

                                lave me all over,
Bathe me O God in thee, mounting to thee. . . .

In "When Lilacs Last in the Dooryard Bloom'd" it is the "Dark Mother" or "strong Deliveress" who performs this function:

Lost in the loving, floating ocean of thee,
Laved in the flood of thy bliss, O Death.

But at last we are given the "Deliverer," and we can therefore correct our earlier formulation: man is fragmentation, unity is woman.

Thus in "Passage to India" we come full circle, which means that in the later poem we have a nonerotic version of Section 5 in "Song of Myself":

Only the lull I like, the hum of your valved voice.

I mind how we lay in June, such a transparent summer morning;
You settled your head athwart my hips and gently turned over upon me,
And parted the shirt from my bosom-bone, and plunged your tongue
    to my barestript heart,
And reached till you felt my beard, and reached till you held my feet.

Swiftly arose and spread around me the peace and joy and knowledge
    that pass all the art and argument of the earth;
And I know that the hand of God is the elderhand of my own. . . .

In fact, the last two lines might well have been repeated in
"Passage to India."

It is more than a coincidence, I believe, that there are verbal
resemblances between Section 5 and the crucial section in "Passage
to India." In the latter the "I" mentions "the Elder Brother found."
In "Song of Myself" the line immediately following the passage
quoted above reads (but only in the 1855 edition): "And I know
that the spirit of God is the eldest brother of my own." I suggest
that both lines have a common emotional source — a younger
son's (perhaps mistaken) belief that an older son is the favorite
of the father. In other words, Walt, envious of the affection Jesse
received from their father, wished to occupy Jesse's favored position. It should be remembered that in several of Whitman's early
prose tales the older brother is the favored child and the younger
son shamefully mistreated by paternal figures, and also that Whitman "forgets" to mention his older brother Jesse in an autobiographical sketch in which he cites by name other members of his
family. Hence the latent content of "Passage to India" appears to
deal with guilt stemming from his rivalry with Jesse as well as
from his ambivalence toward his father. The nature of guilt and
man's defense mechanisms are such that Whitman cannot even
in "Passage to India" acknowledge his ambivalence directly; only
through a variation upon the Prodigal Son motif can he make peace
(or atonement) with the brother-father. Needless to add, Whitman made no such conscious association when he spoke of "the
essential ultimate me" exposed in "Passage to India."

In the return of the son to the father the poet resolves the
psychic conflict, but fails to resolve another conflict, between
Walter Whitman and Walt Whitman, the public figure and the
solitary singer. For the poem concludes with oratorical injunctions
and excessive exclamation points:

Passage, immediate passage! the blood burns in my veins!
Away O soul! hoist instantly the anchor!
Cut the hawsers — haul out — shake out every sail!
Have we not stood here like trees in the ground long enough?

Have we not grovel'd here long enough, eating and drinking like mere
    brutes?
Have we not darken'd and dazed ourselves with books long enough?

Sail forth — steer for the deep waters only,
Reckless O soul, exploring, I with thee, and thou with me,
For we are bound where mariner has not yet dared to go,
And we will risk the ship, ourselves and all.

O my brave soul!
O farther farther sail!
O daring joy, but safe! are they not all the seas of God?
O farther, farther, farther sail!

The sound, however, has neither psychological nor organic justification. "Passage to more than India" should lead to a quiet conclusion like those in "The Sleepers" and "Out of the Cradle Endlessly
Rocking." Instead Whitman attempts futilely to convert and ex-
tend a personal reconciliation and rite into a model for a cultural
transformation. Walt simply never succeeds in incorporating
Walter. The song of the self deals with a universal reality; *"en
masse"* (an ugly and affected phrase) is a faceless, unnamed
abstraction which can be attractive only to those fearful of people
as persons.

    Not only does Whitman fail to present in the thousands of lines
making up *Leaves of Grass* one clearly delineated individual, but
also his poetry, when it is examined chronologically and when one
(rightly) ignores the patriotic and messianic rhetoric, reveals protagonists increasingly in retreat from society. Although never
individualized, crowds of people appear and disappear in poems
like "Song of Myself," "The Sleepers," and "Faces." In these works
we observe social rites, communal activities, banquets, marriages,
funerals. There is at least the suggestion of social interaction. The
crowds shrink to the fleeting lovers, mostly imaginary, of the lonely
singer of "Calamus" friendship. The "I" in both "As I Ebb'd with
the Ocean of Life" and "Out of the Cradle Endlessly Rocking"
plays out his role with nonhuman symbols of human relationships.
The "comrades" of the protagonist in "When Lilacs Last in the
Dooryard Bloom'd" are the star, the lilac, and the thrush. The
occasional poems, written to celebrate topical events and sometimes
even read before an audience, have as protagonist an isolated
observer who has disengaged himself from the very society whose

deeds and greatness Whitman is chanting. What I am suggesting is that the tendency to withdraw in order to contemplate "a spear of summer grass" or the sources of art becomes more marked in his later poetry, although his rhetoric preaches more insistently than ever social action and social involvement. In short, the bard of democracy is always in retreat from democratic society.

Thus "Passage to India" is indeed a swan song. The tensions which lay behind his greatest poetry had worked themselves out, partly because of compulsive artistic repetition. The child that "went forth" had found a mother and, more important, a father. He no longer had need to create the fantasy of a savage (an orphan and deviant) or a heroic impregnator. He was reconciled to never crossing the "bridge." There were no more variations to be played upon his themes, for the tensions expressed in the themes were now quiescent. Without tensions there is no need to seek sublimation in art. Before he wrote "Passage to India" Whitman had achieved some kind of resolution of his conflicts — when this took place we cannot know exactly, nor need to speculate — and the poems show the result: personal serenity, unfortunately, seems to produce a flaccid art.

Nor was the later Whitman "curious": he had nothing more to seek out or to absorb. As the orgiastic rhythms and erotic undertones disappeared, his poetic inspiration also withered except for an occasional reappearance in a poem like "The Dalliance of the Eagles" (1880). When Eros vanishes, art no longer evokes the pleasure principle: occasional poetry stems from the drab sense of duty (the reality principle) of "good gray poets." Public poets are never lawless or eccentric or amorous: they do not make love to their readers; they posture as seers or prophets, and are unfailingly dull.

The public poet is ordinarily not endowed with a rich comic sense. Comedy originates in the dynamics of tensions and often serves as a defense mechanism to shield its creator's disaffections. Further, its affinities to a child's uninhibited playfulness make it seem infantile in so-called maturity. And so the later poems are without the comic braggadocio present in the early editions of *Leaves of Grass*. "The good gray poet" is too decorous to declaim, "Singing the phallus!"

The aging poet hobbled about in the streets of Camden and Philadelphia, a silver-bearded, venerable father, affable, observant, and serene. Although they may have exaggerated somewhat, contemporary commentators noted repeatedly Whitman's serenity. If this was but another "pose," as detractors are too quick to assert, Whitman was an unusually successful actor: it takes toughness not to wear one's heart on his sleeve. And I can see no reason to suspect that the acute eye of Thomas Eakins, a superb psychologist, would have been taken in: Eakins' portrait of the poet is a vibrant tribute to Whitman's contentment in his declining years.

Apparently Whitman was not emotionally shattered when he recognized his waning artistic powers, for he never concealed the fact from the public. Although he was to take several "backward glances," he began the summation of his poetic career in the preface to the 1872 edition of *Leaves of Grass,* one year, it will be observed, after he wrote "Passage to India." This preface is a strange document of admissions and omissions. Whitman speaks of the "impetus," the "imperious conviction," and "the commands of my nature as total and irresistible as those which make the sea flow, or the globe revolve"; but this daemon, we are informed, led him to attempt "an epic of Democracy." "It may be," he admits, "that mere habit has got dominion of me, when there is no real need of saying any thing further," but, he continues, "the earnest trial and persistent exploration" have enabled him "to suggest the songs of vital endeavor and manly evolution, and furnish something for races of outdoor athletes." Such candor followed by such bathetic mentalization! Later he insists that from the beginning he has had but one purpose, "the religious purpose," and that "people, especially the young men and women of America, must begin to learn that religion, (like poetry,) is something far, far different from what they supposed." Without harshness, one must attribute these feeble rationalizations to a weary man whose daemon has fled. Perhaps this was the price of his serenity: the banishment of the daemon.

In the 1872 preface he mentions a sequel to *Leaves of Grass* but at once acknowledges doubts as to whether he can undertake it: "But of this supplementary volume, I confess I am not so certain." In 1876 he abandons the continuation in a muddled passage which is candid but defensive:

It was originally my intention, after chanting in "Leaves of Grass" the songs of the body and existence, to then compose a further, equally needed volume, based on those convictions of perpetuity and conservation which, enveloping all precedents, make the unseen soul govern absolutely at last. I meant, while in a sort continuing the theme of my first chants, to shift the slides, and exhibit the problem and paradox of the same ardent and fully appointed personality entering the sphere of the restless gravitation of spiritual law, and with cheerful face estimating death, not at all as the cessation, but as somehow what I feel it must be, the entrance upon by far the greatest part of existence, and something that life is at least as much for, as it is for itself. But the full construction of such a work is beyond my powers, and must remain for some bard in the future. The physical and the sensuous, in themselves or in their immediate continuations, retain holds upon me which I think are never entirely releas'd; and those holds I have not only not denied, but hardly wish'd to weaken.

If I understand Whitman correctly, he decided to abandon the scheme not because he was in poor health in 1876, but because the subject he proposed, some kind of mystical flight and self-transcendence, was not consonant with the orgiastic sources of his art and was therefore incompatible subject matter for his "sensuous" nature.

In his periodic reviews of his career Whitman invariably advances the wrong reasons for his greatness. *Leaves of Grass* is not, as he alleges in the 1872 preface, "the song of a great composite *democratic individual,* male or female." The book, in the first place, is not a unified work; the poet's arrangements and rearrangements demonstrate that it did not grow organically but was arbitrarily contrived according to a vague scheme. A dozen or more of the greatest poems in the language delineate with profound insight and incomparable art a self that is not so much democratic as universal. To predict in 1872 "races of outdoor athletes" is foolish, but to affirm the sensuous life of the "sweeter fat that sticks to my own bones" is to take arms against the exaggerated gloom of the "waste land" mentality. Only the steady vision of the great artist can take us to the abyss and at the same time renew our faith in ourselves and in life. Whitman does not so much ignore horrors or so-called evils as place them in perspective, perhaps in endurable perspective. He is no prophet, or if he is, he is the prophet of what alienated man can still achieve in the age of the dynamo. Nor is he a philosopher: when he thinks in prose he utters second-rate platitudes. But when he orders his feelings in his great poems, our response is visceral. For as the lonely poet of monologue, of the

inner frontier, of love and death — of our anxieties — he re-
freshes our spirits, and our lives at least for a moment do not seem
fractured and chaotic. Whitman is not a "cosmic" poet but —
what is greater and perhaps rarer — the human poet of the human
comedy. Art, almost alone in a world intent upon other pleasures,
affirms the joys of existence as it defines the problems.

It is only fitting that the "So long" should be uttered by the man
who greeted Whitman "at the beginning of a great career," Ralph
Waldo Emerson: "I rubbed my eyes a little to see if this sunbeam
were no illusion; but the solid sense of the book is a sober certainty."

A SELECTED BIBLIOGRAPHY

Although Whitman until the past decade has been out of critical fashion — that is, he was blithely ignored during the ascendancy and tyranny of the so-called New Criticism — studies of him are considerable in number, if somewhat uneven in quality. For Whitman partisans have often evidenced more zeal than acumen, and his poetry appears to attract commentators intent upon proving a thesis, regardless of the means, or upon elevating Whitman to divine status.

The most important event in Whitman scholarship is the appearance of *The Collected Writings of Walt Whitman,* now being published by the New York University Press. To date (1968) seven of the projected fifteen volumes have appeared: three volumes of *Correspondence,* edited by Edwin Haviland Miller; two volumes of *Prose Works,* edited by Floyd Stovall; *The Early Poems and the Fiction,* edited by Thomas L. Brasher; and *Leaves of Grass: Comprehensive Reader's Edition,* edited by Sculley Bradley and Harold W. Blodgett, who are preparing a two-volume *Variorum Edition of Leaves of Grass.* Other volumes will be edited by Edward Grier, William White, and Herbert Bergman.

The following six books are indispensable:

Allen, Gay Wilson. *Walt Whitman Handbook.* New York, 1946.

————. *The Solitary Singer: A Critical Biography of Walt Whitman.* New York, 1955.

Chase, Richard. *Walt Whitman Reconsidered.* New York, 1955.

Miller, James E., Jr., *A Critical Guide to Leaves of Grass.* Chicago, 1957.

Lawrence, D. H. *Studies in Classic American Literature.* Garden City, 1953.

Matthiessen, F. O. *American Renaissance: Art and Expression in the Age of Emerson and Whitman.* New York, 1941.

Allen's *Handbook* discusses briefly and thoroughly all aspects of the poet's art and life. It is an invaluable tool for critic and biographer. *The Solitary Singer* supersedes all previous studies of Whitman's life.

The definitive biography, it is a model of completeness and judicious-ness. The latter quality is not always present in discussions of an artist who provokes extreme praise as well as violent ridicule.

Chase and Miller present ably the two prevailing critical views of Whitman. Chase emphasizes the artist, Miller the mystic. Chase, while his scholarship is sometimes faulty, often illuminates the text brilliantly; his position is close to those of Kenneth Burke and Leslie Fiedler. Miller explores Whitman's mysticism with more thoroughness than any of his predecessors; Cowley and Chari (see below) are also exponents of this approach.

Although Lawrence is the very model of what academic scholarship deplores, no one can ignore his eccentric essay; he is the rare critic who reads with his guts. It is superfluous to praise once again Matthiessen's monumental work, which has had an extraordinarily beneficent effect upon American scholarship. Under the influence of T. S. Eliot and Henry James, however, Matthiessen is too preoccupied with Whitman's poetic theories and craftsmanship, or lack of it. Whit-man is more skillful and subtle than Matthiessen (or, for that matter, Eliot) allows.

EDITIONS

The Complete Writings of Walt Whitman, edd. Richard Maurice Bucke, Thomas B. Harned, and Horace L. Traubel. Ten volumes. New York, 1902.

This edition was prepared by the poet's literary executors, who compensated for their amateurishness by their devotion to Whitman at a time when he was shamefully neglected by the academic world.

Calamus: A Series of Letters Written during the Years 1868–1880 by Walt Whitman to a Young Friend (Peter Doyle), ed. Richard Mau-rice Bucke. Boston, 1897.

These letters are reprinted, with new ones and excerpts from Doyle's illiterate letters, in Volumes II and III of *The Correspon-dence of Walt Whitman.*

The Wound Dresser, ed. Richard Maurice Bucke. Boston, 1898.

This book reprints many of Whitman's letters written during the Civil War, all of which appear in *The Correspondence of Walt Whitman.*

The Letters of Anne Gilchrist and Walt Whitman, ed. Thomas B. Harned. Garden City, 1918.

Harned's edition clarifies the strange relationship between the widow of Blake's biographer and the poet whom she hoped to marry when, against his advice, she came to Camden in 1876.

The Uncollected Poetry and Prose of Walt Whitman, ed. Emory Holloway. Two volumes. New York, 1921.
    An important collection of miscellaneous writings in poetry and
prose.

Inclusive Edition Leaves of Grass, ed. Emory Holloway. Garden City,
1925.
    For four decades this book by one of the most distinguished Whit-
man scholars has been the best available edition of *Leaves of Grass.*

Walt Whitman's Workshop: A Collection of Unpublished Manuscripts,
ed. Clifton Joseph Furness. Cambridge, Massachusetts, 1928.

*Faint Clews & Indirections: Manuscripts of Walt Whitman and His
Family,* edd. Clarence Gohdes and Rollo G. Silver. Durham, North
Carolina, 1949.
    Although all of the Whitman letters printed here are included in
The Correspondence of Walt Whitman, the letters written by Whit-
man's mother and the other documents are of considerable interest.

Whitman's Manuscripts: Leaves of Grass (1860) — A Parallel Text,
ed. Fredson Bowers. Chicago, 1955.

An 1855–56 Notebook toward the Second Edition of Leaves of Grass,
ed. Harold W. Blodgett. Carbondale, 1959.

Whitman's "Blue Book," ed. Arthur Golden. Two volumes. New
York, 1967.
    These three books are important for the study of the genesis of
Leaves of Grass.

Walt Whitman's Leaves of Grass — The First (1855) Edition, ed.
Malcolm Cowley. New York, 1959.
    In his introduction Cowley argues that the first edition is Whit-
man's masterpiece. His emphasis on the similarities to Oriental
thought has led to what some critics consider a new view of the
poet. (I remain unconvinced that similarities to Eastern philosophy
add to our knowledge or understanding of the poetry.)

*Leaves of Grass by Walt Whitman (Facsimile Edition of the 1860
Text),* ed. Roy Harvey Pearce. Ithaca, 1961.
    In a finely reasoned essay Pearce argues for the superiority of the
third edition. Both Cowley and Pearce challenge the superiority of
the so-called "death-bed edition" of 1891–92, which the poet himself decreed was to be the definitive text of his poetry.

CONCORDANCE

*A Concordance of Walt Whitman's Leaves of Grass and Selected Prose
Writings,* ed. Edwin Harold Eby. Seattle, 1955.

BIBLIOGRAPHIES

Holloway, Emory, and Henry S. Saunders. *The Cambridge History of American Literature.*

Allen, Gay Wilson. *Twenty-five Years of Walt Whitman Bibliography, 1918–1942. Bulletin of Bibliography Pamphlets,* No. 38, 1943.

————, and Evie Allison Allen. "A Check List of Whitman Publications 1945–1960," in *Walt Whitman as Man, Poet, and Legend.* Carbondale, 1961.

Miller, Edwin H., and Rosalind S. Miller. *Walt Whitman's Correspondence — A Checklist.* New York, 1957.

Literary History of the United States, edd. Robert E. Spiller et al. New York, 1948.

Thorp, Willard. "Whitman," in *Eight American Authors,* ed. Floyd Stovall. New York, 1956.
 This book and the preceding one contain splendid critical bibliographies.

COLLECTIONS

The major public depositories of Whitman holographs are: the Library of Congress, the Trent Collection at Duke University, the Clifton Waller Barrett Collection at the University of Virginia, the Henry W. and Albert A. Berg Collection and the Oscar Lion Collection at the New York Public Library, the Hanley Collection at the University of Texas, the Henry E. Huntington Library, the Pierpont Morgan Library, and the Yale University Collection of American Literature.

The Charles E. Feinberg Collection is incomparable, a most extraordinary collection of Whitman manuscripts which Mr. Feinberg has generously made available to scholars.

BIOGRAPHIES

Bucke, Richard Maurice. *Walt Whitman.* Philadelphia, 1883.
 The longest biographical study to appear in the poet's lifetime. Bucke rightly claimed that Whitman was the coeditor.

Perry, Bliss. *Walt Whitman.* Boston, 1906.
 The first academic biography is a most readable study.

Holloway, Emory. *Whitman: An Interpretation in Narrative.* New York, 1926.
 A sound biography, marred only by its romantic treatment of the New Orleans episode.

A Selected Bibliography   229

Catell, Jean. *Walt Whitman: la Naissance du Poète.* Paris, 1929.
    A full-length psychological study which focuses on Whitman's
early years in order to explain many poetic passages.
Canby, Henry Seidel. *Walt Whitman an American: A Study in Biography.* Boston, 1943.
    The best popular account of the poet's life. The treatment of
Whitman's deviancy is unusually sensitive.
Traubel, Horace L. *With Walt Whitman in Camden.* Three volumes.
New York, 1906–1914. Volume IV, ed. Sculley Bradley. Philadelphia, 1953. Volume V, ed. Gertrude Traubel. Carbondale, 1964.
    Day-by-day notations on conversations between a young disciple
and the poet beginning in 1888. Probably three more volumes will
be issued. Although Traubel is no Boswell, these books contain a
wealth of material.

CRITICAL STUDIES

Spitzer, Leo. *"Explication de Texte* Applied to Walt Whitman's Poem
'Out of the Cradle Endlessly Rocking,' " *Journal of English Literary
History,* XVI (1949), 229–249. (Reprinted in *Essays on English
and American Literature* [Princeton, 1962].)
    An exemplary essay written with a breadth of knowledge and
sensitivity.
Schyberg, Frederik. *Walt Whitman,* trans. Evie Allison Allen. New
York, 1951.
    Schyberg's analysis of the various editions of *Leaves of Grass* is a
seminal work. His biographical speculations, while interesting, are
not always convincing.
Bychowski, Gustav. "Walt Whitman — A Study in Sublimation,"
Psychoanalysis and the Social Sciences, III (1951), 223–261.
    A psychiatrist examines the poet and speculates upon the personality structure in an acute diagnosis which goes beyond the earlier
psychological commentaries of Havelock Ellis and Edward Carpenter.
Asselineau, Roger. *The Evolution of Walt Whitman.* Two volumes.
Cambridge, Massachusetts, 1960–1962. (Originally published as
L'Évolution de Walt Whitman [Paris, 1954].)
    Asselineau's is the most exhaustive analysis of the various editions
of *Leaves of Grass* and the best French study of Whitman.
Burke, Kenneth. "Policy Made Personal: Whitman's Verse and Prose
— Salient Traits," in *Leaves of Grass One Hundred Years After,*
ed. Milton Hindus. Stanford, 1955.
    One of the most original and subtle studies of Whitman's imagery.
Although it is often ignored, it represents a new departure in Whitman explication.

Pearce, Roy Harvey. *The Continuity of American Poetry*. Princeton, 1961.

> By all odds the best book on a difficult subject.

The Presence of Walt Whitman, ed. R. W. B. Lewis. New York, 1962.

> This collection contains a fine reading of "Out of the Cradle Endlessly Rocking" by Stephen E. Whicher as well as James A. Wright's admirable article, "The Delicacy of Walt Whitman."

Chari, V. K. *Whitman in the Light of Vedantic Mysticism*. Lincoln, Nebraska, 1964.

> This is the most recent of the analogical interpretations intent upon finding similarities between Whitman and Eastern thought. With his Indian background, Chari is authoritative, but frequently he ignores context and Whitman's art in order to make his points.

Waskow, Howard J. *Whitman: Explorations in Form*. Chicago, 1966.

> Many of Waskow's readings are astute and stimulating. He is especially perceptive in discussing Whitman's voices and forms, but his formalistic approach, while a desirable corrective to the impressionism of many critics, is sometimes too schematic and slights the poet's affect.

Whitman: A Collection of Critical Essays, ed. Roy Harvey Pearce. Englewood Cliffs, New Jersey, 1962.

> A compilation of excerpts from the writings of Matthiessen, Miller, Asselineau, Lewis, Chase, Pearce, Charles Feidelson, Jr., and others.

NONACADEMIC CRITICISM

Pearce (see preceding item) includes in his collection essays by Lawrence, Ezra Pound, and William Carlos Williams, but he omits the following "offbeat" works:

Dahlberg, Edward. *Can These Bones Live*. New York, 1941.

Miller, Henry. *The Books in My Life*. New York, n.d.

————. *Stand Still Like the Hummingbird*. New York, 1962.

Jarrell, Randall. *Poetry and the Age*. New York, 1953.

Morris, Wright. *The Territory Ahead*. New York, 1963.

Dahlberg, writing with the dogmatic gusto of Lawrence, flays the poet. Miller sees himself as the heir of Whitman, Emerson, and Thoreau, and though the nature of Whitman's art eludes him, he is closer to Whitman's spirit than many of the academicians are. Jarrell's "Some Lines from Whitman" is a lovely piece of criticism by a poet whose ear and eye are unfailingly acute. Morris shares Jarrell's empathy, and neither man is afraid to expose his heart.

NOTES

1. *"a long foreground"*

(pages 1–23)

In this chapter and succeeding ones, unless otherwise noted in the text or the notes, I have quoted from the earliest published version of a poem. I have, however, consistently employed the titles given in the last edition of *Leaves of Grass*.

1. In *The Fight of a Book for the World* (West Yarmouth, Massachusetts, 1926), Kennedy, who came to know Whitman as a young man, includes an appendix entitled "A Conspectus of Friends and Foes": there are *"Whole-hearted Accepters"* and *"Bitter and Relentless Foes and Vilifiers"* (pp. 287–288).
2. Horace L. Traubel, *With Walt Whitman in Camden*, III, 452–453.
3. Gay Wilson Allen, "Biblical Echoes in Whitman's Works," *American Literature*, VI (1934), 302–315.

2. *"There was a child"*

(pages 24–40)

1. "Walt Whitman — A Study in Sublimation," *Psychoanalysis and the Social Sciences*, III (1951), 223–261.
2. *The Correspondence of Walt Whitman*, ed. Edwin Haviland Miller, III, 307.
3. Lanier, after writing Whitman an extravagantly laudatory letter in 1878 (see Traubel, *With Walt Whitman in Camden*, I, 208), recanted and attacked the poet in *The English Novel: A Study in the Development of Personality* (New York, 1903), pp. 53, 59–60.

4. Herbert Marcuse, *Eros and Civilization: A Philosophical Inquiry into Freud* (Boston, 1955), p. 169. Reprinted by permission of the Beacon Press; copyright © 1955, 1966 by the Beacon Press.
5. Quoted by Roger Asselineau in *The Evolution of Walt Whitman* (Cambridge, Mass., 1960), I, 276n. Miss Gilchrist's recollections appear in *Temple Bar Magazine,* CXIII (1898), 200–212.
6. Delay's *The Youth of André Gide* (Chicago, 1963) is an absorbing study of the novelist's formative years; the quotation in the text appears on p. 232.

3. *"fathered him . . . and birthed him"*

(*pages 41–65*)

Quotations from "By Blue Ontario's Shore" are from *Leaves of Grass: Comprehensive Reader's Edition,* edd. Blodgett and Bradley.

1. Whitman's short stories have been collected by Thomas L. Brasher in *The Early Poems and the Fiction* in *The Collected Writings of Walt Whitman.*
2. The only detailed discussion of the relationship between Harry Stafford and Whitman appears in my introduction to Volume III of *The Correspondence of Walt Whitman,* where for the first time letters to and from Stafford, as well as other members of the Stafford family, are printed. This correspondence and entries in Whitman's *Commonplace-Book* (in the Feinberg Collection), also published for the first time, clarify this last "Calamus" friendship.
3. The early appearance of a selection of letters from Whitman to his mother, in *The Wound Dresser,* ed. R. M. Bucke (Boston, (1898), undoubtedly played a decisive part, in conjunction with the poet's praise, in creating an idealized portrait of Mrs. Whitman. A few of her letters to her son appear in *Faint Clews & Indirections,* edd. Clarence Gohdes and Rollo G. Silver (Durham, North Carolina, 1949), but these were chosen "with the idea of illustrating the interest in politics and reading which Mrs. Whitman also shared [with Walt]" (p. 183).
4. *Calamus — A Series of Letters Written . . . by Walt Whitman to a Young Friend (Peter Doyle),* ed. R. M. Bucke (Boston, 1897), p. 25.
5. Quoted in Clara Barrus' *Whitman and Burroughs — Comrades* (Boston, 1931), p. 339.

6. See *The Correspondence of Walt Whitman,* I, 185.
7. Edward Carpenter, *Days with Walt Whitman* (London, 1906), p. 43.
8. An acute psychological analysis of *The Red Badge of Courage* by Daniel Weiss appears in *The Psychoanalytic Review,* LII (1965), 176–196.
9. Printed in Gay Wilson Allen's *Walt Whitman Handbook* (New York, 1946), p. 251.
10. Ruth Miller Elson examined over one thousand nineteenth-century textbooks for her fascinating study, *The Guardians of Tradition* (Lincoln, Nebraska, 1964). The passage quoted in the text appears on p. 308.

4. *"The doubts of daytime and . . . nighttime"*
(pages 66–84)

1. *The Heart of Emerson's Journals,* ed. Bliss Perry (Boston, 1939), p. 223.
2. Erik H. Erikson, *Childhood and Society* (New York, 1963), p. 252. Quoted by permission of the publisher, W. W. Norton & Company.
3. Marie Bonaparte's discussion of the "bridge" in *The Life and Works of Edgar Allan Poe: A Psycho-Analytic Interpretation* (New York, 1949), pp. 525–536, is summarized in Paul Friedman's "The Bridge: A Study in Symbolism," *Psychoanalytic Quarterly,* XXI (1952), 51.
4. Bruno Bettelheim, *Symbolic Wounds: Puberty Rites and the Envious Male* (New York, 1962), p. 115. Quoted by permission of The Macmillan Company; copyright 1954, 1962 by The Free Press. Bettelheim's study is useful in an examination of "The Sleepers."
5. If I were to single out one poem to justify my assertion that Whitman's tampering with his verse was unfortunate artistically, I would cite "The Sleepers." Far removed from the emotional context out of which the original poem sprang, "the good gray poet" pruned two of its climaxes: the depiction of the youth wandering about "hotcheeked and blushing" (11. 60–70 in the 1855 edition) and the outburst directed at Lucifer (11. 127–134). Unconcerned (perhaps unaware) that he was destroying the psychic unity of his work, Whitman apparently wanted to make the poem

sexually innocuous and to eliminate material which was too personal to be part of the later image he wished to impose upon his public.

5. *"I celebrate myself"*

(*pages 85–114*)

1. "Song of Myself," admittedly Whitman's most difficult but also his most characteristic and greatest poem, has until recently been admired for its brilliant passages (Sections 5, 11, and 24, for example), and most commentators have detected flaws in organization and structure. The flaws, I suggest, are usually not Whitman's but the failures of the interpreters to "encompass" the poet. Although it would perhaps be absurd to deny that there are occasional weaknesses in a poem of over 1,300 lines, there are very few, it seems to me, and the poem has its own inevitable logic in organization and structure. "Song of Myself" forces us to abandon our preoccupation with traditional forms, just as we cannot hope to grasp the intentions of abstract expressionist painters if we apply to their work the principles of the Renaissance. Too often critics and readers want new art in familiar forms, even though it seems platitudinous to observe that the excitement and immediacy of art depend upon new ways of coping with old problems, and that the nature of reality alters as cultural and personal assumptions and formulations alter.

   Carl F. Strauch, in "The Structure of Walt Whitman's 'Song of Myself,'" *The English Journal*, XXVII (1938), 597–607, made an important contribution to our understanding of the poem in his structural analysis. Later critics have not significantly altered his divisions. The most complete analysis of the poem as mystical experience appears in James E. Miller's *A Critical Guide to Leaves of Grass* in a chapter entitled "'Song of Myself' as Inverted Mystical Experience." There is a perceptive discussion in Roy Harvey Pearce's *The Continuity of American Poetry*, where the emphasis is placed upon the need of Whitman's age "to find an adequate poetic image of its very being . . . the full and complete surrogate for the traditional epic" (p. 72). As my analysis indicates, I am not satisfied either with Miller's "inverted mystical experience" or with Pearce's "proto-epic."

2. *Poetry and the Age* (New York, 1953), p. 110. Quoted by permission of the publisher, Alfred A. Knopf, Inc.; copyright 1953 by Randall Jarrell.

3. In "Walt Whitman, Stranger," *American Mercury,* XXV (1935), 277–285, Mark Van Doren perceptively but too persistently cites the poet's "abnormalities," and claims (particularly in reference to Sections 28 and 29) that psychologists label Whitman an "erethistic, . . . one of those people whose organs and tissues are chronically in a state of abnormal excitement, who tremble and quiver when the rest of us are merely conscious that we are being interested or pleased" (p. 282). Granting the accuracy of the label and its applicability to Whitman, the remark remains pointless, since genius is by definition an anomaly, and the artist is less repressed than the rest of us.

6. *"singing the phallus"*
(*pages 115–139*)

In this chapter in my quotations from "I Sing the Body Electric," I use the greatly expanded version of 1860.

1. *With Walt Whitman in Camden,* IV, 62.
2. *Frontier: American Literature and the American West* (Princeton, 1965), p. 68.
3. *Diary in America,* ed. Jules Zanger (Bloomington, 1960), p. 196.
4. Carpenter and Burroughs are quoted in Clara Barrus' *Whitman and Burroughs — Comrades,* pp. 143, 127.
5. "Policy Made Personal: Whitman's Verse and Prose — Salient Traits," in *Leaves of Grass One Hundred Years After,* ed. Milton Hindus (Stanford, 1955), p. 103.
6. Horatio Greenough, *The Travels, Observations, and Experience of a Yankee Stonecutter* (Gainesville, Florida, 1958), pp. 202–203.
7. The letter which Whitman prepared for O'Connor's signature is reprinted in *The Correspondence of Walt Whitman,* I, 347–349. It is an interesting document in the history of the transformation of the bohemian into the respectable poet.

7. *"the tenderest lover"*
(*pages 140–170*)

In this chapter I have used the 1860 edition of *Leaves of Grass* because it is unquestionably superior to the later bowdlerized versions. When Whitman removed in 1867 some of the better poems in the sequence, he was concerned not with art but with public opinion. I have indicated in my discussion some of the subsequent alterations and omissions, but I have not attempted a systematic analysis — a task which should be undertaken.

1. Frank Harris, *Contemporary Portraits, Third Series* (New York, [1920]), p. 219.
2. Quoted from the earliest version of the tale; see *The Early Poems and the Fiction,* ed. Brasher, p. 74n. The later alterations and excisions surely indicate Whitman's awareness of the possibility that his (dubious) theme might be misconstrued.
3. Quoted by Clifton Joseph Furness in *American Literature,* XIII (1942), 424–425.
4. *With Walt Whitman in Camden,* I, 76–77.
5. This passage is quoted by permission of Charles E. Feinberg.
6. *The Correspondence of Walt Whitman,* II, 97. Stoddard (1843–1909) was a minor poet and essayist.
7. *Walt Whitman's Workshop* (Cambridge, Massachusetts, 1928), pp. 63–64.
8. See *Prose Works 1892,* ed. Floyd Stovall, II, 414–415.
9. *The Heart of Emerson's Journals,* p. 182.
10. *Collected Poems of Henry Thoreau,* ed. Carl Bode (Baltimore, 1964), p. 81.
11. *The Correspondence of Walt Whitman,* II. 151.
12. Quoted in Gay Wilson Allen's *The Solitary Singer* (New York, 1955), pp. 421–422.
13. *Leonardo da Vinci: A Study in Psychosexuality* (New York, 1947), p. 102.
14. *Studies in Sexual Inversion* (New York, 1964), p. 116.
15. *Walt Whitman: A Critical Study* (London, 1914), p. 206.

8. *"the low and delicious word DEATH"*

(pages 171–198)

I have used the 1860 text of "Out of the Cradle Endlessly Rocking, where it is titled "A Word Out of the Sea." For "When Lilacs Last in the Dooryard Bloom'd" I have used the 1865–6 text of *Drum-Taps and Sequel to Drum-Taps,* in the facsimile edited by F. DeWolfe Miller (Gainesville, Florida, 1959).

1. *A Backward Glance* (New York, 1936), p. 186.
2. " 'Out of the Cradle' as a Romance," in *The Presence of Walt Whitman,* ed. R. W. B. Lewis (New York, 1962), p. 68.
3. *Life Against Death: The Psychoanalytical Meaning of History* (New York, 1959), p. 133.
4. *Tropic of Capricorn* (New York, 1961), pp. 288–289. Copyright 1961 by Henry Miller; quoted by permission of the publisher, Grove Press, Inc.
5. "Walt Whitman — A Study in Sublimation," *Psychoanalysis and the Social Sciences,* III (1951), 226.
6. Quoted from the *Saturday Press* in Allen's *The Solitary Singer,* p. 231.
7. *With Walt Whitman in Camden,* II, 116, 122–123; IV, 48.
8. Spitzer's brilliant essay, *"Explication de Texte* Applied to Walt Whitman's Poem 'Out of the Cradle Endlessly Rocking,' "* appears in *Essays in English and American Literature* (Princeton, 1962); the quoted passages are on pp. 32, 33.
9. Powys' discussion of Whitman appears in *Visions and Revisions* (New York, 1915), pp. 281–289.
10. Stephen E. Whicher, "Whitman's Awakening to Death," in *The Presence of Walt Whitman,* pp. 26, 22.
11. This alleged episode is discussed by Allen in *The Solitary Singer,* p. 351.
12. Charles Feidelson, Jr., *Symbolism and American Literature* (Chicago, 1953), p. 22.
13. Burke's study of Whitman's imagery is in the essay cited in note 5 to Chapter 6.
14. *Archetypal Patterns in Poetry* (New York, 1958), pp. 126–127.

9. *"Passage to more than India!"*

(pages 199–224)

For the analysis of "Crossing Brooklyn Ferry" I have used the 1860 text. For the poems written after 1866 I have quoted from *Leaves of Grass: Comprehensive Reader's Edition.*

1. Marx's *The Machine in the Garden: Technology and the Pastoral Ideal in America* (New York, 1964) is an exciting study. The quoted passages appear on pp. 222, 225.
2. *Ibid.,* pp. 220–222.

3. William Bysshe Stein, " 'The Artist of the Beautiful': Narcissus and the Thimble," *The American Imago*, XVIII (1961), 35–44.
4. *With Walt Whitman in Camden*, I, 156–157.
5. *The Correspondence of Walt Whitman*, II, 272.
6. *The Psycho-analysis of Artistic Vision and Hearing* (New York, 1965), p. 75. Quoted by permission of the publisher, George Braziller, Inc.

INDEX